AS CLOSE AS POSSIBLE
Community Residences for Retarded Adults

AS CLOSE AS

Community Residences for Retarded Adults

POSSIBLE

Bruce L. Baker

Professor, Department of Psychology, University of California, Los Angeles

Gary B. Seltzer

Program in Clinical Psychology and Public Practice, Harvard University

Marsha Mailick Seltzer

Florence Heller Graduate School for Advanced Studies in Social Welfare, Brandeis University

Cover illustration by Josephine Croteau, a resident of Oliver House, Southbridge, Massachusetts

Little, Brown and Company, Boston

First Edition
Published November 1977

Library of Congress Catalog Card No. 77-81502
ISBN 0-316-07827-1 (C)
ISBN 0-316-07829-8 (P)
Printed in the United States of America

Dedicated to Gunnar and Rosemary Dybwad

Preface

As I see it, the normalization principle means making available to the mentally retarded patterns and conditions of everyday life which are as close as possible to norms and patterns of the mainstream of society.

Nirje, 1969, p. 181

SETTINGS for retarded people are beginning to cast aside their legacy of segregation and neglect. A more hopeful philosophy seeks to assure retarded people a life "as close as possible" to that of their fellow citizens. Yet these optimistic words mean genuinely opening our communities to persons who are retarded, and when words must become deeds, the record has not been always enviable. In recent years a strong outcry from parents, professionals, and retarded adults themselves, bolstered by significant court action, has led to the exploration of noninstitutional places for retarded individuals to live. Smaller community-based residences have opened throughout the nation as experimental alternatives to the dehumanizing environment of our large state institutions.

This book describes a number of alternative residential models for retarded adults. It is based on a study undertaken to explore the many ways in which retarded adults are beginning to live in and – it is hoped – with communities. A particular motivation for our study was the allocation in Massachusetts of monies for establishing community residences and the initial policy of funding only *one* model – a small, family-style group home. It seemed to us that no matter how effective such a program might be, any single type of program would certainly fail to meet the needs of many retarded individuals. Hence we undertook a descriptive study of alternative residential models, in hopes that our findings would aid in the future planning of multimodel systems.

As Close As Possible, then, reports a survey of community residences across the nation, enhanced by on-site examination of 17 programs. The detailed program descriptions should be of interest to parents, planners, housemanagers, and other professionals who are advocating for or developing similar services. Many of the broader issues raised should be of concern to persons in fields as diverse as community psychology, social welfare, rehabilitation, public health, special education, and administration.

Part I develops some background themes (Chapter 1), followed by a description of our procedures and an overview of survey results from 381 community residences (Chapter 2). Part II (Chapters 3–12) considers in more depth alternative residential models currently serving retarded adults. Part III (Chapters 13–17) expands on several of the more critical issues raised throughout the book. Chapter 17 is a practical series of guidelines for choosing a community residence, informed by our previous findings and directed toward parents.

Acknowledgments

Central to this project were our colleagues Dr. Dennis Shulman, who worked with us in the project's planning, development, and data gathering, and Dr. Alan Brightman, whose critical reading of the manuscript and thoughtful discussions with us were invaluable.

The project was supported by a grant from the Massachusetts Developmental Disabilities Council. It was influenced by many friends, and we can only begin to acknowledge their contributions here. Foremost we are grateful to the community residences that opened their doors to our visitors, and to the many staff members and residents who not only granted us interviews but also welcomed us warmly. Also we appreciate the efforts of the many respondents to our lengthy survey and the cooperation of the state departments of mental health and mental retardation and the associations for retarded citizens that helped us to locate community residences.

The project depended considerably on the perceptions of those who shared field visits with us: Ken Bolyard, Betty Ann Duggan, Hayden Duggan, Teri Martin, and Pam Tropper. Many persons gave freely of their consultation, and we especially thank Ann Berry, Richard Brightman, Dr. Gunnar Dybwad, Dr. Rosemary Dybwad, Dr. Louis Heifetz, and Kurt Wehbring. We are indebted to Gladys Williams and Claudia Schultz for their research assistance, and to Kathi Mannus and Jennifer Carter for typing the manuscript.

Finally we are grateful to Sarah Boardman, our editor, for her encouragement, patience, and many helpful suggestions, and to Jane Sandiford for so effectively seeing the manuscript through production.

B. L. B.
G. B. S.
M. M. S.

Contents

I. Overview

I a mentally retarded person would like to know if there is any other place for us to live then in an institution

Life there is not all fun and games because they get up at five in the morning and take a bath at 5:30 and eat breakfast at six and go to work at jobs that are given to them to do and they don't get a lot of money for doing them. Some of them do not have a job at all and they have to sit all day and wait for the others to come back for lunch at 12:00 and that is a long wait and after lunch they watch their friends go back to work for the afternoon. They come back at 4:00 or 4:30 to get ready for supper and at 9:00 P.M. bed because they get up vey early in the morning. Then they get their mail from home or their brother's and sister's to tell them what is going on at home.

If more people do not take a more active interest in the life of the mentally retarded then we will not have any place to go epcept in an institutional living and that is not fair because we are God's creatures, to be like you are, considered as normal.

This is all vey real to me and all my friends because they do not know what will become of them after their mother's and father's die

Gloria

An unsolicited letter from a retarded adult. . . .

1. Background

The mentally retarded are human beings who are more like other people than they differ from them, no matter the degree of retardation. Their happiness – exactly as that of other people – depends greatly on the houses they live in.

N. E. Bank-Mikkelsen

IN recent years there has been increasing advocacy for comprehensive services for developmentally disabled children and adults. The continuum of services envisioned would engage an individual from infancy on, through an interrelated series of educational, recreational, vocational, and residential programs. Although it is difficult to separate the sphere of *residential services* from the other three services, it can be argued that where people live, in particular, should form the basis of any service delivery system (Kugel and Wolfensberger, 1969). When a retarded person no longer lives with parents and is not yet able to live on his or her own, social agencies customarily intervene to provide some other place to live. The question of where these people might live is certainly not a new one, and its history has been fraught with fears and prejudices, and with good intentions, which, in hindsight, have seemed misguided. This book is about the recent creation of residential alternatives to the institutional practices of the past. Its focus is on residences for adults, since there are many fewer alternatives for children, and these raise a host of separate issues.

A dominant view today is that residential settings for retarded adults should approximate family homes, be integrated with neighborhoods, and make use of generic community resources. This view results from an increasing distaste for segregated institutions, and the fact that these newer alternatives are called *community residences* highlights their hoped-for contrast to the separateness and impersonality of the large institutions. However, these goals are too general and provide few specific guidelines to community residence planners. Little has been written to date exploring the relative merits of various types, or models, of community residential living or even describing how existing residences operate. Thus now that there is a variety of programs, the need for evaluation and comprehensive planning for the future is clearly indicated.

Our study attempts to delineate the most significant models that have developed as alternatives to the isolation of traditional institutions and solitary home maintenance. We intend only to describe rather than to evaluate these models, although some reaction to the programs we have studied is unavoidable. In this chapter we will briefly consider the emergence of the community residence movement and several contrasting philosophies manifest in various community residence programs.

Institutional Nonservices

As the door locked behind me, I stepped into a room of bare cots, naked bodies and unintelligible voices. Some of the bodies strolled about or danced, waving their hands, grunting, shouting; others sat on the floor with folded legs, staring silently and emptily. There were 18 men, aged 15 to 30; some had bodies of old men and others those of children. They had slept without pajamas and they had not yet been dressed, but they milled about as though they had been milling for decades in that room with its flimsy cots and puddles of urine.

Wendy Kimball, 1972

Change is difficult, but change is necessary. We've got to close that goddamned place down.

Geraldo Rivera, 1972

During the past century the predominant mode of service to retarded people has been nonservice – either leaving parents to cope unaided or encouraging them to segregate their retarded offspring in institutions "for their own good" and for the good of a frightened and suspicious community. A comfortably accepted myth held that the big "state school" in the country was really just that, a school that was somehow "best" for those attending. Only recently have graphic descriptions of total institutions and their deleterious effect on human life been forced into the public consciousness (Goffman, 1961; Blatt and Kaplan, 1966; Nirge, 1969; Wolfensberger, 1969c; Blatt, 1970; Rivera, 1972).

Generally institutions for retarded people are large, located away from population centers, and overcrowded. Over half the institutions in the United States house more than 1,000 people each (Butterfield, 1969). Yet institutions continue to be the dominant (non-) service choice of professionals. The situation was depicted as follows in 1969:

More than 200,000 people, nearly half of whom are children, now live in over 150 institutions for the mentally retarded in the United States. Another 20,000 retarded reside in approximately 500 known private facilities. Tens of thousands more wait out their time in institutions for the mentally ill; nearly 10 percent of all residents in public mental hospitals are retarded. The number of institutionalized mentally retarded increases by over 3,000 every year . . . . Even though fewer than 5 percent of the mentally retarded in the United States reside in institutions, more money is spent to maintain them than is spent for any of the public programs which serve the remaining 95 percent.

Earl Butterfield, 1969, pp. 17–18

Despite the overwhelming financial cost of maintaining retarded persons in residential institutions, estimated at $1.6 billion in 1970 (Conley, 1973), residents of institutions are nearly always denied adequate privacy, education, training, and even medical care. In the worst of institutions residents live in sex-segregated, unsanitary, and dehumanizing conditions. And even in the best of institutions, residents would find few persons eager to change places with them, even for a day.

Relocating Residents in the Community

At Waverly, a careful study of the discharges for twenty-five years showed that a very small proportion of the discharged male morons had committed crimes, or had married or become parents, or had failed to support themselves, or had become bad citizens . . . . We have begun to recognize the fact that there are good morons and bad morons.

Walter E. Fernald, 1919, pp. 119–120

While for most retarded persons institutional placement has historically been a point of no likely return, there were always a few residents trickling back to the community. As early as 1919, Walter E. Fernald, who was a leading spokesman for the segregation of the retarded, conducted a follow-up study of retarded people who had left the institution. He discovered to his surprise that many were making a very successful adjustment in the community. During the following years numerous researchers sought to identify characteristics that could be used to predict postinstitutional adjustment, attempting to determine the common attributes of those individuals who had successfully left the institution behind them.

One limitation of these prognostic studies was a narrowness of vision; for example, researchers often equated successful community adjustment with the length of time an ex-resident remained outside the institution, making little allowance for the quality of life experienced in the community. Moreover, reviews of this literature (Windle, 1962; Eagle, 1967; Clark, Kivitz, and Rosen, 1968; and Cobb, 1972) concur that, in addition to their methodological flaws, these studies suffered from an overconcentration on the individual's characteristics, paying little attention to the community settings to which the individual returned.

These studies were carried out in the tradition of the impairment model, which sees an individual's failure to adjust in any setting as a personal shortcoming rather than as a result of situational factors. More recently there has been an increasing willingness to see that the extent of an individual's handicap may relate partly to the reactions of others to him or her. However, even today there is little research being done on the interaction between the personal and situational variables that promote successful adjustment of retarded individuals in a community. While planners of community-based alternatives might be quite aware that characteristics of the community setting are crucial in determining who will succeed and who will fail, they have very limited substantive knowledge to draw on for guidance. Nevertheless, decisions to release residents are made, and, during the past decade, an increasing number of residents have been relocated in the community.

To trace the origins and evolution of the community-residence movement comprehensively would send us in many and varied directions – as diverse as the civil rights and women's movements, the application of behavior modification to the retarded, the rising costs of health care, the halfway house movement in mental health, or the debate about IQ tests. Yet two major influences, which indeed are partly a reflection of these many diverse trends, are the revolution in service provisions in the Scandinavian countries, and the increased legal advocacy for civil rights and resulting court decisions in the United States.

Impetus for Locating Services in the Community

We are safe in saying that as far as possible, they should be considered and treated just as ordinary persons, our equals and friends, are treated, and not singled out as special objects of pity. This is too often forgotten.

Samuel G. Howe, 1866, speaking about the blind

Scandinavian Example

The benefits of changing the locus of residential services for retarded adults from custodial institutions to community-based homes have been recognized for some time (e.g., Dybwad, 1959). However, the actual development of personalized, modern, and comprehensive community-based services during the 1960s in Scandinavian countries spoke louder than many previous words. Bank-Mikkelsen (1969) and Grunewald (1969) described how Denmark and Sweden reevaluated their residential models and consequently began to place settings near population centers to provide their programs with a full complement of backup services. Existing institutions were remodeled, regional centers were built, and small community-based hostels were established. At the same time, medical, educational, and vocational services were expanded and a national 3-year training program for staff members was established.

In Denmark and Sweden national legislation helps to ensure that retarded people are afforded their civil rights, while consumer groups advocate for needed services. Parent groups have figured quite prominently in the growth of services by monitoring existing services, often beginning new ones, and then turning them over to the state.

Numerous influential planners in the United States have visited Scandinavia. They returned with generally glowing reports of tasteful community dwellings that were airy and rich in color, accommodating diverse programs in a system that views these services as a right, not a privilege. They returned embracing the philosophy of *normalization* as well.

Normalization

By far the most important product of the Scandinavian experience for reconsideration of services in the United States has been the articulation of the normalization principle. First proposed by Nirje (1969) and Bank-Mikkelsen (1969) and later expanded by Wolfensberger (1972), normalization means "making available to the mentally retarded patterns and conditions of everyday life which are as close as possible to the norms and patterns of mainstream society" (Nirje, 1969, p. 181). While this notion was not a new one, it has become the major philosophical impetus of the community residence movement. However, it has remained a philosophy for the most part, with little written about how the principle translates into action. (For an exception, see Wolfensberger and Glenn, 1973.)

A not infrequent problem in the rush to import and adopt this seemingly humane and simple notion has been a greater attention to the words than to the message. Normalization has often been misinterpreted to mean that the mere provision of a normative environment, such as a typical home in the community, will automatically be beneficial to retarded people. An obvious danger in this interpretation is that needed supportive services will not be developed. Providing conditions that are as close as possible to mainstream society should imply consideration of specific individual needs and the provision of training, supervision, and support as needed. Nirje's further development of the concept stresses this latter, and more realistic, view.

The application of the normalization principle will not "make the subnormal normal" but will make life conditions of the mentally subnormal normal as far as possible, bearing in mind the degree of his handicap, his competence and maturity, as well as the need for training activities and availability of services . . . . the awareness that mostly only relative independence and integration can be attained (is) implied and stressed by the words "as close as possible."

B. Nirje, 1970, p. 63

Court Decisions

Normalization is a relative concept. It is understandable that viewpoints on just what is desirable, or "possible," have clashed often during the 1970s in the courts. Plaintiffs have been single institutionalized individuals or groups of thousands combined in class action suits, while defendants have typically been professional caregivers and/or the state agencies that employ them. However, the court decisions have generally favored the plaintiffs, upholding the rights of civilly committed individuals and mandating rapid change.

Court actions in two areas are particularly germane to the community residence movement. First, many decisions and consent decrees have asserted a constitutional *right to treatment* of civilly committed retarded persons and have spelled out in considerable detail what institutional treatment must entail. For example, in a final order and opinion in a major case in Alabama (*Wyatt* v. *Stickney,* 1972), the court set 49 individual standards and guidelines concerning physical surroundings, nutrition, staffing, habilitation, and transitional services. While rulings vary among states, their consistent thrust is toward more humane institutions. Moreover, since high costs are involved in altering institutional plants and practices to comply with court rulings, planners are becoming more open to alternatives.

Second, it has been provided that every mentally retarded person has a right to treatment in the *least restrictive alternative,* which is often interpreted to mean the provision of community-based alternatives to total institutions. For example, among the requirements of an oft-quoted class action suit on behalf of over 5,000 residents of Willowbrook in New York *(New York State Association for Retarded Children* v. *Carey,* 1975) was the development of sufficient community alternatives to reduce the institution's population within 6 years to 250 persons.

Therefore, drawn by the example of the Scandinavian system and the spirit of normalization (and urged more than a little by the courts), many states have rapidly opened community residences. Before turning to specific models and programs in later chapters, we will briefly preview some of the various philosophies that influence many decisions about what the retarded person "needs."

Program Philosophies

Why train a retarded person to fit into an abnormal outside community where he will feel stress and run a high probability of being exploited? Why force a retarded person to live like that because many "normal" people live like that? We see our challenge not to bring the retarded to the community but rather to bring a sense of community to the retarded.

Co-worker Interview, Camphill Village (see Chap. 8)

Various perspectives have guided the program development in community residences, although as we have noted, the most influential has been *normalization,* with an emphasis on making settings similar to typical homes and providing autonomy and daily responsibilities for the residents. Wolfensberger (1969b) advocated the establishment of small community-based residences, each with a specific function, all widely dispersed among neighborhoods and staffed by live-in houseparents rather than by shifts of caretaker personnel. Residents were to be encouraged to utilize already existing services in the community for education, work, health care, and recreation. Elsewhere Wolfensberger (1971) suggested that normalizing conditions could also be met in a variety of individual residence models, such as boarding a retarded adult with a local family, individual foster care, or adoption. He also argued for additional backup services to help retarded people continue to live with their own families – services such as vacation homes, respite centers, and crisis assistance units.

The influence of several other perspectives can also be seen in community-based programs. The view that settings should provide retarded people with *protection and benevolent guidance* has not been entirely discarded in the move away from the large institution. While all programs must make some accommodation for protection, a number of models derive their daily practices in large part from this central theme. These include sheltered villages, many foster care homes, and some group homes for older adults.

Another view focuses more on the interpersonal climate a setting should strive for, termed by Sarason (1974) a *psychological sense of community*. Sarason concluded that the main criterion by which any program should be developed and assessed is whether it promotes a sense of belonging, mutual responsibility and purpose, and the experience for individuals to be a part of a group on which they can depend and to which they can contribute. While all community residences consider this criterion at times, for some group homes and sheltered villages it is the central concern influencing program decisions.

A final view held by some community residences is that a setting should provide intentional *training* for the resident – opportunities for skill acquisition in activities of daily living to increase his or her ability to function independently. Again, although training is a consideration voiced by most programs, it is the primary emphasis in some models, such as dormitories related to workshops or programs that prepare institutionalized residents for community living (see Chaps. 9 and 10).

Although all these perspectives have some merit and could be embraced in a single program, it is typical that a community residence is influenced mostly by one or two of these views. In fact, conflict between programs or among staff and residents in a given program sometimes results from different persons operating from different perspectives, often without being clear what these are. Ideally, for a retarded person to be placed in a program where the emphasis coincides with his or her particular needs, a number of program models would have to be accessible in any given geographic region.

Planning Comprehensive Systems

In Greek mythology we encounter a somewhat overly friendly character by the name of Procrustes. He wanted very much to be a good host to weary wayfarers, and when a traveler journeyed past his dwelling, Procrustes would insist that he stay the night with him. After some wining and dining, Procrustes would show his guest to his bed. Trouble was, there was only one bed, of one certain size, and Procrustes was a perfectionist. The bed just had to fit the guest. So if the guest was tall, Procrustes chopped off his legs until guest and bed were exactly of the same size. If the guest was too small, the host strapped him into a rack and lengthened him out a few inches. Obviously, by doing things his own way, Procrustes was prepared for all comers.

Wolf Wolfensberger, 1969

Impetus

The development, implementation, and coordination of multimodel systems is an enormous task that requires extensive planning. An early impetus for such planning on the state level was provided in 1963 by federal legislation that made grants available to states for planning comprehensive action to combat mental retardation (PL 88-156). Numerous task forces were established, and planners and lay citizens alike began to confront issues that previously had rarely been addressed. The need for community residential services was noted in most resultant state plans, although the specifics of implementation have varied widely among states.

Obstacles

One obstacle to developing comprehensive systems has been that state guidelines, at least initially, have usually promoted one specific program model that is influenced by the terms of court rulings, the particular bias of prominent spokespersons, and funding and other political realities. For example, Massachusetts, under a mandate to "fund the transition of 3,000 residents from the state schools to the community" in 4 years (Greenblatt, 1972) limited funding to group homes with houseparents and a maximum of nine residents, eight of whom must have come from an institution (along with a number of additional restrictions). Just across the border in Rhode Island, the only option available was semi-independent apartments, developed by a local agency to avoid the strict zoning regulations governing group homes. Hence a resident who required the structure and supervision of a group home would likely succeed in Massachusetts but fail in Rhode Island, while conversely, a resident ready for greater independence might succeed in Rhode Island and fare less well in Massachusetts. It is noteworthy that both states in recent years have expanded options to include group homes and semi-independent apartments.

Another obstacle to developing comprehensive service systems has been the reality that in most states some community facilities already exist, and bringing these together into an emerging system is probably more difficult than beginning anew. California, for example, as its primary model, licenses and supervises "family care" homes with six or fewer residents. Yet this state has also relied heavily on a great many "board and care" facilities, each housing 30 or more persons. These are essentially private, profit-making enterprises, typically unlicensed, with untrained staff (Edgerton, 1975). Often jealously protective of their autonomy, these programs are not readily integrated into a comprehensive system.

First Regional Plan

The nation's first region-wide plan of community residences was developed in eastern Nebraska, where there were few existing noninstitutional services. Through the successful political activities of parents and other citizens, the Eastern Nebraska Community Office of Retardation (ENCOR), a private, nonprofit corporation, provided a network of 10 models of community residences for adults and children, including children's hostels, adolescent hostels, adult training hostels, adult board and room homes, apartment clusters, supervised living units, coresident apartments, independent living, behavioral development residential hostels, and developmental maximization units (Wolfensberger and Menolascino, 1970). Within such a system, an individual's chances of having his or her particular needs met are obviously increased. Multimodel systems in other states and regions are evolving and are constituted differently. However, regardless of the specifics, a system with multiple options is necessary to maximize the chances for each retarded person to live successfully in the community.

As Close as Possible

Our study of the community residence movement was undertaken as a quest for diversity. As we have suggested, it seemed to us that to make available conditions for the retarded as close as possible to mainstream society would mean to create programs that reflect the considerable variability of that society. It would also mean creating settings with features designed to meet the special needs of retarded persons. And it would certainly mean creating training programs to help the retarded individual learn skills to enable him or her to move still closer to that nebulous construct of mainstream society. Further, it should mean helping that society itself to move closer to increased acceptance of differences. The challenge of these plans and provisions – and then of knowing each individual's abilities, needs, and desires well enough to make an appropriate placement – seemed both exciting and overwhelming. Therefore our descriptive study of existing programs was carried out in the spirit of examining what is available from the perspective of the comprehensive and effective system that could be developed.

2. Methods and Models

The Government is very keen on amassing statistics. They collect them, add them, raise them to the N*th power, take the cube root and prepare wonderful diagrams. But you must never forget that every one of these figures comes in the first instance from the village watchman, who just puts down what he pleases.*

Sir Josiah Stamp

IN considering methods for studying community residential models, we faced a dilemma. It appeared from newspaper accounts, our own experiences, and reflections about reasonable possibilities that a great many variations must exist in facilities and programs across the country. To visit all or even most of them would have been impossible. Hence we sent out a questionnaire nation-wide to survey and examine as many facilities as possible. A questionnaire, however, captures little of the richness and subtlety of a program or the quality of life of its residents. Therefore a more thorough on-site observational study was made of 17 residences in the Northeast. The survey data reported in this chapter reflect the national scope of the community residence movement. Also, the data provide a demographic backdrop against which we will subsequently view the selected community residences that we visited.

Survey Methods

Selection of Community Residences

In the spirit of exploring as many viable residential models as possible, our selection criteria were broad. We considered a facility as a community residence if it had been open more than 6 months, accommodated no more than 80 retarded adults, and regarded itself as an alternative to an institution.*

Survey Questionnaire
The 74-item questionnaire is included as Appendix I. The questionnaire sought information in the following eight areas:

1. History of the residence
2. Physical plant
3. Resident population
4. Staff and organizational structure
5. Rules and policies
6. Day and evening programs
7. Financial arrangements
8. Community relations and resources.

The questionnaire also asked the respondent to send any additional information about the residence that was available, such as newspaper articles, progress reports, photographs, or a budget.

Questionnaire Returns
Questionnaires were sent to 1,140 addresses between April and September 1973. The return rates are shown in Table 2-1. About 50 percent of the questionnaires were completed and, of these, 381 met the criteria for further analysis.

Community Facilities Surveyed

The recency and growth rate of the community residence movement are striking. The great majority of community residences have opened since 1960. Of the few that opened earlier, a number were group homes for former mental patients or older adults and while they served some retarded persons, they were not specifically oriented toward the retarded. Figure 2-1 shows community residences surveyed according to the year they opened, underscoring their rapid expansion in recent years.

*To obtain a list of community residences, letters were sent in the spring of 1973 to the Departments of Mental Health and Retardation and to the Associations of Retarded Citizens in every state; many letters were followed by phone calls. Replies were received from 49 states and the District of Columbia, although seven states reported they had no community residences at that time. Questionnaires were sent to community residences identified in the states, from lists received from associations and to others known to our staff. Also, the questionnaire asked for names and addresses of other community residences known to the respondent, thereby continually adding to the list. A preliminary letter explained the purpose of the project, advised that a questionnaire was to follow, and requested involvement. The questionnaire followed this letter by several days with a stamped, self-addressed envelope included for return. All residences that did not respond within 3 weeks were prompted at least once by mail.

Table 2-1
Return of the Survey Questionnaires

		Number of Questionnaires
Originally sent out		1140
Returned blank, no community residence	116	
Possible community residence pool		1024
Completed questionnaires returned		518
Questionnaires not included in survey statistics		
Primarily for children	46	
Program operating for less than 6 months	6	
More than 80 residents	11	
Comprehensive systems	6	
Inadequately filled out or not a community residence	48	
Arrived too late	20	
Questionnaires included in survey statistics		381

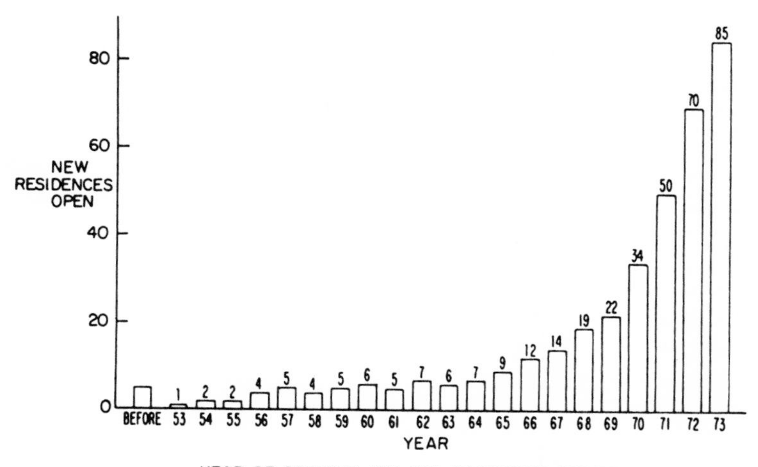

Figure 2-1
Year of opening for community residences in survey. (It should be noted that this figure may overestimate the growth rate of the community residence movement. By graphing opening dates only for residences surveyed, no account is given of other facilities that have already closed. Certainly a number of residences opened in earlier years and failed to stay in operation, while a few residences that opened in the year or two before the survey have already closed. Hence to the extent of the failure rate [unknown to us] the figure overestimates the growth rate of community residences.)

There is notable diversity in this movement. For example, a considerable array of available housing in communities has been adapted to serve as community residences. Most frequently used are large, old houses (54 percent), but community residences are also located in apartment buildings, apartment units, ex-hospitals, ex-hotels, farm houses, town houses, and even trailer camps, motels, and convents. Only 15 percent of community residences are located in new houses, and only a few of these were built especially as community residences.* These facilities vary in size, from places for one resident to comprehensive systems for hundreds. Considering location, community residences can be found in the smallest village or the largest city (Table 2-2), each in some way reflecting its larger surroundings.

Table 2-2
Location of Community Residences by Size of Municipality

Community Residence	N	Percent
Village (2,500 or fewer)	69	17.20
Small town (2,600–10,000)	78	19.45
Large town/small city (11,000–30,000)	67	16.71
Small city (30,000–100,000)	88	21.95
Large city (100,000 or more)	99	24.69

The considerable diversity in physical facility, size, and location is paralleled in other areas as well. The purpose and philosophy of a program, its sponsorship and decision-making processes, the criteria by which a resident is accepted, or the length of time residents are normally expected to stay vary widely, and each choice in some way determines the unique quality of life in a particular program. Variability, then, is an exciting hallmark of the community residence movement, but it is a frustrating characteristic as well, for comparisons that highlight important program features necessitate some classification of community residences.

Classification of Facilities into Models

All community residences are characterized by a group of retarded adults living with staff supervision in a facility that is smaller than the sprawling institution. Our search for one critical factor, or set of factors, to evaluate these facilities was futile, so our resultant classification requires some explanation. We sought to classify community residences into models based on variables that are reliably assessed and potentially most influential in determining the qualities of programs. Also, we tried to retain categories of models already in use in the field.

The majority of facilities were classified as *group homes,* a term that actually has been often used synonymously with community residences.

*Specific frequencies are sometimes omitted in the interest of readability, and statistics presented in the text are generally rounded to the nearest whole number. A table of exact statistics for the various models will be found in Appendix II.

These were subdivided according to size (number of residents served). Size is widely assumed to have a critical influence on the community residence program, and various state guidelines impose size limits, so it seemed desirable to categorize by size and then study how the programs relate to this variable. Thus group homes were classified as *small, medium,* and *large,* with a separate category, *mini-institution,* for programs so large that many persons would question the appropriateness of calling them community residences at all. Smallness, indeed, is basic to most people's conception of a community residence, and particularly typical of small and medium group homes is an emphasis on the philosophy of normalization.

With the exception of *sheltered villages,* which are a decidedly different entity, just about every facility could, in fact, have been called a *group home,* and divisions could have been based solely on size. However, there are some facilities where other variables, such as sponsorship and funding procedures, population served, or staffing pattern are sufficiently unique that they warrant separate consideration. For example, even though a foster family bringing several retarded adults into their home might resemble a small group home, their unique sponsorship and funding procedure probably affects their program; furthermore, the model of *foster family care* has long been recognized in the field as distinct from group home care, so despite some similarities to small group homes, we classify it separately. Similarly, when a group home is administratively linked to a sheltered workshop with an emphasis on an integrated work and living skills program, we have classified it specially as a *workshop-dormitory.*

Also, some group homes serve special populations, such as older adults only or mixed populations, including former mental patients. While these community residences could also be included in the general group home classification, our assumption is that a population that is unique will create other variables that will have more influence than size. There are many questions worth considering regarding characteristics of programs in community residences that have a particular population. Hence *group homes for older adults* and *mixed group homes* are considered separately. Finally, a small number of group homes has intentionally stressed independence by having staff present less than 24 hours a day, and it seemed important to consider these *semi-independent* facilities as a separate model and to examine the correlates of reduced staffing.

We have therefore categorized the community residences surveyed as follows, with the number of community residences in a category in parentheses:

1. *Small Group Home* (SGH), serving 10 or fewer retarded adults (132)
2. *Medium Group Homes* (MGH), serving 11 to 20 retarded adults (66)
3. *Large Group Homes* (LGH), serving 21 to 40 retarded adults (23)
4. *Mini-Institutions* (MI), serving 41 to 80 retarded adults (5)
5. *Mixed Group Homes* (Mix), serving retarded adults and former mental hospital patients and/or ex-offenders in the same residence (18)

6. *Group Homes for Older Adults* (OA), serving only older retarded people and often nonretarded people as well in group homes or rest homes (38)
7. *Foster Family Care* (FOS), serving five or fewer retarded adults in a family's own home; families are not governed by a board of directors, and they collect monthly payments for the care of residents (55)
8. *Sheltered Villages* (SV), providing a segregated, self-contained community for retarded adults and live-in staff in a cluster of buildings usually located in a rural setting (9)
9. *Workshop-Dormitories* (WD), serving retarded adults, where the living unit and a work training program are associated administratively and sometimes physically (16)
10. *Semi-independent Units* (SI), providing less than 24-hour supervision of retarded adult residents (19).

Two related program models that will be discussed but are not included in our survey results are (1) *community preparation programs* that prepare retarded adults for more independent living arrangements and usually operate within a public or private institutional setting and (2) *comprehensive systems* that operate several different models simultaneously through an umbrella agency. In such systems residents can move from one model to another as their needs and abilities change.

Comparisons Among Models

In Part Two the common characteristics of each community residence model will be discussed in detail. Now we will briefly consider some overall characteristics of community residences as well as how these models compare in terms of residents, staff, program, and turnover rate and subsequent placement.

Residents

The average resident is 35 years old and equally likely to be male or female. There are significant differences among models in age of residents, but not in sex.* The age difference is not surprising, however, since one model (group homes for older adults) had, by definition, older people. Yet it is interesting to note that the mean age was below 30 years for small group homes, workshop-dormitories, semi-independent units, and sheltered villages.

Residents were most likely considered moderately retarded (42 percent) or mildly retarded (32 percent). Severe retardation was infrequent (12 percent). Occasionally residents either were not retarded, or the retardation level was unclear, while a small percentage were multihandicapped.

*When differences are reported among models or are shown in figures, statistical tests (e.g., analysis of variance) showed that variability this great or greater could have occurred by chance less than one time in a thousand ($p < 0.001$). Therefore we feel confident that overall the models do differ in these areas. However, we cannot draw any further conclusions about differences between any particular two models without additional testing.

A *level of retardation* score for each community residence is based on a staff rating of each resident's level as mild (2), moderate (1), or severe (0) retardation. Hence a low score on this scale means severely retarded. The average level of retardation for each model is shown in Figure 2-2. Semi-independent, mixed group homes, and group homes for older adults have residents who are less intellectually retarded. A generally lower level of functioning is found in residents of foster care and sheltered villages, and this is important to remember when considering the programs in these settings (see Chaps. 7 and 8).

Almost half the residents came to the community residence from a state school for the retarded (48 percent); others came from their families (28 percent), a foster home or other community residence (13 percent), a hospital (9 percent), or the community (2 percent). Residents in group homes for older adults, sheltered villages, and workshop-dormitories most frequently came to the community residence from their families. In all other models residents came most frequently from a residential institution, in part reflecting the recent court decisions mandating alternatives to state institutions.

To some extent, differences among models in resident age, level of retardation, and previous placement reflect differing admission criteria. The most frequently cited admission restrictions relate to sex, age, work potential, behavior problems, and health. The extensiveness and variability of these criteria are illustrated in Table 2-3, a partial list of criteria in effect in community residences studied.

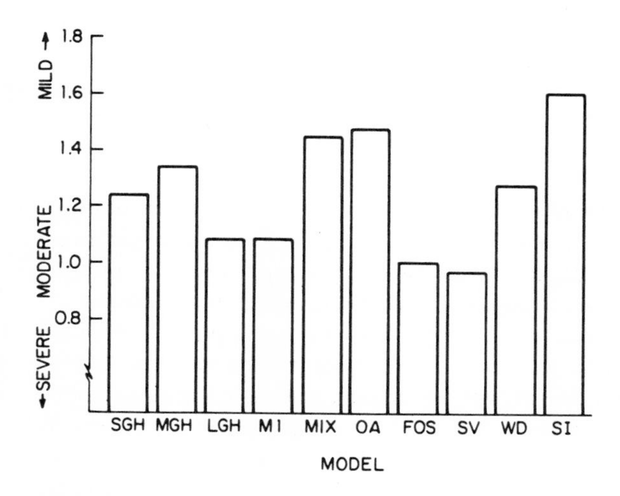

Figure 2-2
Level of retardation by model (lower scores indicate greater retardation).

Table 2-3
Some Admission Criteria Used by Various Community Residences

Some Admission Criteria Used by Various Community Residences
Over 18
At least 16
Under 50
Under 35
Must work in the community, in the training center, or in a sheltered workshop
Potential to benefit from the program
From the geographic area
Able to take care of personal being and possessions
Able to take active part in family-type program
Primary diagnosis: mentally retarded
Mildly or moderately retarded
Seizures, if present, are under control
Ambulatory and able to care for personal needs
Selected by other residents
Motivation to live and work in the community
Complete medical and dental examination
Physical stamina and health adequate for strenuous, full-time employment, verified by a physician's report
IQ falls within the approximate range of 60 to 80
Auditory, visual, speech, or orthopedic handicaps are admissable as long as the admissions committee does not judge them to be detrimental to job placement and vocational success
No history of delinquency or police record
Free of psychotic tendencies; e.g., hallucinations, delusional thinking, bizarre and/or uncontrollable behavior
Free of suicidal ideation
Demonstrates conformity to and understanding of the legal codes
Has a social security card

Staff

On the average, community residences had almost one staff member for every two residents. The staff-to-resident ratios varied significantly by model, from the least-staffed mini-institutions (1 staff member to 3.7 residents) and large group homes (1:3.4) to the most-staffed small group homes and sheltered villages (1:1.7). Unfortunately, our questionnaire did not distinguish between full-time and part-time staff, so these ratios overestimate the full-time equivalent staff that is available. The average community residence had two live-in staff members. The ratio of live-in staff to residents also varied significantly by model, with the larger facilities having fewer live-in staff members per resident. Although some type of live-in staff is usual in community residences, there are facilities that alternate shifts so that no staff person resides at the community residence; the particular staffing patterns vary widely among community residences and will be explored in subsequent chapters.

Program

Our greatest concern is with the community residence program itself, or how a resident experiences daily living. We want to be able to weigh the resident's autonomy against the inevitable restrictions, productivity against idleness, and growth against stagnation. We want to understand the extent to which the resident is an agent in his or her own life or is simply a passive recipient of the good will of others, and we certainly want to see what happens when a sense of community with others replaces the all-too-predictable isolation that occurs in institutions. The statistical picture that emerges from 381 community residences, representing 4,991 residents, suffers as much as it gains from the quantity of evidence. The individual resident, or even community residence, becomes lost in numerical averages and must wait for the closer delineation of models in later chapters to be, at least in part, found again. Here we will consider the broad parameters of community residence programs that in some ways shape a resident's day. We will compare the various models in terms of furnishings, rules and policies, resident responsibilities, and work placements.

Furnishings

As we examined the furnishings and allocation of space within community residences, we found that there is usually some consideration given to privacy and ownership of personal possessions as well as to provision of space for group interaction. Overall, community residences present a marked contrast to the institutions they work to replace; most have comfortable furnishings and many have inside locks on bathrooms (56 percent) and bedrooms (32 percent) for privacy. In the average community residence the 13 residents themselves own about two televisions, seven radios, three record players, and one musical instrument. Yet quasi-institutional dimensions remain. Residents have more privacy but typically still share a bedroom with another person. Bathrooms are not always homelike; about a quarter of community residences have bathrooms with more than one toilet. And while residents seem to have use of the telephones, only one resident in 65 has his or her own telephone.

While some lack of personalization and privacy necessarily accompanies group living, the trend in more recently opened facilities has been to move even further toward a homelike atmosphere than the previous descriptions imply. Small and medium group homes and semi-independent homes, due to both their philosophy of normalization and the generally more homelike potential of these smaller settings, have created the least institutionlike atmosphere. Of course, creating an environment that looks like other people's homes is only a first step – albeit an important one – toward normalized living.

Autonomy

Despite the widely voiced philosophy of normalization, community residences place considerable restrictions on residents' behavior, as shown in Table 2-4. Most have some curfew and bedtime, and deadlines of 10:00 P.M. or earlier are common. Alcohol consumption is often not permitted. Although most community residences permit residents to entertain guests of the opposite sex, many report restrictions on the place and/or time of these visits. Restrictions are likely somewhat greater than indicated in Table 2-4, since those places that profess to have "no policy" often have an unwritten code. Finally, for the resident seeking a vacation or overnight leave yet another restriction arises: In 83 percent of community residences, such leaves can be taken only with permission from someone.

An *autonomy scale* was derived from a combination of policies regarding entertaining the opposite sex, alcohol use, curfew, and bedtime. Autonomy was found to be highest in semi-independent community residences (Fig. 2-3). In group homes resident autonomy diminishes as the size increases, and in mini-institutions autonomy is lowest. The sheltered village affords residents a relatively high degree of autonomy, albeit within a more protected environment. The theme of autonomy and provisions for risk taking recurs throughout this book as we examine various models in greater depth.

Responsibilities

Program philosophies that stress normalized living or training opportunities should result in residents assuming increased responsibility for routine daily chores. The majority of residents do carry out household tasks or share this responsibility with the staff. Table 2-5 shows household responsibilities, ordered from highest to lowest resident involvement. Residents are most likely to be involved in routine inside tasks of cleaning bedrooms, setting the table, and doing dishes; they are least likely to be involved in tasks that require more skills, often outside and where errors are not as reversible, such as preparing meals and shopping.

Despite increased resident responsibility over that allowed in large institutions, for each task there is still a sizable number of community residences in which staff members assume responsibility exclusively. In some instances resident infirmity might preclude greater involvement; however, generally there seems to be more room to move toward a greater sharing of responsibility. Thus a *responsibility scale* was determined by combining the variables in Table 2-5, and this scale significantly differentiates the models, as shown in Figure 2-4.

As with autonomy, residents are found to assume the most responsibility for household tasks in semi-independent community residences. Residents assume the least responsibility in group homes for older adults; in fact, most models with older residents generally have residents performing fewer duties.*

*The correlation was $r = -0.51$, $p < 0.001$ between age of residents in a community residence and the amount of responsibility.

Table 2-4

Resident Autonomy: Policies Regarding Drinking Alcohol, Entertaining Nonresidents of the Opposite Sex, Curfew, and Bedtime

	Type of Restriction (percent)				*No Explicit Restrictions (percent)*		
	Not allowed	*Certain rooms*	*Certain times*	*Time and room restrictions*	*No policy*	*Policy leaves it up to resident*	*Total Percent with Restrictions*
Can residents entertain nonresidents of the *opposite* sex within the house?	5.6	27.5	7.8	29.4	16.6	13.1	70.3
						Policy allows drinking	
Are residents permitted to drink *alcohol* within the house?	60.7				18.8	20.4	60.7
	Curfew						
	8 P.M.	*10 P.M.*	*12 A.M.*	*Other*			
Residents are expected to be in the house by	16.8	34.5	6.7	24.9	17.1		82.9
	Bedtime						
	8 P.M.	*10 P.M.*	*12 A.M.*	*Other*			
Residents are expected to go to bed by	1.3	49.2	7.4	14.5	27.6		72.4

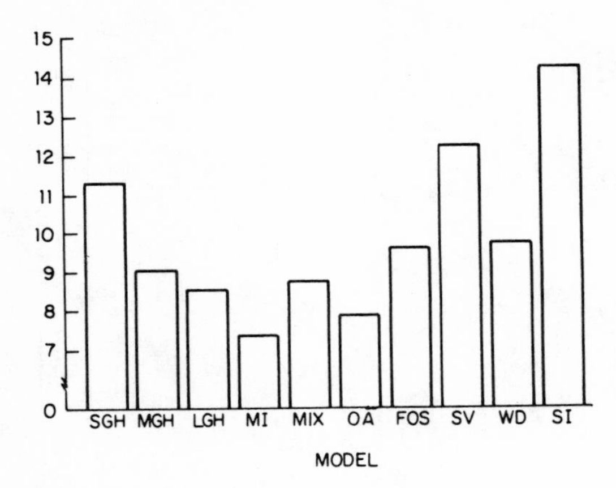

Figure 2-3
Resident autonomy scale by model.

Table 2-5
Household Responsibilities, in Order of Decreasing Resident Responsibility

	Percent of Community Residences		
	Residents exclusively	Staff and residents	Staff exclusively
Cleaning bedrooms	51	33	16
Setting the table	55	28	17
Doing dishes	43	37	20
Cleaning living and dining rooms	37	35	27
Cleaning kitchen	29	41	31
Doing laundry	32	33	36
Serving meals	23	39	38
Maintaining grounds	19	43	38
Preparing meals	10	41	49
Shopping for supplies	7	37	57
Shopping for food	4	33	63

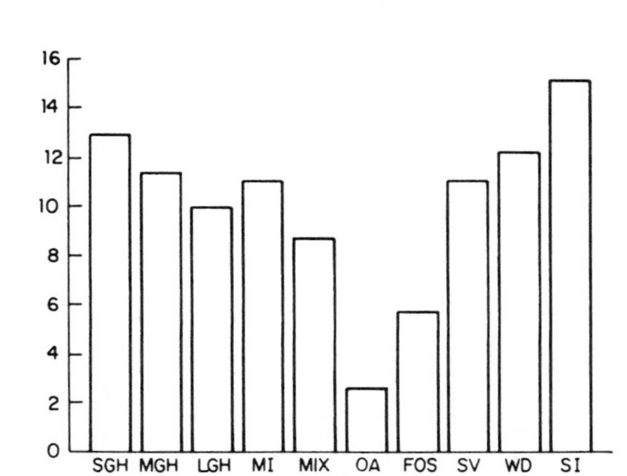

Figure 2-4
Resident responsibility scale by model.

Also, larger community residences with more staff might be expected to have more duties carried out by staff and therefore less resident responsibility. However, no relationship between size and responsibility was found; indeed, the small foster family care homes seem to involve residents relatively little in daily tasks.

Work. The extent to which residents can be engaged in a meaningful daily activity will be an important determinant of the community residence movement's growth and viability. While some residents are in competitive employment (Table 2-6), the largest proportion of residents work in sheltered workshops or other training programs. Unfortunately, a large number of residents have daily programs with little or no work relevance.

Table 2-6
Percent of Work Placements of Residents

Competitive employment	16
Sheltered workshops	43
Day activity centers	13
Work at community residence	10
No work placement	18

A combined *work scale,* shown in Figure 2-5, varies with community residence models. Residents in semi-independent community residences score highest in work, with high work scores also in small and medium group homes. Workshop-dormitories, by definition, have most residents in a sheltered workshop program and therefore score high. For residents in mini-institutions there seems to be relatively little outside work involvement. Finally, just as

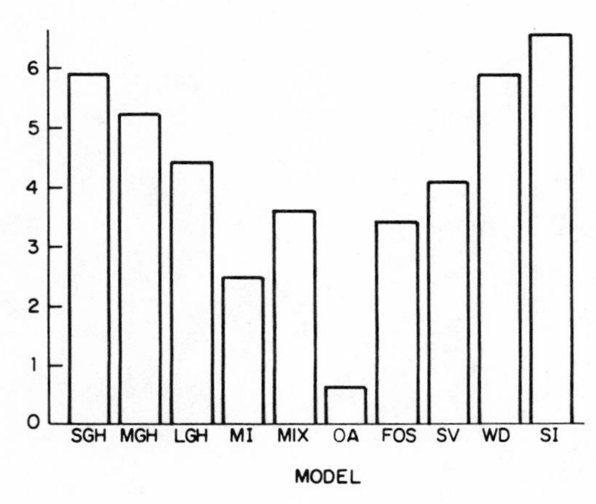

Figure 2-5
Resident work scale by model.

group homes for older adults severely limit resident autonomy and daily household responsibility, they provide little in the way of constructive daytime work placement.

Turnover Rate and Subsequent Placement. Three philosophies about the length of residence in community residences prevail. Most commonly, the community residence is viewed as a permanent home for residents (46 percent). However, in other community residences, this decision is made on an individual basis (26 percent) or the stay is limited to 6 years or less (28 percent). In fact, most community residences (82 percent) reported some ex-residents. Final discharge decisions are usually made by the staff or consulting professionals; residents are reported to have the main voice in discharge decisions in only 9 percent of community residences and to have *some* involvement in just half.

A *turnover score* was determined for each community residence, calculated as the number of ex-residents per place per year.* On the average each year, 56 percent of residents leave, or the average resident stay is only 1.8 years, a surprisingly short time given the views many community residences hold toward permanence.

This rate of turnover does not relate to the length of time a community residence has been open. However, it does relate strongly to the type of model. Figure 2-6 shows the variability of turnover by model.

The highest turnover is in mixed group homes. Remember, though, that both retarded residents and former psychiatric patients reside in mixed group

*For example, let us consider a community residence with a capacity for 10 residents that has been open 3 years and has 18 ex-residents. This averages to 6 ex-residents per year; since there are 10 resident places, the turnover score is 0.6 (or 6/10). If this is multiplied by 100, it converts to a percent and tells us that this community residence has a 60 percent turnover each year.

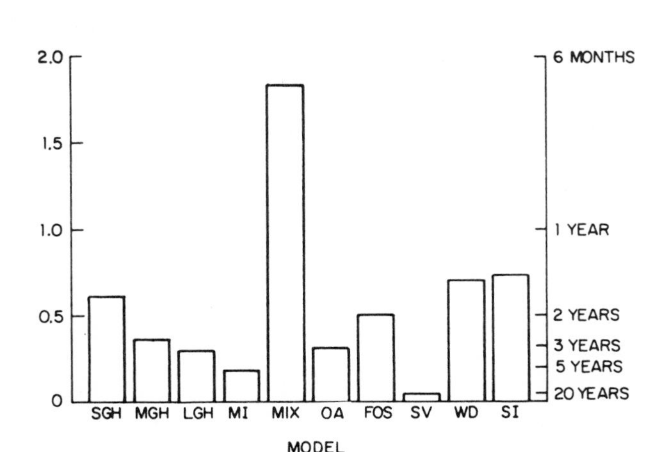

Figure 2-6
Resident turnover scale by model.

homes. Discharged rehabilitated psychiatric patients probably account for the especially high turnover in this model. Turnover rates in residences for just the retarded are highest in semi-independent residences and workshop-dormitories. Turnover was minimal in mini-institutions and sheltered villages.

Like most social services, community residences do not have well-developed follow-through plans; for example, only 35 percent carry out any automatic follow-up within 6 months of discharge. Nonetheless, community residences had a rather good idea of where most ex-residents were living. The types of living arrangements for ex-residents are shown in Table 2-7.

Table 2-7
Percent of Ex-resident Placements

Living independently	19
Returned to family	19
(Other) community residence	14
Foster family care	4
Returned to community residence	2
State institution or hospital	22
Elsewhere, unreported or deceased	20

In an average group of five residents leaving a community residence, one moves into independent apartment living, one returns to his or her family, one moves into another sheltered facility in the community, one moves into an institution, and one is unaccounted for.

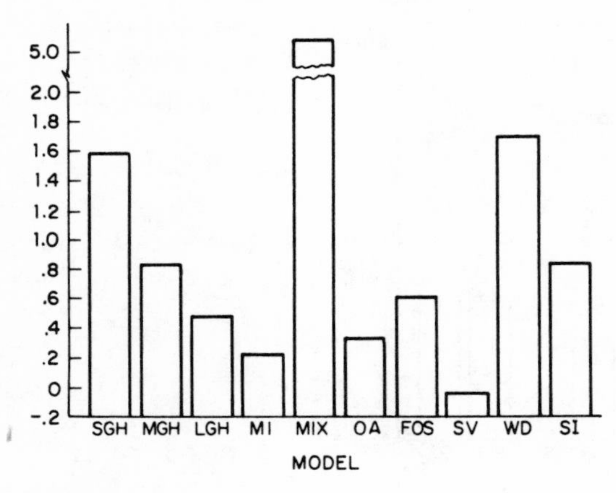

Figure 2-7
Resident desturn (destiny × turnover) scale by model.

These ex-resident placements were combined into a *destiny scale,* a weighted index of the degree of independence represented by the placement.* However, due to high variability, differences between models were not significant.

By combining the turnover rate and the degree of independence achieved in each placement (turnover × destiny), Figure 2-7 reflects both the quantity and quality of ex-resident placements.

Apart from mixed group homes, the most successful flow of residents appears to be in the workshop-dormitory and small group home; the most likely placement for ex-residents from these models is to their own families. As group home size increases, however, the quantity and quality of ex-resident placements decrease somewhat. Also, most frequent ex-resident placement in group homes for older adults and sheltered villages (elsewhere or unreported) is not reflected in Figure 2-7, since it was uncodable; it appears, though, that the main way persons exit from these facilities is by dying.

Summary

This overview of community residences reveals some differences between models. We have generally seen that the more recently developed models (e.g., semi-independent, small group home, workshop-dormitories), which are most often based on philosophies of normalization and/or training, are

*The destiny scale is a measure of ex-resident placements from a community residence, scaled according to the extent of independence represented by the placement. The weights chosen, more so than for other composite scales, represent our particular value system. In any case, destiny was calculated as follows: percent of ex-residents in own apartment ×(5); percent of ex-residents with family or another community residence ×(3); percent of ex-residents in foster care or returned to the community residence ×(1); percent of ex-residents in a hospital ×(−3); percent of ex-residents in institutions for the mentally retarded × (−5). Mortality rates are not reflected in the destiny scores, for although destiny after death may be variable, it is as yet uncodable!

more apt to serve young residents, provide a higher degree of autonomy and resident involvement in community residence responsibilities, ensure a daytime work placement, and discharge residents sooner and to more independent living arrangements. However, in all the categories we considered there are still gaps between the expressed normalization philosophy and actual practice. As group homes become larger, life within them is apt to become less normalized as well. Those facilities for more than 45 residents, which we call mini-institutions, were consistently low in autonomy, work involvement, and turnover. Sheltered villages, foster family care homes, and group homes for older adults were more likely to be permanent placements, although their daily programs varied considerably. These findings raised many further questions, which were probed at on-site visits, during which staff and residents were formally and informally interviewed, daily routines were observed, and field staff members shared, however briefly, the experience of living in the facility.

Visits to Community Residences

In selecting residences to visit we tried to choose programs that seemed from the questionnaire (or other knowledge) to represent the model favorably. All the 17 facilities contacted about visits agreed to participate.*

This project was not an attempt to evaluate the residences, but simply to describe some of the existing programs. Interviews and observations were intended to lead to a better understanding of the quality of daily life for residents and staff. Also, an account was made of the "typical day" and its concomitant rules, policies, decision-making procedures, daily living responsibilities, and experiences outside the residence. For example, we were especially interested in how community residences resolve questions of autonomy and risk taking and how residents react to restrictions on their autonomy. We were also interested in how the programs adapted for residents of various ages, levels of functioning, or prior experiences. Also, through questionnaires and interviews, attitudes of the participants toward the community residences were sought.

Staff members were interviewed about the philosophy behind the program, their goals for residents, their own felt needs, and their attitudes toward both

*These residences were located in Massachusetts (7), New Hampshire (1), Rhode Island (1), Connecticut (1), New York (3), Pennsylvania (3), and Michigan (1). Visits were made by four two-person (male/female) teams during July and August 1973. Nine residences were each studied by a team for four consecutive weekdays at the beginning of the summer and by the same team for an additional 4-day sequence (including a weekend) approximately 1 month later. Six other residences were visited for only one 4-day period. Two additional visits were made by two staff members for 2 days each in fall 1975.

Visiting teams sometimes lived at the residence, usually ate meals there, and attended most on-going meetings and residence activities. They received a receptive welcome in every facility, and only in rare instances were they excluded from full participation in activities. It was clear from the visiting teams' experiences that community residence staffs are eager to discuss their programs, share ideas, and seek support.

the job and more general issues in the field of retardation. The effects of staffing patterns and personal characteristics of staff members on the program's success were of special concern. Eighty-one residents were interviewed about their satisfactions, dissatisfactions, and desires concerning areas such as moving to the residence, daily life in the residence, work, and leisure time. In some cases, ex-residents were interviewed about their preparation for leaving and experience of moving out of the community residence. A detailed history of the residence was obtained, as well as information about sponsorship, funding, the physical plant and its furnishings, and the neighboring community. When possible, community attitudes were assessed directly by interviewing neighbors and/or community shopkeepers nearby.

In the section that follows, we turn to a more detailed look at the various community residence models and the issues raised by each. We will begin with the most prevalent model, the group home.* In this section, descriptions of models are divided into the following topics: (1) place and people, (2) program, (3) community, and (4) sponsorship and funding. In some models, however, not all topics were found to be significant and therefore are not discussed.

*To preserve anonymity for the settings visited and for persons interviewed, the policy was established to use pseudonyms for the community residences; the two exceptions are Camphill and Transitional Services, very large programs that would be identifiable in any case due to their uniqueness. Permission was obtained to use the real names of these programs.

II. Models: A Closer Look

Section 1. Group Homes

THE models described in this section are all variations on the basic model of the group home, the most widespread community-based alternative for retarded adults. Although there is much diversity among group homes, these programs are characterized by a group of retarded individuals residing in existing community dwellings, with live-in supervisors who help them cope with the exigencies of daily life. Given that the interest in community residence programs grew out of an aversion to enormous, impersonal, and isolated institutions, it is understandable that the primary alternative advocated has been small, familylike dwellings located most often in existing community homes and residential neighborhoods. The emphasis, indeed, in most group homes has been on a normalized environment, in which the natural comforts and supports of "living as others do" would help residents to get over the psychological stresses that had attended institutional life.

Aside from scattered earlier efforts, the movement to develop group homes for retarded persons is generally traced to the mid to late 1960s. These programs looked for guidance to the Scandinavian system described in Chapter 1 and to the psychiatric halfway houses in the United States. Short-term transitional facilities for patients moving from the mental hospital to the community had been opening over the previous decade, so that by 1963 Raush and Raush (1968) were able to survey 40 psychiatric halfway houses and see a "movement" in the rapid, though undirected, growth.

Halfway house was, by then, a familiar term, with images of transitional facilities providing short-term guidance, respite, and therapy to persons halfway away from the institution's confines and customs (Glasscote, Gudeman, and Elpers, 1971). The expectation was that ex-patients would soon move the additional half way to independent living (although actually a number of these facilities became more permanent boardinghouses). The terms in the movement away from institutionalization of retarded persons, which was to follow, reflected somewhat different expectations. The facilities were to be group homes or residences, with the implicit expectation that they might well be long term or permanent, but with a commitment that they would not be institutional.

As states drew up guidelines for group homes, a major distinction arose in the number of residents such a facility might accommodate. New York, for example, distinguishes a group home (7 to 12 people) from a group residence (13 to 25 people). Massachusetts limits a group home to 9 residents; Nebraska limits a hostel to 12; Washington defines a group home as 20 or fewer residents; while in Michigan facilities having 25 to 50 residents are considered group homes. Yet there is little evidence available about how life in a group home varies with size. We have categorized 226 group homes according to their size.

The *small group home,* considered in Chapter 3 and representing over one-third of community residences surveyed, has been promoted by adherents to the normalization philosophy. Most images raised by the word *institution* are dispelled by the picture of a comfortable house on Main Street, where 10 or fewer retarded adults live with two staff members sharing daily responsibilities.

Certainly this picture is still quite unlike the way most other people live, but for many it may be as close as possible, and its characteristics warrant careful study.

Larger facilities *(medium group homes, large group homes,* and *mini-institutions)* have potential drawbacks, since they may approach the impersonality, restrictiveness, and custodialism of the institutions they seek to replace. Yet these larger programs have potential benefits as well, such as more differentiated and specialized staff roles. We will consider these models in Chapter 4.

Finally, the *mixed group home,* including persons who are former psychiatric patients, ex-offenders, and retarded persons, offers both advantages and dangers in the opportunity for retarded persons to view a wider range of other kinds of behavior. We will consider this model briefly in Chapter 5.

The following exchange took place between an interviewer and Frank, a resident of a halfway house.

INTERVIEWER: Do you think it's a good thing to have more houses like this one?

FRANK: A lot of kids from the school want to move out here and make it by themselves. They're bored at school. Most of the bright ones are gone – they're going to close down that place . . .

INTERVIEWER: You called the people at school "kids"; are they children or adults?

FRANK: While they're at the school they're kids; you're an adult only when you get out here.

INTERVIEWER: What are the things you do really well?

FRANK: Making salads, cooking, working; I'm a good friend.

INTERVIEWER: What are the things you're not so good at?

FRANK: I screw things up once in a while – it's in my mind. I don't know how to take a vacation. They'll have to teach me.

---

3. Small Group Homes

A community residence is categorized as a small group home quite simply if it is small (between 6 and 10 residents) and if there is a group living in a single dwelling; 132 programs in our study met these criteria. A distinguishing characteristic of this model is the staffing pattern. Most often, a small group home is staffed by two houseparents or housemanagers, typically a young married couple, and a third staff member, a relief person or an assistant housemanager. Sometimes, too, a house director is hired on a full-time or a part-time basis to handle administrative matters. Full-time house directors are employed most often when a sponsoring corporation operates or intends to operate more than one home.

The average small group home had been open for 4 years. In keeping with their general philosophy of integration with the community, small group homes are usually situated in residential neighborhoods. Their programs attempt to provide daily living experiences as similar as possible to those of nonretarded persons. To the extent that they teach residents, small group home programs tend to emphasize the mastery of activities of daily living, relying heavily on day placements for work-skill training.

Place and People

Small group homes tend to be situated in large, old houses in urban residential and suburban areas. Fully 74 percent are located within one-half mile of public transportation, thus providing residents with the opportunity for increased mobility to other parts of the community and to their work placements. There was an average of eight residents living in each small group home. Usually, two residents shared a bedroom. The mean age of these residents was 29, significantly lower than the overall average in the survey.* Thirty-five percent of

*In this and subsequent chapters all differences reported between the model and the pool of other models were statistically significant ($p < 0.01$).

residents were considered by staff to be mildly retarded, 48 percent moderately retarded, and 13 percent severely retarded. The remaining 4 percent were handicapped, nonretarded individuals. More so than in other models, residents in small group homes tended to come from institutions for the mentally retarded (55 percent).

Program

Most small group homes are philosophically and programmatically oriented toward the principle of normalization. The espousement of this philosophy does not necessarily provide specific guidelines for in-house programming, but it does provide a common language to those involved in the community residence movement.

In small group homes, there is about one staff person for every two residents, creating the potential for excessively close supervision of residents' activities. In actuality, however, residents in small group homes have a significantly greater degree of personal autonomy and responsibility for household tasks than do residents in many other types of community residences (see Fig. 3-1). Almost 80 percent of residents were involved in a work-oriented day activity, another normalized feature of small group homes (see Table 3-1).

Table 3-1
Work Placements of Residents in Small Group Homes

Competitive employment	21%
Sheltered workshop or educational program	51
Day activity center	16
No work placement	12

The movement of residents through small group homes to other facilities is evident in the model's turnover rate. Each year an average of 62 percent of residents in small group homes have moved out of the community residence to a variety of community and institutional settings (Table 3-2). The model of small group homes has contributed to the process of deinstitutionalization and to the integration of retarded adults into the community.

Community

Small group homes involve the community in the operation of the house to a significantly greater extent than all other models combined. A variety of local groups provided the impetus for beginning these community residences, including nonprofit corporations, parent groups, and concerned citizens. In the process of opening, 83 percent of the houses made efforts to prepare the surrounding communities for their presence, talking primarily to parent groups, neighbors, and city government representatives. However, 40 percent of community residences met with some opposition from the communities, typically neighbors' complaints and zoning disputes. Community members are

Table 3-2
Flow of Residents Through Small Group Homes

Percent of residents who previously lived at:	
1. State or private institutions for the retarded	54.7%
2. Family	29.8
3. Foster family	3.3
4. Another community residence	3.5
5. Hospital	1.9
6. On own in community	1.7
7. Other or not known	5.1
Percent of ex-residents who went on to live at:	
1. Own apartment	24.0%
2. Family	26.5
3. Foster family	5.1
4. State or private institutions for the retarded	15.4
5. Another community residence	9.4
6. Hospital	3.5
7. Other or unknown	16.1

often involved with small group homes on an on-going basis as volunteers or board members.

Sponsorship and Funding
Fully 87 percent of the small group homes reported that they operated under the aegis of a corporate structure, administered by a board of directors. Financial support for these houses was derived primarily from state funding and residents' payments. The average monthly fee paid by residents in small group homes at the time of our survey was $170.

Conclusion
Small group homes were found to be quite high relative to other models in those program dimensions held to be important by the normalization principle: autonomy, staff-to-resident ratio, responsibility, and work. However, the small group home model deserves critical reexamination because of the 19 percent of ex-residents who have returned to institutions and hospitals (see Table 3-2). This fairly high "failure rate" raises questions about the appropriateness of such a model for all residents. Since small group homes account for the largest proportion of community residences, descriptions of two small group homes are presented in detail on the following pages. In addition, information from two other programs will be integrated into the later discussion of issues. In reading about these community residences, it might be useful to consider the following questions:

1. How is the program philosophy of normalization put into practice in every-day life?

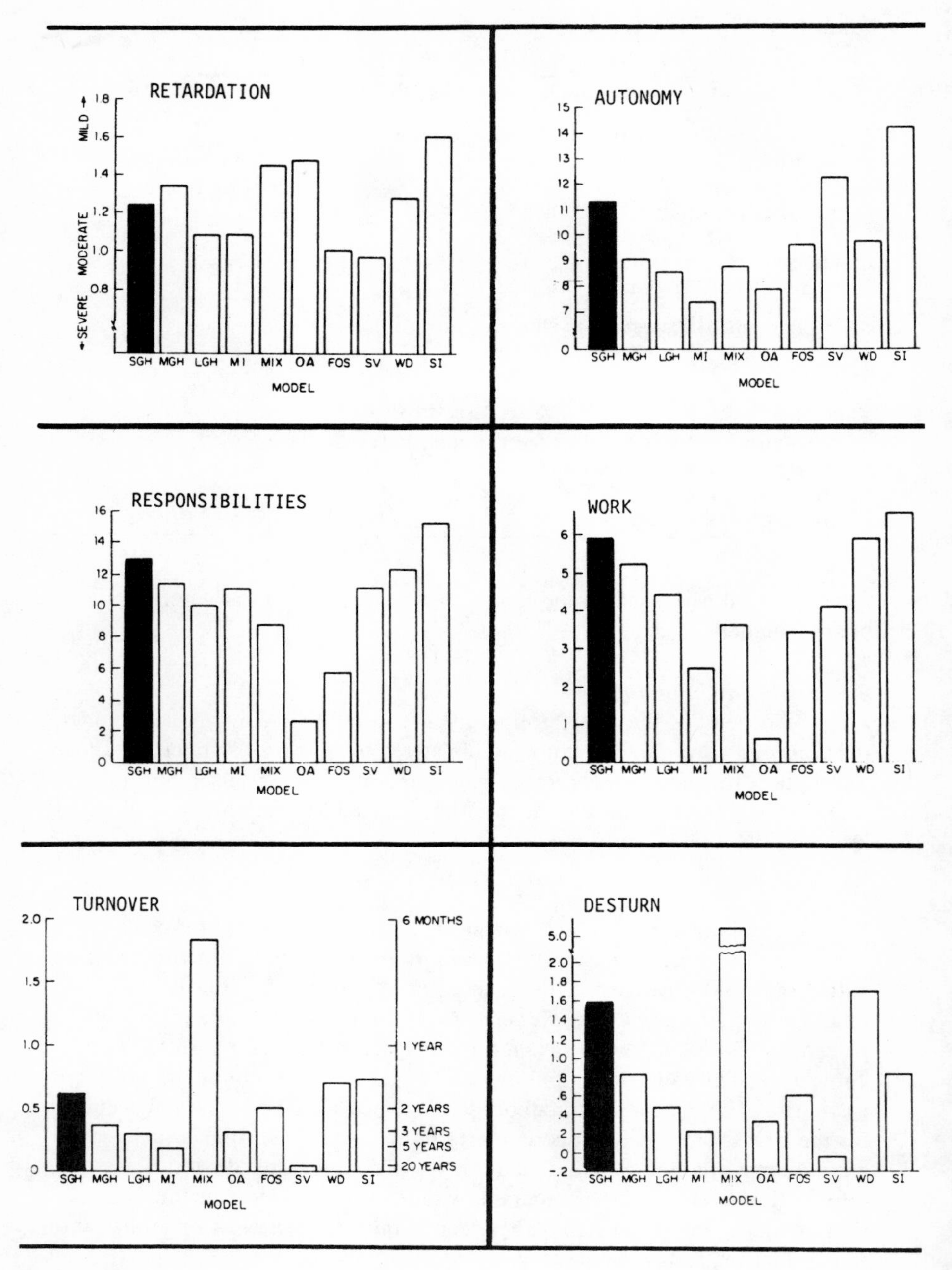

Figure 3-1
Major scales by model.

2. How does the self-definition of a small group home as either a permanent or a transitional facility influence the program?
3. What assets and liabilities are inherent in the staffing pattern of small group homes?
4. How does the interface between the community and the small group home influence the residents?

Arcade House

Setting

Located in an eastern seacoast city of 43,000 people and near a large metropolitan area, the house on Arcade Street had become home for nine male and female residents and three staff members. (For the sake of clarity we will call this home Arcade House even though it had no name, only an address.) The state had only recently allocated hundreds of thousands of dollars to promote the rapid proliferation of small group homes primarily to accommodate persons from state schools. The corporation that sponsored this home had been formed in response to the state's mandate. Arcade House was the first of seven proposed small group homes to be sponsored by this corporation, composed of professionals and lay people from the surrounding towns.

Once the elegant residence of a prominent fire chief, Arcade House sits on the corner lot of a now lower-middle-class neighborhood. Within two blocks of the house are supermarkets, laundries, restaurants, and public transportation. The house, which is by far the largest on the block, has an attached four-car garage equipped with a stage and floor-to-ceiling velvet curtains. Once used as a theater for garden parties, the garage is now used for storage and recreation.

The house itself has 18 rooms, five of which are bedrooms for the nine residents, and two of which are bedrooms for the staff. The house is in excellent condition, spacious, and comfortable. The living room, newly furnished and set aside for reading and quiet music, is infrequently used by the residents. Instead, they gather either in the sun room, which is filled with plants, or in the television room. The dining room is large, the walls covered with hand-painted murals of the New England seacoast; dinners are served at a table that seats fifteen. The kitchen is also large and affords space enough for four persons to eat breakfast seated at the table at any one time, as well as ample room to prepare large meals.

Sheila's and Karen's Room. Once the master bedroom of the house, the room is large and sunny. With pink curtains and flowered wallpaper, it is lovely and inviting. Especially luxurious is the blue-tiled bathroom opening directly off the bedroom, an extra feature that Karen puts to good use. Karen's side of the room (and most of the bathroom) is filled with makeup, skin creams, shampoo, and hair curlers. The carefully arranged bottles and tubes remind us that Karen's physical appearance has become increasingly important to her since leaving the institution.

In marked contrast is Sheila's side of the room. Her dresser, night table, and TV stand are filled with adolescent romance and travel books, one of which she reads each evening before going to bed. Sheila's love of books increases as her reading improves. She attends a night school class at the institution where she formerly lived.

What is distinctive about this room is Sheila's and Karen's imprint – they have made it personal and cozy, and a visitor can sense their pride.

Staff

The staffing pattern of Arcade House is typical of the small group home model: There is a full-time housemanager, Nancy; a part-time staff person, Sam (her husband); and a relief housemanager, Dave. All three live in the residence. Nancy takes responsibility for most of the day-to-day operation of the house, as well as for counseling residents and teaching them skills. She describes her job as "helping people to get acclimated to community living and offering them challenges so they can realize their potential." For her, as for many, the least satisfying aspects of the job involve the lack of privacy and limited time for herself. She emphasizes that, because of the taxing emotional involvement with the residents, she would like to participate regularly in some activity outside the house; leaving the scene and having another interest would help her maintain a more objective perspective about her role as a housemanager.

Her husband, Sam, was hired to work part time (evenings and weekends) in the residence and is free to attend graduate school during the day. Sam's attitude toward his work is frank and disquieting. He says he took this job to provide a satisfactory work situation for his wife and would have no interest in working at the house were it not for her needs. He mentions that he typically spends no more time with the residents than the residents spend with each other, and that ideally he would like his role to be "nothing more than another person living in the house." He emphasizes this stance by saying that since he began working at the house, he has neither learned nor wanted to learn any new skills that would allow him to perform the job more adequately. He does not believe that the house should provide any formalized treatment and thus feels that just being himself is sufficient. His only formal responsibilities are bookkeeping and attending board meetings.

The other staff member, Dave, was hired to spend approximately 10 hours a week on the job to relieve Sam and Nancy. Actually, he spends more time in his role because he lives in the house and has become involved with the residents in a personal way. He seems to assume the male role model that Sam intentionally avoids. Dave feels that three single individuals would function more effectively as house staff than would a married couple and one single person because the couple brings to the job the added problems of a marital relationship.

Residents

At the time of our visit, nine residents lived in Arcade House, five men and four women, ranging in age from 22 to 53 years (average, 35). Eight individuals had previously lived in institutions for the mentally retarded, while Frank came directly from his parents' home. The residents varied considerably in their level of retardation, with Vineland Social Maturity Scale scores in the range of 29 to 95. Dick was clearly the lowest functioning person in the house. He had a very limited vocabulary, was unable to travel in the community on his own, was awkward in his gait, and often referred to himself as being "9 years old." At the other extreme was Frank, who had previously lived with his family and who was unusually well acquainted with the local community. Frank was frequently observed reading the sports section of the newspaper, signing up for local community activities, and taking long walks to visit friends. The skill development of the other residents fell at various points between these two extremes.

It is important to note the changes in Dick's and Frank's community adaptation after they had lived at Arcade House for 7 months. Dick progressed. He began to orient himself to the community and was beginning to recognize the subway stop near his workshop. His vocabulary expanded, and he became less desirous of the role of small boy of the house. His increased assertiveness provides testimony to the fact that lower functioning individuals can adjust and make progress in small group homes.

Frank, on the other hand, was less successful. Having been out of work for some months, he spent most of his time taking long walks or hanging around the house. Although he had tried to maintain first a competitive job and then sheltered employment, he quit because he was bored with the work. Since lack of employment was a violation of one of Arcade House's most stringent rules (the necessity for maintaining a regular daytime activity), the house staff members were becoming increasingly uncertain about Frank's future in the house. Even the possibility of placing him in an institution was being considered, despite his high level of community functioning. This paradoxical finding of a low functioning person making a better community residence adjustment than a more able peer was observed repeatedly. We were again alerted to the fact that success or failure is determined less by the individual than by how he or she fits into a particular program. With this in mind, let us examine the Arcade House program.

A Typical Day

8:00 A.M. — Two women eat breakfast at the kitchen table while a third cooks some eggs. One man searches through the refrigerator for some bologna to make a sandwich for lunch. Nancy, the housemanager, stands and hastily drinks a cup of coffee before driving her husband Sam to school. The other residents sit in the sun room, talking about the subway ride to work and the stops they will pass.

9:00 A.M. — Eight of the residents have left for the workshop, leaving only Frank, who is unemployed, at home. He leafs through the morning newspaper.

10:00 A.M. to 4:00 P.M.	The house is quiet and empty, except for Nancy and Frank. They are in and out all day, Nancy doing errands and Frank taking long walks.
5:00 P.M.	The residents are now home from work. Two (a man and a woman) set the dining room table for dinner, while two women help Nancy prepare the roast beef. A few residents are in their bedrooms, resting after work. Dave and the remaining two men listen to rock and roll records upstairs.
6:00 P.M.	The residents and staff are still at the table, lingering over their ice cream, talking in small groups. Sheila and Karen are discussing the rodeo they plan to attend this weekend, while most of the others mention incidents from their day at work. Nancy interrupts the conversations to mention that the board of directors of the sponsoring corporation of the house will meet here tonight – everyone will have to pitch in and clean up. With only a little reluctance, they all get up from the table to begin.
7:00 P.M.	The dining room and kitchen are clean. Frank reads the sports page of the paper and occasionally talks to another man who sits and smokes. Two others work on a jigsaw puzzle in the large garage, while a woman gingerly handles a stack of 78-rpm records left in a pine cabinet in the garage by the previous owners of the house. A record player can be heard from one bedroom and a TV from another. The sounds of country music and a situation comedy mix strangely together.
8:00 P.M.	The board members begin to arrive, and they congregate in the dining room with the staff. All nine of the residents remain upstairs, in their bedrooms or the TV room, during the entire meeting.
11:00 P.M.	The house is quiet; the meeting is over and the board members have left. Most residents have gone to sleep, but the sounds of the TV can still be heard. The staff members straighten up the dining room and talk about the meeting.

Program

The staff of Arcade House note that program goals are still in the process of being developed. This process takes the form of negotiation between the house staff and the members of the corporation, because the housemanagers believe that house rules and policies should be formalized by approval of the board of directors. As a result the board tends to make conservative decisions on these issues, but that does not discourage the staff from involving the board in the policy formulation process. Issues that have arisen include the extent to which residents will be supervised while in the community residence and the kind of sexual behavior that will be tolerated. In both of these areas, residents' autonomy had been restricted as a result of the compromises reached by the staff and board of directors. Residents of Arcade House, then, do not make the *major* decisions about issues that affect them, although they do have control over the less significant decisions of daily life, such as the planning of recreational activities.

In contrast to the reduced autonomy afforded to residents is the considerable shared responsibility for performing the tasks necessary for maintaining the house. Residents take care of their own bedrooms, and each has a weekly housecleaning job. Nancy prepares all weeknight dinners; residents assist by setting the table and washing dishes. Residents practice cooking skills by preparing their own breakfasts, lunches, and weekend dinners. Although the major weekly shopping for the house is done by Nancy, she delegates to the residents the responsibility for purchasing small items. Residents learn cooking and shopping skills as they perform them; there is no formalized teaching or individualization of responsibilities except in the degree of assistance Nancy gives to each resident.

When delineating the program goals of a community residence, a major influence should be the policy on length of stay of the resident. The staff of Arcade House was in conflict over this issue: For some residents the house was to be a permanent home, for others it was to be transitional, and which residents actually fell into each category seemed as yet undefined. Since rules and policies were negotiated between the staff and the corporation members and then imposed on *all* residents, it would seem especially important to be clear as to whether the placement generally was to be permanent or transitional. In fact, the absence of monitoring, planning, and carefully formulated, individualized service plans with thoroughly specified long- and short-term goals differentiated Arcade House from a more ideal transitional community residence.

The lack of well-formulated strategies for securing day placements was also a deficiency of the Arcade House program. Although several of the residents seemed to be appropriate candidates for competitive employment, all eight who had previously lived in institutions were employed at sheltered workshops. The house staff felt that all residents could profit from some initial experience in sheltered employment; yet, after working in these settings for many months, all but one (Dick) felt that they would prefer some other kind of job in the community, such as taking care of children, working for a radio station, or working in a candy store. In response to these wishes, the house staff was thinking of locating potential employers in the community.

Frank's plight highlights the potential problems a small group home risks when its work and program philosophies are not carefully articulated and implemented. Although possessing the prerequisite skills for living successfully within the house and working in the community, Frank clearly needed more independence and on-site job skills as well as training in assertiveness and decision making. Had Arcade House articulated its policy either to be a permanent residence or to be a transitional one, more care could have been taken in selecting residents whose needs could best be met there.

Community

Approximately 6 months prior to our visit, the corporation purchased the house and hired the houseparents. The day before they moved out, the previous owners informed several neighbors that a group of retarded adults would be the new occupants. In response, the next-door neighbor quickly organized a meeting of community people and representatives of state and local government to be held at Arcade House. Then they scheduled an open meeting at the city hall so that neighbors would be able to vote to determine whether the small group home would be permitted to open. At the city hall meeting, the houseparents presented a slide show highlighting differences between life in an institution and in a community residence. In addition, they offered to create a neighborhood advisory board to enhance communication between the community and the residence. Despite the apprehension of many neighbors, when a vote was taken, the majority of those present indicated support for the house.

Subsequently, resident interaction with the local community was limited to friendly relations with a few neighbors. There were no community volunteers, and the neighborhood advisory board, negotiated before the opening of the residence, was never established. When interviewed, many owners of stores patronized by residents were unaware of the community residence's existence. This low community profile was partially due to the residents working outside Arcade City and maintaining most of their social contacts with other handicapped people, either from their workshop or from the institution in which they lived previously. Residents at Arcade House have brought their institutionalized peers to the community residence for weekends and have attended dances and night classes at the institution. The strong commitment to continuing this institutional involvement is demonstrated by the residents' traveling for up to 2 hours on public transportation to reach the state school. Despite this apparently strong tie, all the formerly institutionalized residents of Arcade House said that they preferred living in the community.

Arcade House's key link to the community was through the residents' families. Six residents have maintained an active relationship with their families, who live either nearby or in the same city. Dick's mother is a member of the sponsoring corporation, and other families interviewed remained informed about their child's and other residents' progress. Most residents go home on weekends, attend family functions, and go on vacations with parents and siblings – an absence from Arcade House that permits the staff some relief, but burdens them, on the other hand, with assuming the surrogate family role for those who remain behind. It seemed that most residents view their families' homes as their true home, a perspective that could hamper further moves toward independent housing but which may still be advantageous in that it provides residents the local stability that a community residence with a transient house staff tends to lack.

Sponsorship and Funding

As stated earlier, Arcade House is sponsored by a local nonprofit corporation formed specifically for the purpose of operating this community residence and potentially six others. The executive board of the corporation takes responsibility for the selection of staff and residents, maintenance of community relations, and formalization of general rules and policies in conjunction with the house staff. The board delegates the responsibility for the day-to-day operation of the house to the staff. Because Arcade House is part of the state system of community residences, it receives state funding for staff salaries. In addition, the state's Developmental Disabilities Council provided start-up funds for the purchase of furniture, appliances, and other necessary housewares. Finally, residents paid a monthly fee of $120, a set fee that came from such sources such as Social Security, veterans' benefits, and wages.

Conclusion

One of the key problems facing the corporation of Arcade House involves the short-term commitment of the staff. The three in-house staff members plan to remain on the job for one more year; the house director, a full-time employee, plans to leave at the same time. Although it is assumed that members of the corporation will continue to be involved with Arcade House beyond the 1-year period, no single staff person has made a long-term commitment to the house.

Arcade House is still in a formative stage of development. Many questions are left unanswered: When a resident enters Arcade House, can he or she ever expect to move out? What will happen to the resident who chooses not to find a job? Do the housemanagers have enough time and energy to deal simultaneously with the problems posed by residents and the problems within their marital relationships? Should the board of directors determine in-house policy, or should this be solely the domain of the staff, and should not the residents be consulted in the policy-making process?

Halfway House

Setting

Midway up Henry Street is a brown stucco wood-trimmed house. It is of moderate to large size. Weeds are visible on the front lawn and are pushing their way through the winding asphalt driveway, where an old Dodge pick-up truck is parked. In front of the somewhat dilapidated garage stands a second-hand bike, missing its front fender. Although the lawn is not neatly manicured and the house is not freshly painted, a real estate agent might list the home as "ideal for a couple with means and a large family." Approaching the front porch, one notices the comfortable-looking Salvation Army–type couch and armchair. This halfway house for six retarded men, with no sign or name, blends well with the other houses on Henry Street.

Situated in Green Meadows, a city with a population of less than 25,000, Halfway House is located about half a mile from the city's center where, almost daily, the residents patronize the numerous shops, banks, the post office, and YMCA. Green Meadows appeared to be receptive to having halfway houses within its scenic, primarily middle-class neighborhood, and there are other homes in the city serving residents who are labeled as alcoholics, drug addicts, and delinquents. Although there is public transportation available in the city, there is none within the immediate area of the house; consequently, residents walk to most destinations within about a mile, and staff members typically drive residents when they need to go farther.

The interior of Halfway House is decorated in contemporary thrift-store-specials style, somewhat run down, but clean and comfortable. The appliances are in excellent condition, including the used dishwasher that the residents chipped in to buy for $40. Each of the three floors in Halfway House contains what could be a separate apartment, although each floor does not have a separate entrance. The first floor has a living room, dining room, and kitchen used commonly by residents and staff. In addition, there are three bedrooms and a bathroom for the four residents on this floor. The second floor apartment, which has a living room, kitchen, bathroom, and two bedrooms, is used primarily by staff and affords them more privacy than is typical in small group homes. On the third floor is an apartment that offers the two residents most ready to move into their own apartment the opportunity to practice independent cooking, shopping, budgeting, and cleaning.

Halfway House had been in operation for two years when we visited. Through the combined efforts of the local Association for Retarded Citizens and the director of the Department of Mental Health's local catchment area, the house had been bought and the staff positions filled. The staff decided to inform the community about the small group home by placing an article in the community newspaper; the residents moved in without incident.

Staff

One week prior to our first visit the original houseparents at Halfway House moved out of the residence, and one week prior to our second visit the new staff moved in. The relief staff member provided coverage and continuity during the month between the two sets of houseparents. This transitional period provided us an opportunity to observe a not infrequent occurrence in the life of a small group home.

A negotiated set of responsibilities was characteristic of the original house staff. One of the original houseparents, Bill, assumed the administrative and community outreach responsibilities. He dealt with public agencies, employers, and the residents' potential landlords. Also, he spent time counseling residents and teaching them community skills, although he considered these aspects a secondary responsibility. His wife, Helen, and the relief person, Greg, also had well-defined roles which they exchanged with each other after about a year and a half. Initially, Helen's responsibilities included cooking instruction, shopping, and budgeting, while Greg's role was teaching academic skills. Helen and Greg exchanged responsibilities for two reasons: First, both were feeling a bit bored with their respective teaching areas and felt that a change would improve the quality of teaching; and second, Greg believed that the residents would benefit from learning that cooking and cleaning were legitimate responsibilities for men as well as for women.

Helen and Bill felt that they were very effective in their roles as houseparents throughout the first year and a half. However, during the final 6 months on the job, pressures built up significantly. Their own 9-year-old son was not getting enough of their attention, and they, as a couple, did not have enough free time to themselves. The baby they were expecting would be sure to demand even more time. Helen and Bill conjectured that had the staffing pattern been different, they perhaps could have remained in their jobs longer and been more effective. Bill would have preferred a staffing pattern in which two sets of house staff alternated with each other. Helen, too, felt that more backup staff would have relieved some of the daily pressures that ultimately hastened their departure.

The new houseparents, Karen and Rick, were friends of Helen and Bill, and they had frequently visited Halfway House. Their decision to replace Helen and Bill as house staff was well deliberated, and they had the resultant luxury of knowing the residents over an extended period of time before moving in. Still, Karen perceived that their most immediate problem as houseparents would be gaining trust and respect from those residents who resented their presence. When they did become the replacements for Helen and Bill, they found that the previously friendly attitude and fluid rapport established with the residents had changed to distrust and resentment.

Overall, Karen felt optimistic about her plans for her job as a houseparent. She did not anticipate that she and her husband would have trouble working together and believed that she could adjust easily to the lack of privacy. Both Karen and Rick felt the house needed more rigorous programming, planning, and supervision. Rick wanted to intensify special education programming, and Karen intended to implement some behavior modification programs. Yet they did not intend to institute any formal differentiation of roles within the house, envisioning a fluid and dynamic interaction between them.

The two sets of houseparents each espoused somewhat different program ideas, foreshadowing the impact changing house staff would have on the residents. The impact of staff change is felt all the more intensely when two (a couple) of the three staff people leave a small group home at once. Rick and Karen had what seemed to them to be well-articulated goals for the residence – what remained to be seen was the agenda that the residents had in mind for Rick and Karen.

Over a dinner we shared with the residents of Halfway House, they talked about some of their feelings related to the transition in house staff. Rick and Karen had not yet moved in.

ARCHIE: One thing, you can't beat Helen and Bill, that's one thing.
VICTOR: They're leaving on account of the baby.
ARCHIE: It's cause it's much too crowded here.
VICTOR: Too much.

ARCHIE: It got crowded and that's why they moved over there. It would have been too crowded over here with the baby. Right?

*GREG:** I think that was part of it. They wanted to have time to be with the baby.

INTERVIEWER: How did you learn that they were leaving?

JAY: They told us.

ARCHIE: They told us they were going to leave about a month before.

GREG: Victor, are you sad to see them go?

VICTOR: I was glad to see them go on account of the little child. Now they have a baby plus the boy. With this house the way it is, they . . . .

ARCHIE: In a way I hate to see them go, but there's nothing I can do.

JAY: They're so nice, you know.

ARCHIE: Bill was so nice, and she was so nice too. There's nothing I can do about it. I hate to see them go, but what can you do?

GREG: You can still see them.

INTERVIEWER: How do you think it's going to affect the way you live here?

ARCHIE: Everything's gonna change since they are through.

GREG: Will things be better or worse?

FRANK: Worser.

VICTOR: Well, I think Rick and Karen will be better.

GREG: How come, Vic?

VICTOR: Because everything will be nicer, and the rules will change and things like that.

JAY: It will be OK. They're different people, you know.

ARCHIE: I think they're going to be good people, though. They'll bring their big dog, too.

VICTOR: A short-haired German shepherd. They also have a baby.

GREG: What do you guys think of having a baby around? (Laughter)

JAY: Crying out at night and everything. Everything else keeps you awake, why not a baby too?

GREG: It ought to be pretty good when they move in. Karen is a nurse, and that will be good when you guys aren't feeling good.

ARCHIE: Oh, that's why she goes to that . . . what do you call it? Her nursing place.

GREG: The important thing is that you guys make them feel at home right away.

JAY: Yeah. Help them. But you'll be here, Greg, won't you?

GREG: Yes, but not all the time. I figure they'll probably need plenty of help from you guys too.

INTERVIEWER: What did you guys think would happen when you first heard that Helen and Bill were leaving?

JAY: We didn't know exactly what would be our future, you know. We were used to them.

ARCHIE: When I first heard that they were going, I said, "Oh, no." Just like that, I said, "Oh, no." I said, "We're going to miss you," and he said, "You can come over and see us whenever you want to," and I ain't gone over there since yet. Just once, when Greg told me to bring the check to Helen.

*Greg is the relief person. All others are residents.

GREG: Have you guys seen Helen and Bill's baby?
VICTOR: I saw it in the car.
ARCHIE: It is kind of cute, isn't it?
FRANK: Was it nice?
VICTOR: I remember the first time I want to see it. I saw Bill and her together and the baby. That was it. The baby had blond hair.

Residents

The most salient characteristic of the six male residents (the capacity is eight) in Halfway House seemed to be the differences among them. While Bobby held his makeshift microphone and bellowed out the date he imagined the spinning 45-rpm record to have made the hit parade, Chuck was meticulously painting in the defined spaces of his paint-by-number clown replica. Outside, Victor was sweating from his bicycle trip up and down the driveway, while Frank was actively engaged in a game with the neighborhood children. When Archie returned home from a clothes-buying spree, Jay inquired mockingly why he had wasted so much money on underwear that no one could see. The clothes buyer was not sure of how much he had spent since he had handed the salesperson a 10-dollar bill and trusted that his change was correct – impression management seemed more important to him than money.

Residents of Halfway House all came directly from institutions. They were eager to leave these institutions, offering reasons such as, "It was like a battlefield there"; "I was bored there"; and "I decided to live on my own." Only one of the residents (perhaps the most intellectually capable) felt that he was not happy now because he was "lonely without women."

Helen and Bill originally expected residents to be more capable than they now perceive them to be, even though all the residents had fairly sophisticated self-care skills before moving into the house. In fact, residents' scores on the Vineland Social Maturity Scale were in the range of 55 to 83, somewhat higher than those of residents in the other small group homes visited.*

Sunday at Halfway House

10:30 A.M.	Archie and Jay are sitting and talking to each other in the living room, while Chuck eats his breakfast alone. All other residents and staff are still asleep.
11:30 A.M.	Everyone is awake now. The early risers, now finished with breakfast, are watching TV in the living room and talking

*This discrepancy between initial expectations and current perceptions is especially important because it was almost unanimously voiced by staff interviewed in other community residences as well. High initial self-help skills and social maturity as measured by most instruments are less than perfect predictors of residents' abilities to solve problems, deal with contingencies of group living, and negotiate in the community. There is perhaps a greater potential for disillusionment with relatively high functioning residents who show initial promise of rapid and smooth movement toward independence. After these residents spend months and sometimes years in the community residence, time marked by repeated and unpredicted failings, however minor, it is understandable that houseparents would progressively feel disappointed and somewhat personally to blame.

to an ex-resident, Hank, who has dropped by. The dining room seems to be the hub of activity: Frank eating breakfast, the houseparent folding laundry, and the other staff members talking among themselves. Victor takes his breakfast alone in the kitchen.

12:30 P.M. Some residents, staff members, and friends are cleaning the garage, while another group stays inside, watching TV and leafing through the *Sunday New York Times*. Archie waits on the porch to be picked up and taken to an uncle's birthday party.

1:30 P.M. The house is quiet except for the sounds of the Marx Brothers on TV. Three residents are out of the house on errands or visiting. The others prepare to go to the beach. Two dogs chase each other through the house.

2:30 P.M. The sounds of Laurel and Hardy fill the nearly empty house; two ex-residents, Hank and Barry, half doze and half watch. Chuck sits alone in his room. At the sound of the ice cream truck's bell, only staff members run out to buy.

3:30 P.M. The TV group has changed channels to a Lon Chaney movie. The houseparents are in the yard, and the rest of the men are still out visiting or at the beach.

4:30 P.M. Finally the TV is silent! No activity inside except for one resident, Frank, who is cleaning the kitchen, ready to prepare supper. A group of residents and staff sit talking in the yard.

5:30 P.M. While the residents and staff eat supper together, friends of the staff watch TV in the living room, seemingly comfortable yet separate from the activity of the house.

6:30 P.M. In the kitchen, some staff and residents discuss a problem one ex-resident, Hank, is having. Meanwhile, the friends of the staff continue to watch TV with Bobby while Chuck sits nearby, staring into space. In the dining room, Jay counts his pills and transfers them to a pillbox.

7:30 P.M. The baseball game is on TV, capturing much attention. On the front porch Hank angrily discusses his living situation with some residents. Archie stands out on the street talking with the ice cream man.

8:30 P.M. The game still dominates the living room. All the residents are watching by now, except for Chuck who sits alone in the yard.

9:30 P.M. Chuck, who has been sitting in the yard now watches TV; as he watches he slaps his leg in a bizarre manner. All others have retired to their bedrooms, except for Victor, who rides his bicycle in the back yard.

10:30 P.M. All residents are asleep by now, except for the solitary TV viewer, Jay.

Program

Halfway House, as the name implies, is a transitional facility between the institution and independent living. This goal of transition is envisioned for all residents, despite the fact that its attainment will take varying lengths of time for different individuals. Staff members realize, however, that unless they continue to recruit what they perceive as "higher level" residents, the goal of providing a temporary residence will not be realized; places will progressively be taken by "permanent" residents instead.

During the 2 years that Halfway House has been open, five men have moved out. Two have returned to the institution, one at his own request and the other to have plastic surgery, after which he will return to the house. A third ex-resident, Barry, moved to a boarding house and is employed at the local sheltered workshop. Two other ex-residents, Hank and Jack, share an apartment and are competitively employed.

Residents at Halfway House have a great deal of independence and autonomy. There are no house rules, and the only restrictions are those based on the needs of each individual, such as limitations on drinking for one resident, Frank, who had been arrested for disorderly conduct, behavior that occurred whenever he drank in public. Also, every resident is involved in all phases of in-house responsibilities except for grocery shopping.

Frank and Archie are competitively employed at a local motel as helpers to the chambermaids. They often work together and express similar feelings about their jobs: "There are no bosses standing over you, and they don't tell you what to do." Archie was previously employed at the local sheltered workshop, but was "flunked out" due to an alleged lack of ability. He has, however, continued to succeed at his current, more demanding job. The other four men are working at the sheltered workshop, although they expressed some dissatisfaction about their work there. Three men resisted going to work, complaining bitterly about how boring the work was.

Hank and Jack are ex-residents of Halfway House and have been friends for many years. They moved from the institution to Halfway House together, and after living there for a year rented their own two-bedroom apartment. Hank, 35 years old, is a mechanic's helper at a car dealership in town. He plans to work there until he retires (at age 65). Jack works in an ice cream and sandwich shop as a handyman. He is also very satisfied with his job and spends his free time bowling in a league.

Both men feel that their stay at Halfway House prepared them well for independent living, by teaching them time and money skills, housework, cooking, and "how to meet people." Although both said they were pleased to live independently, Hank feels that Jack does not have sufficient respect for his privacy. In fact, Hank suspects Jack of rifling through his drawers and even stealing some money.

It is interesting to note that the issue of privacy never came between them when they lived in the institution – where there is little privacy – or when they were roommates in the group home. But now, when they have achieved an independent status, this issue has become important. Deinstitutionalization, it would seem, continues beyond the point of moving into one's own apartment.

Community

One noteworthy characteristic of the residents at Halfway House is their very well-developed repertoire of leisure time activities. For example, Victor has taken swimming lessons at the YMCA; Bob collects rock and roll records; Chuck paints by numbers; and Jay reads *Popular Mechanics*. Together, the men go swimming, fishing, and "hang out" at a sandwich shop. For all these activities, they have been able to use preexisting community facilities, rather than relying on specialized services for handicapped people. This situation can be attributed to the efforts of Bill, who during his years as houseparent spent much time developing community contacts. Because he and his wife planned to remain in this city for many years to come, their relationships with townspeople were as members of the community, rather than as transients living there only because of a job. Bill joined the softball team, and Helen was involved in activities in their son's elementary school.

Almost every community member we interviewed was enthusiastic in their praise of Halfway House and the residents – more so than in any other setting visited. Included in these interviews were employers of the residents, professionals in mental retardation, an ice cream truck driver, and the proprietors of several local businesses. The immediate neighbors, however, presented generally neutral and uninformed opinions of Halfway House, stating that they did not interact with the residents more than any other family on the block. Here we have an example of what might be considered a normalized integration into a modern community: positive relations with some persons, and few, if any, contacts with anyone else.

Sponsorship and Funding

The financial characteristics of Halfway House are different from those of Arcade House in that Halfway House is not a part of the state system of community residences. Each houseparent receives a full-time separate salary; couples are not paid as a unit.

The sponsoring group is the local Association for Retarded Citizens. At the time of our visit, Halfway House residents paid $130 per month; out of this, $15 per week was spent for food and small maintenance costs, and another $15 was paid to the corporation to pay house bills. Members of the corporation rarely interacted with residents, nor were they a part of the day-to-day operation of the house; rather, they delegated all such responsibility to the house staff.

Issues Particular to the Small Group Home Model

Arcade House and Halfway House, both classified as small group homes, each have their own distinctive characteristics – differences and similarities that speak to more general issues about this model. Where relevant in our discussion, we will draw from our visits to two other small group homes, North House and West House.

Community Involvement

The avenue of entry into the community differed for Arcade House and Halfway House, and this difference foreshadowed the relationships these houses maintained with their respective communities. Halfway House, by announcing its arrival post hoc in the newspaper, began its "Here we are" relationship with the community, a posture that had repeated itself many times during the 2 years the house had been open. Arcade House, on the other hand, was met with immediate community reaction that effectively made it separate and oppositional to the community, even though it was "allowed" to open. At the time of our visits, Halfway House residents used the local YMCA and the community swimming pool, while Arcade House residents went to a social group for retarded citizens in a city 45 minutes away or returned to the state school for dances. Halfway House residents were regular customers of the ice cream man and volunteered to clean at a local coffee shop, while Arcade House residents rarely used the local banks and post office and knew few shopkeepers. Halfway House residents were all employed locally, while Arcade House residents traveled into the metropolitan city for work.

Yet to attribute Halfway House's more responsive relationship with the community solely to the initial entrée (or to resident or staff characteristics) would be somewhat misleading; we need to examine, as well, the differing receptions that each community offered to the small group homes. While Green Meadows had already successfully absorbed five halfway houses for different disability groups, Arcade City had gone on record in other cases as being against halfway houses for any disability. Some advocates argue that, given the many battles that small group homes have to fight in getting established, changing community attitudes to effect a semblance of integration may be a battle too difficult and too long to warrant the effort. Others argue that the retarded have as much of a right to live in a community as the neighbors who oppose them, and therefore that community opposition represents an attempt to abridge the civil rights of the retarded, an attempt that should not be met with passive aquiescence. Certainly, there has been an effort to select more receptive towns. And while a resistant community can often be made less so by a community residence's presence, this process may be at the expense of the residents.

Physical Setting

The programmatic and psychological messages of a community residence are spoken as much by the physical setting as by the words of staff, brochures, and schedules. Halfway House's stated goal for residents was a transition to a more independent setting, and the furnishings within the house clearly paralleled the type of decor that residents living independently on marginal incomes could expect to afford. Arcade House, on the other hand, had plush carpets and modern furniture, appealing, but well beyond the income bracket of the residents, as if to say, "Stay around, you'll never afford me on your own." Halfway House further suggested transition by offering separate apartments for the more independent residents and a separate unit for the staff. Privacy and independence – a life of one's own – were values conveyed by the allocation of space to residents and staff alike. The benefits to both seemed substantial. Arcade House had more than ample space, especially given the four-car garage, to move in this direction if it so chose, but, like the other two small group homes we visited, there was a strong programmatic emphasis on the "family group," with its implicit message to staff and to residents of "deny yourself for the needs of the group."

Staff Morale and Turnover

Complaints of a lack of privacy and of time to oneself, while commonly voiced in all models, were loudest here. For these married couples, who were both in the same job, who had minimal living space and no home to retreat to and who were on duty almost constantly, there often seemed no escape. The Halfway House staff members were in a slightly better position in that both couples were somewhat older and married longer than the other couples interviewed. They had considerably more commitment to an involvement in the local community; each person was paid a separate and equal salary; they had a more separate living unit; and both couples had children of their own. Still, they too expressed dissatisfaction with a number of aspects of their jobs and resultant life-style.

In three of the four small group homes visited (the exception was Halfway House), at least one member of the staff said that if given the opportunity to do it over, he or she would *not* take the job again. In contrast, not one staff member from any other program visited felt this way. In effect, the small group home's staffing pattern ensures a short-term *institutionalization* of staff (who live and work in the same place) as it attempts to *deinstitutionalize* the residents. Staff members, demoralized by the experience, have a rapid turnover, about once every 2 years; and, of course, turnover of houseparents in a small group home represents a change in a much greater proportion of the total staff than in other models with larger staff and/or unmarried staff people.

This staffing pattern creates other problems, especially regarding actual and felt effectiveness. Staff members in small group homes serve a generalized rather than a specialized function. They must respond to all needs of residents and cannot deal intensively with any one need without ignoring others. The results were obvious in the four small group homes we visited. Not one of these settings simultaneously provided instruction to residents in new skills, satisfied their emotional needs, and effectively integrated them into the general community. Instead, each house seemed to attempt to specialize in one of these areas (e.g., West House had an educational program, while Halfway House emphasized community integration), but none fulfilled all vital functions. It seems that the small group home staffing pattern cannot cope with the enormously demanding goals it sets.

Over a 1-year period, one small group home, North House, made significant changes in its staffing pattern. Two successive sets of houseparents had come and gone, finally being replaced by three single people, called housemanagers. The single housemanagers, who had defined responsibilities, seemed to be functioning quite competently and happily in their roles. Also, in-house programming had developed considerably because a psychologist had been hired to provide services to residents and consultation to the staff; thus the need for specialized staff had been acknowledged and was being provided in this small group home, certainly to the advantage of the residents.

Sex-Related Policies

A recurring question, raised mostly by house staff, was whether a residence should be coed. Given the prevailing ethos that a small group home is to be "family style," are residents in a coed community residence supposed to relate as brothers and sisters? The question is not intended to be facetious; the two small group homes visited that were coed (Arcade House and North House) were, in fact, perplexed about how to treat the sexuality of residents. All the small group homes visited expressed a need to provide sex education for residents. However, Arcade House had, indeed, provided a sex education course and was now considering ceasing instruction since residents had, naturally, begun to experiment with their new (or perhaps not so new, but at least now verbalized) knowledge. The reaction of the staff at Arcade House was to institute a dress code (no pajamas and/or nightgowns out of one's bedroom) and to designate a common room for socializing, since bedrooms had become off limits for guests of the opposite sex. External pressures such as consideration of what the neighbors would think often became the rationalization for the implementation of rules to inhibit sexual activity. Single-sex houses, such as Halfway House, had not instituted these restrictive rules, perhaps because they did not have to deal with the issue daily. Obviously, the issues of coed housing, sex education, and sex-related policies are complex.

House Policies and Risk Taking

Policies regarding in-house responsibility varied. For instance, residents in Halfway House had more responsibility for their daily living than persons in the other small group homes visited. Supper at Arcade House was far more appetizing and elegant than at Halfway House (on a given evening, Arcade House serves roast beef while Halfway House has chili), but Arcade House residents have little involvement in the menu selection and meal preparation. In these and other areas the staff at Halfway House facilitated the development of resident interests and skills by allowing them the dignity of risk taking in their daily living activities as well as by individualizing each resident's programs.

A related question is, Who should formulate house policies? In Arcade House, the house staff forced the sponsoring corporation into developing house policy, while Halfway House avoided sponsorship involvement with in-house policy.

At North House it was advantageous that the corporation (in particular, the director) was intimately involved with house policy, given the rapid turnover of houseparents. However, the nature of this involvement in Arcade House seemed to be detrimental to the growth of the residents. As long as small group homes continue to be run by transient staff, it seems essential that members of the sponsoring corporation remain actively involved with in-house policy. However, Raush and Raush (1968) in their study of psychiatric half-way houses found that lay persons were *less* likely to take risks than were professionals, a finding borne out in the experience of the small group homes we visited. It would obviously be desirable to have more permanent staff and more individualized policies for each resident – issues that will be reconsidered in Chapter 14.

4. Larger Group Homes

A distinguishing characteristic of larger group homes is their program diversity. Such program variability, if developed to best meet the needs of a client population, might be able to maximize the services available to the resident who, for example, would benefit from either (1) a more specialized or more generalized staff or (2) a more diverse or more similar peer group. However, the larger group home models have not always arisen from a careful assessment of the needs of a given group of potential residents. More often, a model is selected on the basis of such factors as the availability of a facility, the bias of a sponsoring group, zoning restrictions, or the guidelines of a state bureaucracy. Consequently, the variability existing in the programs of different models of group homes is largely unplanned.

This chapter will consider group homes that are larger than those we have designated as small group homes (Fig. 4-1). In the survey, there were 94 facilities with 11 to 80 residents; these were designated as follows: medium group homes, 11–20 (N=66); large group homes, 21–40 (N=23); and mini-institutions, 41–80 (N=5).

The five facilities that were large enough to be designated mini-institutions might have been excluded from the sample, but they were included to give a more accurate picture of the relationship between group home size and program.

There are several potential advantages to a larger facility:

1. The greater number of staff members could allow for more well-differentiated roles and some specialized functioning. Also, duty shifts could result in better staff morale than in programs where houseparents live in and assume more all-inclusive responsibility. The net result may be better resident training.

2. The larger number of residents could allow for subgrouping according to individual needs, and specific programs could be developed for given subgroups. For instance, the "need" of one resident in a small group home of eight for sex education, a special workshop, or a pool table might remain unmet, while a

Figure 4-1
Possible sites for large group homes.

similar need of four residents in a large group home of 32 could inspire development of a special program.

3. The larger facilities could be less expensive per resident to operate.

There are obvious potential disadvantages to a larger facility as well. Not only is a medium or large group home a bigger financial and administrative undertaking, it is also less likely to integrate as a "normal" home within a community. With these considerations as a background, we will examine the larger group home models.

Medium Group Homes

By a medium group home, we refer to the 66 facilities in our sample serving 11 to 20 residents. As we have noted, some states' guidelines make the presence of medium-sized facilities more likely by setting upper limits on size, falling within the 11- to 20-resident range. The largest number of medium group homes in our sample were in Washington (13) and Nebraska (8).

Place and People

Medium group homes most frequently use large old houses, although a variety of buildings such as ex-hospitals, ex-convents, and apartment houses are also used. The average size of 15 persons per residence is not really representative of this model; in fact, the medium group home distribution is bimodal. Many houses have 11 or 12 residents and are philosophically and programmatically very similar to smaller, family-style group homes. Many others have about 20 residents, with larger physical facilities and more complex staffing patterns.

As with smaller group homes, two staff members live in each residence. However, on the average, only five staff members work at each medium group home, or one for almost every three residents. This staff-to-resident ratio is significantly lower than the 1:1.7 for small group homes. (However, the survey did not distinguish well between part-time and full-time staff, and some staff members in both small and medium group homes work only part time.) While no typical staffing pattern emerges, a number of medium group homes with 11 to 14 residents have two houseparents, one or two part-time relief persons, and possibly one cook or housekeeper working part time. Thus while serving 50 percent more residents than the small group home, these medium group homes operate with a similar staffing pattern.

Medium group homes with 20 residents are apt to have a more varied staffing pattern and include some additional staff who can provide specialized training in self-help, community living, vocational training, and other skills. One such group home, for example, has a director, two teams of husband and wife live-in houseparents (the first for 4 days and the second for 3 days), a job developer (10 hr/wk), a counseling social worker (10 hr/wk), a part-time maintenance man, and a cook. Others are likely to have activity or recreation therapists, especially for weekends. The cost of this kind of staffing is no greater, per resident, than in small group homes, and the alternating shifts may help maintain houseparent morale.

Program

The residents in medium group homes were slightly older and slightly, although not significantly, less retarded than those in small group homes. Nevertheless, greater restrictions than in other models are imposed by house rules governing alcohol use, bedtime, curfew, and entertaining the opposite sex. It seems likely that the diminished staff ratios have led to stricter imposition of house rules.

There is considerable contrast among medium group home staffing patterns. For example, consider two facilities, which we will rename Urban ARC and Family Home. Urban ARC serves 15 residents in a large old house. Most are mildly retarded, with some residents labeled moderately retarded. One resident is competitively employed, while all but one of the rest are in a sheltered workshop placement. Family Home serves 13 residents, somewhat more retarded than in Urban ARC, though with a similar work pattern; three are competitively employed; the remainder are in sheltered workshop or day activity placements.

Yet these two similar facilities have remarkably different staffing. Urban ARC has two full-time and eight part-time staff members, filling roles of houseparents (2), home supervisor (1), residential services director (1), substitute houseparent (4), cook (1), and housekeeper (1). Other staff members, such as counselors or maintenance workers, are occasionally used. (There are also four social workers, two workshop counselors, two psychologists, three counselors, and a dietitian outside the house who provide some service to Urban ARC.)

Family Home, on the other hand, is a private residence. Mr. and Mrs. H. bought an 18-room ex-convent next to their former home, moved in with their three teenage sons, and began a group home for retarded persons. "Mom" and "Dad," as they are called by residents, have only a part-time laundress to help, and Mr. H. has a full-time job elsewhere. Several outside social workers and vocational counselors have input as needed. However, Family Home is essentially just that – a family-style group home.

The amount of responsibility given residents for in-house daily chores and the number of residents competitively employed (20 percent) did not differ from small group homes. However, there was great variability in competitive employment. Fully 57 percent of medium group homes had none or only one person competitively employed. The overall work score was, consequently, significantly lower than for small group homes, reflecting a greater percentage of the remaining residents spending their days in activity centers or at the house rather than in sheltered workshop or educational placements. This difference in work may result from different admissions criteria or may indicate the increased difficulty of finding placements for almost twice as many residents.

Sponsorship and Funding

Medium group homes typically have boards of directors. While the average monthly fee of $177 per resident at the time of the survey was quite similar to that in small group homes, the total per-resident operating cost of medium group homes was reported to be significantly *lower* ($4,080 versus $5,690). However, in assessing real total costs per resident, consideration should be given to turnover rates and ex-resident placements; i.e., how long a resident must be served and how independent he or she becomes after moving out. The average resident stay in a medium group home was 2.7 years, compared with 1.6 years for small group homes, a difference that approached significance ($t = 1.69$, $p < 0.10$). Furthermore, the placements of small group home ex-residents tended to be more independent, so the combined *desturn score* (destiny times turnover) for small group homes was significantly higher than for medium group homes. From this perspective, then, the higher per-resident cost of small group homes would be justified (Fig. 4-2).

Conclusions
Although we raised the possible advantages in providing individualized services that larger group homes could have over smaller facilities, the survey data indicated that these potentialities are generally not realized. The typical medium group home had a poorer staff-to-resident ratio, less autonomy for residents, fewer residents in competitive jobs, and a lower per-resident budget than a typical small group home. Nevertheless, there are isolated examples of medium group homes that seem to use their larger size to creative advantage.

Kingston Residence

Setting
Kingston Residence is located in a major metropolis. It is in a neighborhood composed of small apartment buildings, with a variety of small ethnic stores and interesting boutiques nearby, as well as medical and recreational facilities. A subway, stopping one block away, provides access to other parts of the city. Kingston Residence is a medium group home, serving 16 mildly and moderately retarded adults. Its purpose is to provide a transitional home for residents. To this end, the in-house programming focuses on building independent living skills and on community reintegration.

Kingston Residence is an excellent example of intentional planning to maximize resident development in almost every sphere. The physical facility combines the qualities of group home and apartment living to ensure both a supportive atmosphere and personal independence. On the first floor of this five-story apartment building is a large living room, a dining room, kitchen, and office; the finished basement has a television set and a Ping-Pong table. Residents use these rooms to meet casually in small groups. On the upper four floors are eight apartments, one of which is for staff. Each apartment (for two or three residents) has a living room, bedroom, bathroom, and kitchen area; these units are quite small but certainly not atypical for the city in which Kingston Residence is located. In fact, apart from Halfway House, this is the only group home we visited in which the physical facility was designed to simulate the expected future living arrangements of residents.

Residents
Kingston Residence accepts persons who have handicaps in addition to retardation. This flexible admissions policy, in marked contrast to that of the four

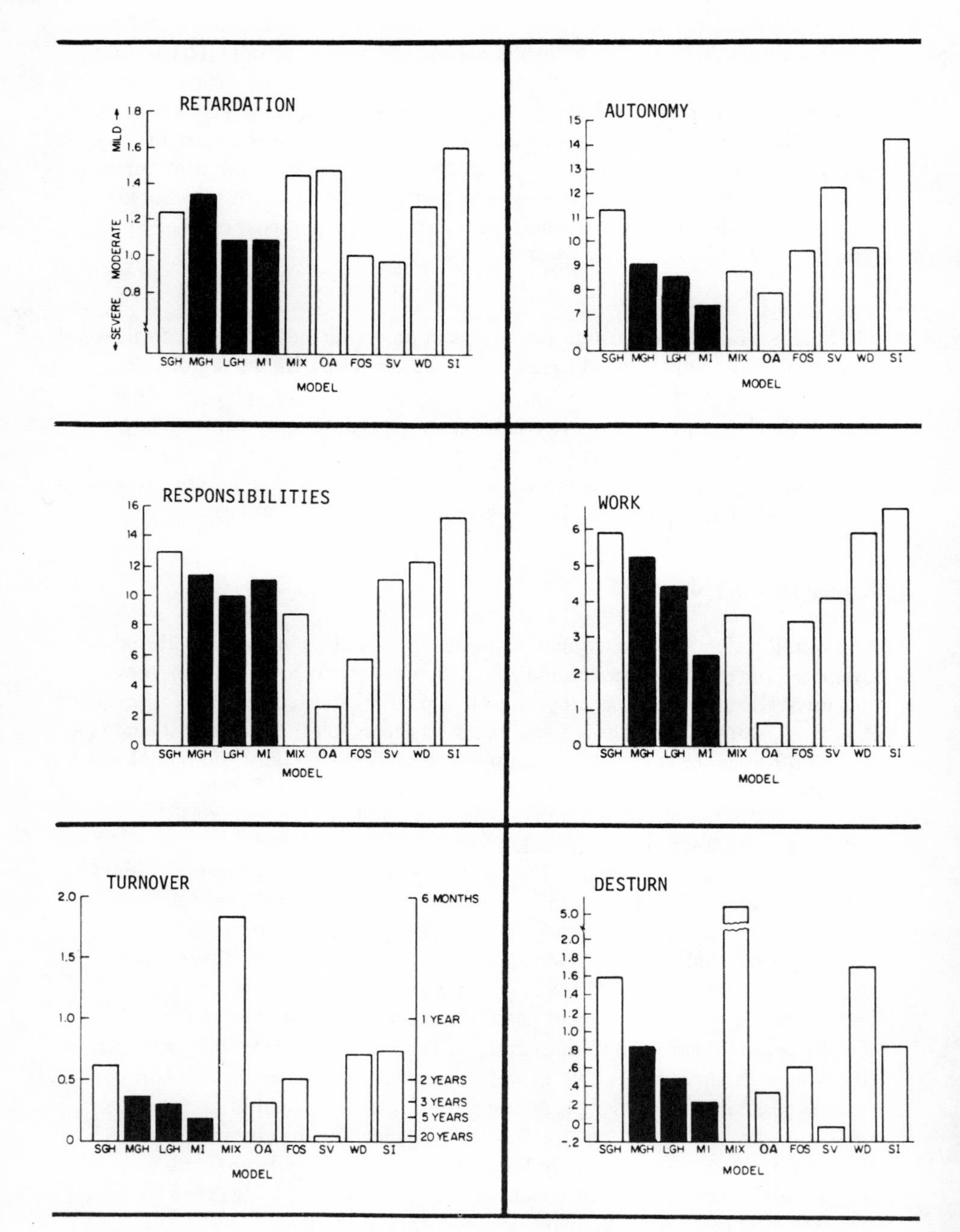

Figure 4-2
Major scales by model.

small group homes we visited, allows for the inclusion of two deaf people, one resident who has a history of theft, and one who has severe emotional problems. The mixed racial composition of the house parallels that of the city. Also, one apartment is set aside for a married couple, the remaining apartments being occupied by either men or women.

Most rules are formulated on the basis of individual needs; there is no set curfew or bedtime, visitors are allowed in bedrooms until midnight, and there are no restrictions on drinking alcohol at the house. Residents have keys to their own apartments, and they leave the house during the day: eight go to sheltered workshops, three go to a clerical work training program, three go to competitive jobs, and two go to public school classes. The apartment-style living at Kingston does not seem to promote isolation but rather allows for a flexible interaction between residents in common rooms, always with the confidence that there is a private area to which they can return. A sense of humor characterizes the atmosphere at Kingston Residence. The staff members respond to resident problems without panic, keeping small dissatisfactions from becoming major issues. Minor complaints brought to staff are dealt with quickly, and then the staff are sure to involve the unhappy resident in the conversation at hand. We witnessed staff and residents laughing together frequently, obviously enjoying one another's company.

Staff

This program has evolved over the 2 years in which the residence has been operating. The present director, Eric, assumed his position 1 year before our visit. He had been employed previously for a number of years by Kingston's sponsoring agency in various programming capacities and was asked to assume the directorship of the residence because of some dissatisfaction with the quality of the program at that time. In fact, the program at that time sounded very much like the typical medium group home reflected in the statistical data presented earlier. The staffing pattern at Kingston Residence had included a housemother who slept at the house five nights each week, college students who provided weekend relief for her, a counselor who was responsible for in-house programming, and a director. The problems with this staffing pattern had included the inconsistency inherent in the short-term involvement of college students as well as limited capacity for individualizing programs for residents based on their needs. Eric made the following changes:

1. Another housemanager was hired to provide relief for the housemother for the entire weekend, and their roles were expanded to include supervision of all apartment living skills.

2. The counselor's hours and responsibilities were altered to meet the residents' needs better. At the time of our study the counselor was working on weekdays from 3 P.M. to 11 P.M. and teaching the residents skills needed for community reintegration, especially use of outside resources. Also, he was responsible for money management for the house and preparing progress reports on individual residents.

3. A cook-nutritionist was hired to instruct residents in cooking and shopping skills and to assist ex-residents in setting up kitchens in their own apartments.

4. A better liaison was established with outside agencies to provide residents with services. For example, a counselor from the Office of Vocational Rehabilitation assisted in job placement and a social group worker ran an optional Tuesday night recreation program.

As a result of these changes, there are enough staff members with discrete responsibilities to be able to respond to the residents' individual needs.

Program: Skill Teaching

Typical of many programs, teaching of living skills previously had been conducted in one particular way for residents with diverse needs, and incentives for performance had been absent altogether. The staffing changes were largely a consequence of the redesign of this program toward a constantly changing one in which the residents' needs dictate what is taught. By tracing the development of the cooking program over this period of time, the program orientation can be highlighted.

During the first year of operation of Kingston Residence, all residents ate together in the common dining room; there were kitchens in each apartment but residents were prohibited from using them. Realizing this extreme contradiction with the expressed purpose of the residence (to prepare residents for future independent living), Eric instructed the staff to begin teaching residents basic cooking skills, one apartment at a time, so that they could prepare meals independently in their own kitchens. Three months later all residents cooked in their own apartments, and Eric began to evaluate the *quality* of their cooking skills. He found that there was great diversity in resident performance: Some apartments were clean and meals were well prepared, while others were filthy with bugs and mice and had poorly planned menus.

It was at that point that Eric hired the cook-nutritionist; he charged her with the task of developing a systematic cooking program. She observed each resident and, after making an assessment, identified those who were having the most difficulties. She proposed that this group begin eating in the common dining room again, preparing meals as a group in the adjoining kitchen. She began her supervision at 4:30 P.M. daily and worked with the group through preparation, dinner, and cleanup. Several of the group reached a level of proficiency that allowed them to return to their individual kitchens for meals, freeing up some of her time to work with ex-residents in their independent apartments.

To complement the cooking program, standards were also developed for apartment cleanliness. Staff members assessed the residents and established that all had the skills to keep their apartments clean, but they found that regular performance was poor in a number of cases. Consequently, each apartment was evaluated daily and the charted results of this evaluation were displayed in the living room. Any apartment that earned three top "grades" in cleanliness in 1 week was rewarded with either a free movie or $5 per person. Although only recently instituted, this incentive program has had good results.

Conclusions

This description, while brief, highlights the realized potential of the medium group home model. The larger space has been used variously to provide for socialization and privacy and to parallel residents' future living arrangements. The development of programs has been in accord with residents' individual needs, and specialized staff are used in specific ways.

Two other important factors need to be mentioned. First, Kingston Residence is part of a developing system of services sponsored by a single non-profit corporation, which, as of this writing, includes a clerical work training program and in the near future will include a residence for severely retarded adults and a series of retail businesses operated by retarded adults under supervision.

Second, Kingston Residence is an expensive program, with an annual budget in 1974 of $132,000. The resulting per-resident cost is $8,250, which is twice that of the typical medium group homes surveyed. This budget is 2 years more recent than those budgets represented in the survey data, and we would naturally expect an increase in costs over this time. However, there is such a substantial difference in the cost of operating Kingston Residence that we can recognize these differences as real, in spite of inflation. Although state funding partly supports these costs, a substantial portion of the budget is covered by resident payments. The monthly fee for residents in school or in work training programs is $350, paid out of Supplemental Security Income benefits. Working residents contribute 50 percent of their monthly take-home pay, or $200, whichever is less. The director emphasized the necessity of a large operating budget to avoid mediocrity in services. Also, an expensive short-term program may well result in a lower expenditure per resident over the long run if residents do indeed go on to develop independent skills.

To conclude, we return to the issue of the size of group homes. Kingston Residence could not provide the quality and scope of services we observed if there had not been 16 residents to provide the capital to support the specialized staff. Yet this program did not impress us as impersonal, a quality often attributed to larger residences. Perhaps the combination of individual apartments in a group home results in an ideal combination of privacy and support, allowing for larger numbers of residents to be served at once.

Large Group Homes

We turn now to facilities serving 21 to 40 residents. No large group home was visited, and therefore what follows is based exclusively on the 23 facilities surveyed. As with medium group homes, we can hypothesize that large group homes could have potential advantages. For example, a person living in a group home of this size might be able to associate closely with a small group of residents with similar interests, abilities, and needs. Yet the larger size might also result in many negative program characteristics, and a resident might find the atmosphere in such a facility institutional and depersonalized, conducive neither to stimulating interpersonal relationships nor to promoting specialized training. It is this latter characteristic that tends to emerge from the survey data.

Place and People

The typical large group home surveyed had been open for 4½ years, and it occupied a very large old house with almost 30 rooms. Also, this type of facility was more likely than a small or medium group home to be found in larger cities.

As with smaller homes, the large group home had an average of two live-in staff members; it had only about six additional day staff members, thereby yielding a staff-to-resident ratio of 1:3.4. The numbers of day staff, professional staff, and live-in staff per resident were each significantly lower in large group homes than in all the other community residences combined.

Although not distinguishable from residents in small and medium group homes in age and sex distributions, residents in large group homes tended to be more severely retarded. Thus it appears that large group homes have fewer staff members to care for individuals with somewhat greater skill deficiencies, and a more custodial atmosphere is often the result.

Program

As compared with small group homes, large group homes have stricter rules and give the resident less responsibility for daily routines. While one-fifth of the residents are competitively employed (as in smaller models), other residents are significantly less likely to be placed in a sheltered workshop or in a training or educational setting.

Within the larger group home model there is the potential for considerable variability in program quality. Many facilities, in fact, are reminiscent of the institutions they are trying to replace. One, for example, stresses daily supervision, medication, and the provision of laundry and cleaning facilities; employee regulations end with the demand "Never leave clients unattended." Other facilities, however, allow for and encourage greater independence, despite their size. One former apartment house with 31 residents has only two residents in each five-room apartment, thus providing spacious living quarters and minimal direct supervision. Individual and small group activities are encouraged in an atmosphere of reasonable autonomy: telephones are in the residents' names, residents have keys to their own apartments, they may entertain nonresidents of the opposite sex between 6 A.M. and 2 A.M., alcohol is permitted, and there is no curfew. Several other large group homes provide structured training programs and are developing independent apartments for residents to move into after acquiring the behaviors specified for more independent living.

Community
Despite the fact that larger group homes were potentially more intrusive in a neighborhood, the staff members and boards of directors had exerted significantly *less* strenuous efforts to prepare the community for their presence than did the small and medium group home models. This finding seems to be in keeping with a relatively lesser concern with normalization, and the related behavior it dictates, than was evidenced in smaller models.

Conclusions
The variability in this model precluded the choice of a single program to describe in detail. Therefore this brief look at large group homes should not be taken as conclusive but rather as a starting point for further inquiry. The model described next, mini-institutions, will also be considered briefly because only five facilities are represented.

Mini-Institutions

The mini-institution serves 41 to 80 residents, and because of its large size, this model often falls outside most conceptions of a community residence. However, since we did not gather data on large state institutions, mini-institutions provide a comparison group of sorts, against which we can examine smaller facilities. It becomes clear that although life in mini-institutions is markedly more restricted than in smaller community residences, it still seems much less restricted than life in the large state institutions.

Place and People
Mini-institutions have an average of 58 residents living in former hospitals or specially constructed modern facilities. There is great variability among the five settings sampled, but they have a few factors in common: relatively few staff members per resident, limited organized involvement with the outside community, and considerably restrictive rules and policies. Indeed, mini-institutions ranked lowest of any model on these variables. The staffing pattern, while consistently thinner than in all other models, was nonetheless quite variable (see Table 4-1). And while all facilities reported some involvement of outside professionals, these were primarily medical personnel. Indeed, most strikingly missing in these staffing patterns were trained staff members to educate the residents in community living or vocational areas (although several facilities stated that their aides tried to assume these functions).

Program
Although we have classified these facilities as mini-institutions because of their size, even these five represent an interesting array of program models. They are

Table 4-1
Staffing Patterns in Four Similarly Sized Mini-Institutions

A.	B.
50 residents Average fee: $135 Staff: 6 1 owner 2 cooks 1 driver 1 housekeeper 1 maintenance (4 live-in staff members)	50 residents Average fee: $205 Staff: 10 2 co-owners 6 houseparents 2 cooks (0 live-in staff members)
C.	**D.**
51 residents Average fee: $297 Staff: 21 1 administrator 1 secretary/arts and crafts 1 licensed practical nurse 14 nurse's aides 3 cooks 1 maintenance (0 live-in staff members)	58 residents Average fee: $350 Staff: 26 3 administrators 2 social service 3 licensed practical nurses 10 nurse's aides and orderlies 1 houseparent (live-in) 4 cooks and dietitians 2 bus drivers 1 maintenance (1 live-in staff member)

self-labeled as a boardinghome, a nursing home, a rest home, a community living center, and a foundation. One sees its function as providing a homelike and supportive environment for mentally retarded young men who are steady wage earners and stresses a planned program of personal and social adjustment training during leisure hours; another facility sees its function as accommodation only and runs a rather standard boardinghouse; yet another, in a tiny rural town with no public or community residence transportation, operates as a pretty much self-contained, although thoughtfully planned, total institution.

Regarding autonomy, a resident will find in any one of these settings restrictions such as a ban on the use of alcohol, a curfew, and a bedtime of 10:00 P.M. or earlier. These restrictions are found both in a facility with predominantly severely retarded residents and one with mildly retarded and borderline individuals. The well-intentioned benevolence behind such restrictions is reflected in the following statement: "Residents are permitted to visit (outside) for any length of time, as long as we know who they are with and approve."

With regard to work, mini-institutions do not fare much better. Although overall the proportion of competitively employed residents is similar to that of each of the smaller models (21 percent), this is misleading, for three facilities had 0 percent competitively employed, one had 16 percent, and one had 88 percent. This latter setting had work placement as its main focus and carefully selected residents using a number of criteria to ensure successful placements. Most residents had little work involvement, with the proportion of residents whose employment was only "at the residence" the highest of any model, and the overall work score was the lowest of any model, except group homes for older adults.

We should note that this seemingly custodial picture is sketched in contrast to smaller community residences. In fact, these mini-institutions appear to offer a better quality of daily life than do the typical large state institutions. Even though mini-institutions were less homelike than smaller models, a degree of privacy was afforded to all residents, with only two or three residents per bedroom, in modern facilities. This contrast with the bed-to-bed layout of the cavernous institutional ward is further enhanced by the finding that residents in the mini-institution model often own their own television sets, record players, and radios. One facility is described as "modern but homey . . . decorated in early American . . . with a large fireplace in the living room which we use quite often in the winter," while another speaks of gardening, bicycling, crafts, and helping to defuse community opposition by regular shopping trips.

Too, the paucity of work placements is seen as problematic by at least some administrators of mini-institutions. One such administrator has been involved in developing a small sheltered workshop in the town, which presently can accommodate only 10 of his 50 residents but there are plans for expansion. Another mini-institution has plans to build on the grounds a two-bay garage to maintain its own vehicles and to prepare residents for employment as service station attendants.

The mini-institution provides a sharp contrast to the smaller models discussed earlier; however, it is important to note that the better quality of the small group home would have been all the more dramatic if the comparison had been to the large state institution rather than to the somewhat restrictive but still more humane mini-institution.

The equivocal experience of life in a mini-institution is reflected well in a report by Birenbaum (1974). The setting, called Gatewood, is a large new motel-like structure, located in an ethnically heterogeneous working class neighborhood. The 63 male and female residents live two to a bedroom, two bedrooms connected to a bath; there are large common dining and living rooms.

Gatewood is an institution of sorts, *and yet* contrasts well with the former home of these people – a state school built for 3,000 housing 5,000, with 47.5 sq ft of sleeping area per individual (although Health Code regulations require 80), 1 toilet for 10 residents, and 1 shower for 40. The sex-segregated institutional dining hall seats about 500!

And yet at the state institution, these residents had a certain status, holding helper jobs in the service shops. In the first months at Gatewood, while an inexperienced staff evaluated residents for possible sheltered workshop placements, persons who had formerly been quite busy on delivery trucks, in shoe repair shops, and in the kitchens simply sat. The lack of jobs was a bitter disappointment, and waiting for meals became a common way of killing time.

And yet residents now had a monthly allowance and a newfound opportunity to spend money, and spending became a major activity. But budgeting, purchasing, and transportation skills were lacking and untaught. *And yet* . . . .

The story and contrasts continue. The mini-institution, like any other program, looks better or worse, depending on what aspect of it one looks at and the comparative standard.

Group Home Size and Residents: Further Considerations
The group homes presented thus far have been categorized according to size. In this section, we will present correlations between group home size and selected program characteristics to identify which program variables are related to size and which are not. In addition, the relationship between selected resident characteristics (including age, sex, and level of retardation) and program variables will be discussed. These correlations are included in Appendix II.

Resident Characteristics. Sex of residents (percent of males in the community residence) does not relate to program variables, but age does. Homes with older residents tend to have a higher proportion of residents from institutions, more continuing institutional involvement, and fewer staff members per resident. Residents in these homes assume fewer daily responsibilities, are less involved in outside work, and are less likely to leave the residence for other living arrangements. This diminished programming with increasing age is highlighted further in Chapter 6, where we examine group homes specifically for older adults (which were not included in this analysis).

Contrary to expectations, the degree of retardation relates only slightly to house policies and programs. Houses where residents are more retarded tend to receive lower responsibility, desturn (quality and quantity of ex-resident placements), and work scores, although these relationships are not strong ones. Within work, less retarded persons are more likely to hold competitive jobs, but there is no relationship between retardation and sheltered employment.*

The level of retardation did not relate significantly to the number of staff members per resident, to autonomy, or to involvement of the house with the community or the institution. The extent of resident retardation per se, then, tells us only a little about the functioning of a group home.

Setting Characteristics: Size. Group home size is unrelated to the resident characteristics of sex, age, and level of retardation. As we have seen throughout this chapter, group home size *does* relate to house policies and programs. Group homes that are larger tend to (1) have fewer direct and professional staff members per resident; (2) allow the resident less autonomy and responsibility for daily chores, and; (3) have fewer residents in work training experiences.

*In general, competitive employment seems to relate to either the perceived potential ability of residents (the younger and less retarded being more apt to be employed) or the location of the community residence (more competitive employment as population area increases). Sheltered and educational placements, on the other hand, are unrelated to the level of retardation and are evenly distributed across population areas; placement mainly reflects the house policies and the efforts of the staff. Sheltered placements are related to house size, reflecting the greater ability of smaller facilities to place most of their residents.

Although the average resident fee increases with group home size, the actual budget per resident decreases, because larger homes meet a higher proportion of their budget from fees alone. The cost savings in larger facilities is at the expense of staff members to work with the residents and hence may be somewhat self-defeating. Since facilities are larger, residents are less likely to move out into more normalized situations (and hence more likely to remain a cost burden somewhere).

In considering these relationships to size, we should first note that a larger facility need not, per se, be more custodial. There is a shared feeling among those promoting the normalization philosophy that smaller facilities are better, so it stands to reason that these persons would have become more involved in developing smaller facilities. It may well be that if these same administrators and staff members were transferred to a larger facility, they would or could make it much less custodial. This is to say that correlation does not imply causation – the correlation with size may not reflect fixed consequences of house size as much as it reflects the actions of those who develop small or large facilities.

It should be remembered that a group of any size can only approach, but never really attain, normalized mainstream living. Further compromises with the ideal may be warranted if a somewhat larger facility can allow people to group according to individual preferences and can provide individualized and specialized training through a larger and more differentiated staff. We have seen from Kingston Residence that a medium group home that is appropriately staffed and operated by those with a program orientation toward normalization can provide very good training and not become as custodial as many larger facilities in our sample seem to have become.

5. Mixed Group Homes

MIXED group homes are programs that include both mentally retarded individuals and former mental hospital patients, persons with problems of alcoholism, and/or adult ex-offenders. Houses clearly oriented toward the retarded, even if they have one or two residents with other primary diagnoses, are *not* called mixed group homes. Rather, the 18 mixed group homes in our sample had an admission policy that intentionally included other disabilities and, in fact, retarded persons were usually in the minority. Our discussion of this model is necessarily brief, because it is based on the survey alone; we did not visit a mixed group home.

There is virtually no evidence of the effects on a retarded person of living in a mixed group home, and opinions vary widely. Wolfensberger (1972) argued against mixed facilities, stressing that community reactions will be more negative to retarded residents by virtue of their association with other deviant groups. He predicted that the retarded residents themselves would come to model deviant behavior from other residents. On the other hand, the Transitional Services program (which is discussed in Chapter 12) has stressed the advantages of mixing people with different disabilities, noting that retarded persons learn skills from those more intellectually able and that disturbed persons benefit from the emotional stability and patience of the retarded.

The Texas Plan to Combat Mental Retardation (1966) left open the question of "joint centers" for the mentally retarded and the mentally ill, noting potential advantages and calling for an empirical investigation of the relative effectiveness of joint and separate centers. Hence six (33 percent) of our mixed group homes are in Texas and are called "halfway houses for the mentally restored, mentally retarded, and alcoholics." Another seven (39 percent) are found in New Jersey, where the state plan also permits this option.

Of all our models, the mixed group home is closest to the psychiatric halfway house, a transitional facility called by Raush and Raush (1968) ". . . a way station in the career of the 'sick' or 'convalescing' patient." Psychiatric halfway houses serve predominantly as short-term homes for former mental hospital residents, and foster an easing back into the community through a sheltered setting. There is often individual or group therapy, sometimes recreation, yet rarely a program of planned teaching. The assumption is that residents have the necessary abilities but that intrapsychic difficulties impede performance; hence residents need psychological therapy and/or simply a place to live while spontaneously recovering. This psychiatric (or medical) model on which halfway houses are customarily based poses some potential disadvantages for the retarded individual who may be in need of more intentional skill learning.

Survey

Place, People, and Program

Not surprisingly, compared with all other community residences, many more mixed group home residents came from mental hospitals and the community, and many fewer came from schools for the retarded. The number of retarded residents were in the range of 12 percent to just over 50 percent. Yet the survey questions did not differentiate between retarded residents and others, so we can say little directly about how the retarded person fared within this model (Fig. 5-1).

The average mixed group home had 18 residents, and although the range was from 4 to 45 residents, most fell within the medium group home range (e.g., 11 to 20). (See p. 79 for a comparison of mixed and medium group homes.) The mean age of 41 years was higher than that for all the other community residences combined. While a slightly higher proportion of residents held competitive jobs (27 percent versus 15 percent for other community residences pooled, $t = 1.79$, $p = 0.08$), the remainder were far more likely to have no work placement at all or to work only at the home itself; hence the overall work score was relatively low (Fig. 5-1).

It is striking then that the turnover rate exceeded that of all other models; while the average resident stayed for 2 years in other models, the length of stay in mixed group homes was just over 6 months. This is similar to the median stay of 4 to 8 months reported for psychiatric halfway houses in Raush and Raush's (1968) survey. Since relative to other models a significantly higher proportion of ex-residents moved into their own apartments (40 percent versus 18 percent; $t = 2.39$, $p = 0.02$), the desturn score for mixed group homes was highest of any model, almost five times that for other models. As noted, however, we can conclude nothing from these results about turnover for the *retarded* residents in these facilities.

Conclusions

The picture that emerges from these statistics and from some mixed group homes' self-descriptions is of a facility that is both separate from the

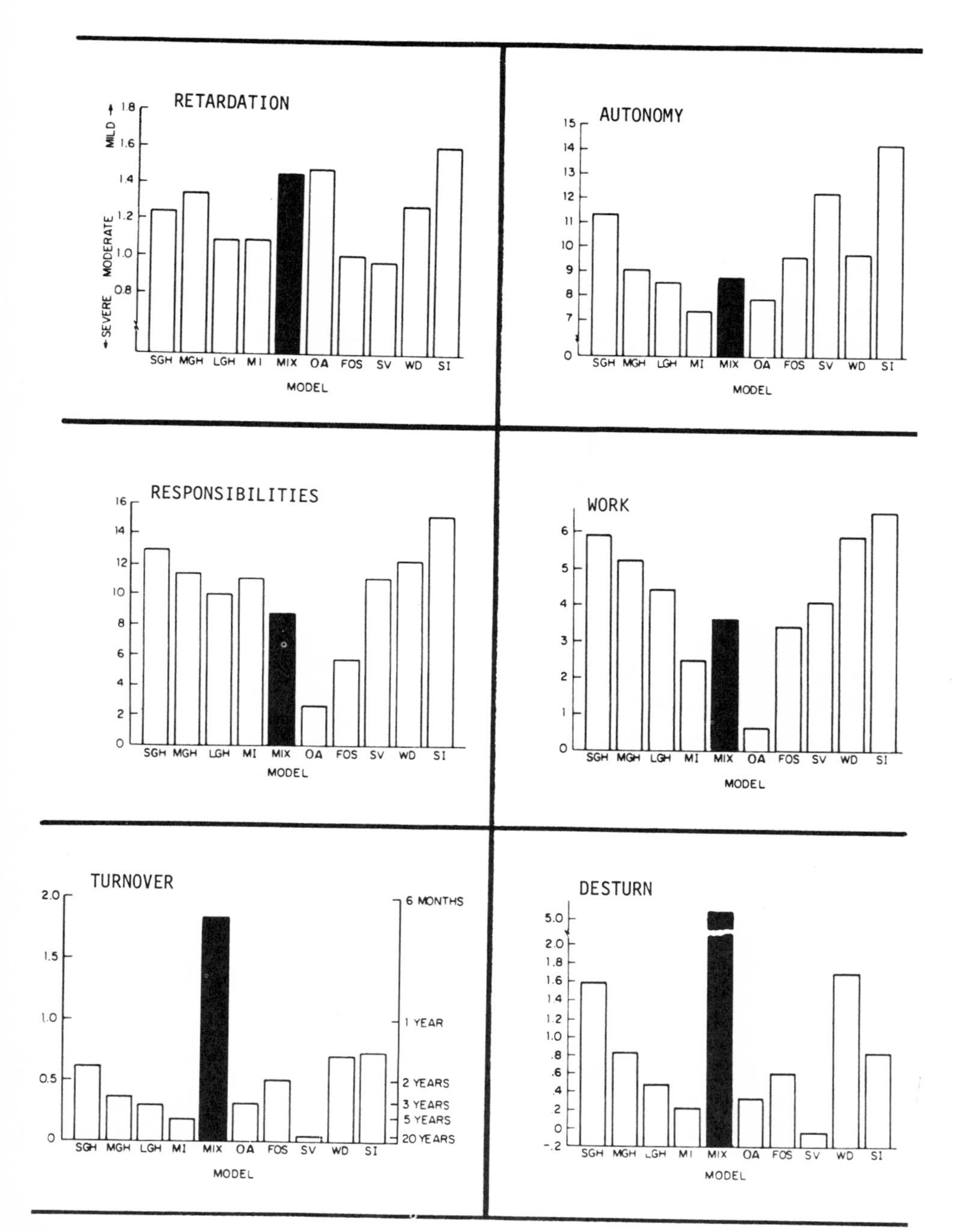

Figure 5-1
Major scales by model.

community and somewhat protective of its residents. These homes provide a short-term decompression from institutional living or a respite for noninstitutionalized persons experiencing emotional problems. They are commonly a halfway station between an institution and the outside world, although sometimes they are a preventive placement for persons already in the community. Some mixed group homes view their role as intentionally therapeutic and structure group therapy sessions, resident government meetings, and other forums for residents to deal together with each other.

The residents, living together as a family, meet three times a week for classes. Monday night is regular group therapy conducted by the staff psychiatrist . . . . During this session, residents openly talk about their personal problems and feelings.

A house government meeting is held on Tuesday nights. That meeting is held by the residents for planning of outside activities, including skating parties, YMCA participation, hikes and picnics.

From a newspaper article on
Odessa Halfway House, Odessa, Texas

Group sessions are held twice weekly to discuss problems arising from relationships at the Center and/or on the job. A weekly House government meeting provides an avenue for learning self-determination by the residents. These meetings consider rules and the staff-resident interrelationships.

From a brochure of The Underwood Hall
Rehabilitation Center, Amarillo, Texas

More commonly, residents avail themselves of psychotherapy outside the house, and the house itself functions very much as a boarding facility. (A number describe themselves as boardinghouses or rest homes.) In contrast to the above therapeutically oriented mixed group homes is a boardinghome described in our questionnaire. The staff members are simply the owner and his wife, and they do sole planning of what recreational activities there are. The philosophy is summarized by answers to the following questions:

Most descriptive of house: House for sheltered care.
Joint staff and residents meetings: No.
Placed in work situations: None.
Staff: Owner and wife.
Recreational activities planned: By owner.

From a questionnaire from a
"rest home" for persons with mixed disabilities

As noted earlier, most mixed group homes are privately owned, with the owners constituting the primary staff, although they sometimes have cooking, maintenance, and/or relief help. There is considerable variability in staffing, from highly staffed, therapeutically oriented homes to minimally staffed boarding facilities. It becomes clear that the retarded individual in need of skill training is less likely to find it intentionally provided in mixed group homes as they are presently constituted. Also, a guided entry into community resources and job (or job training) placement may be lacking. In fact, a program oriented toward "therapy" (especially encounter, or sensitivity, groups) may not only miss the needs of many retarded persons, but be destructive of self-esteem and otherwise adaptive defenses. Yet the borderline retarded individual with good community survival skills may find useful therapeutic help in some mixed group homes – or at least the opportunity to live with and learn from a greater variety of people. It should be noted that the most apparent drawbacks of a mixed group home for a wider retarded population stem much less from the mixing of disabilities than from the prevailing psychiatric emphasis.

The isolation and protection of mixed group homes are themes that will be highlighted in Section 2 which will explore models for which the philosophy of normalization is not a major influence in program development.

Comparison with Medium Group Homes

The mixed group home is similar to the medium group home in size as well as other variables such as staff-to-resident ratio, type of physical facility, location, and amount spent for each resident; hence a comparison of these models was made.

The mixed group homes had been open longer ($t = 1.86$, $p = 0.07$) but had prepared the community less for their presence ($t = 2.01$, $p < 0.05$); the present community involvement of the two models is similar, but mixed group homes were less involved with institutions (e.g., for medical care) ($t = 2.52$, $p < 0.02$). Too, mixed group homes were much more likely to have an owner (59 percent) than were medium group homes (8 percent) ($x^2 = 20.3$, $p < 0.001$) and hence not be linked to boards of directors, community groups, or mental health facilities.

The resident in the mixed group home appeared somewhat more like a temporary boarder, with less provision for either work or leisure. Within the mixed group home, residents had less responsibility for daily housekeeping tasks ($t = 1.89$, $p = 0.07$) and, because of the dearth of training-related work placements, had lower work scores ($t = 2.11$, $p < 0.05$). Also, residents were less likely to possess their own television sets ($t = 2.62$, $p < 0.02$), radios ($t = 3.09$, $p < 0.01$), and musical instruments ($t = 2.77$, $p < 0.01$).

Section 2. Protected Settings

THE models described in this section – group homes for the elderly retarded, foster family care, and sheltered villages – are quite different in many ways. They include small houses and complete villages, programs for only one person or up to 80 persons, and residents who are both young and healthy and those who are elderly and sometimes infirm. Some places have spacious lounges and expensive furnishings, while others are quite humble. Perhaps even if there is a common thread running through this patchwork, it is hardly worth noting relative to the contrasts that stand out. Nonetheless, it has seemed to us that despite the differences, the themes of *separation and protection* bind these models together in important ways.

The aim of segregation to protect the retarded and the community *from each other* was paramount in the late nineteenth and early twentieth centuries, and vast institutions were erected as monuments to these aims.

A moment's thought, and the fact is plain that unprotected feeble-minded women of full physical development are in constant danger themselves, and are always a menace to society – a twofold reason why custodial care for this class should be the paramount idea in the State's provision for the feeble-minded. Thus their proper care and protection is a twice blessed charity, in that it blesses the recipient of the State's bounties and blesses society by the removing of a great evil therefrom.

Winspear, 1895, p. 163

Former eugenic notions and sexual fears diminished over the years until protection became less of a celebrated cause, although even without a rationale the institutions persisted (Wolfensberger, 1969c). As we have seen, recently begun group homes usually adhere to the principle of normalization, which argues that the retarded should be allowed to live as close as possible to life in mainstream society rather than be separated from the community. However, the issue of protection persists, if philosophically underground, for even the normalization principle must, to be realistic and humane, add the words *as close as possible.* The question is not one of foregoing all protection for retarded persons but rather, How much? In what ways? For whom? For how long? and Toward what ends?

The sheltered village squarely advocates a considerable degree of protection, for separation and shelter are its defining characteristics. As such, this model evokes echoes of Winspear's words and visions of ever-increasing size and inhumanity. Yet as we will see in this section, separation, while perhaps still difficult to accept in principle, can sometimes be both humane and growth promoting in practice. To be sure, sheltered villages are not community residences, nor do they claim to be, and some of the comparisons we will make should be qualified by this point. Yet sheltered villages compose an alternative model that is well worth consideration.

The models of foster care and group homes for older retarded people predate the normalization movement in this country, and both tend to see protection and guidance of residents as higher priorities than do other group homes.

Group homes for older adults have been isolated from the community and have drawn a protective veil around their residents, in part because of real diminished vigor and infirmity but mainly, it seems, because of notions about old age. If the retarded person in our society is seen as needing care and protection, and the older person is seen as needing much the same, then a facility for older retarded people, no matter how vigorous its residents, seems doubly trapped by our stereotypes.

These themes in foster care are not as obvious and, in fact, not as strong. Indeed, foster care evolved for other deviant populations as an alternative placement to institutions and has been widely used to move retarded persons "back to the community." Yet as we examine the foster homes in our sample, we get less of a sense of individuals in the community, than of protected guests being cared for in some type of isolation. No other model has the potential variability of foster care, since it is minimally monitored and depends almost entirely on the philosophy and actions of the owners, and certainly some are growth promoting. For a variety of reasons, however, this model seems generally characterized more by a protective benevolence relative to the group homes that are guided by normalization ideals.

---

6. Group Homes for Older Adults

MANY older persons who are discharged from state schools or who previously lived at home are placed in special group homes, defined by a minimum age for residents. Others are placed into homes for nonretarded elderly persons. By group homes for older adults we mean community residences that are exclusively for retarded people over the age of 50 years and homes that mix retarded and elderly nonretarded people.* These two types of program appear to be strikingly similar in most ways and therefore will be treated as a single model.

While variously classified as group homes, nursing homes, rest homes, etc., most of these facilities are protected settings; much is done for residents, and they are closely bound to the house, having limited contact with the outside community. The residences seem to be safe and comfortable, albeit not very stimulating (Fig. 6-1). Their "low key" programs are perhaps justified for some elderly persons, but may prevent more capable residents from leading a fuller life.

*The age of 50 years has been chosen as a cutoff point for elderly retarded people despite the fact that the age of 65 years is more commonly used for elderly nonretarded people. This decision is based on the fact that retarded people at any age are less capable than their normal counterparts and that society views them as being even more impaired than is warranted, resulting in a cumulative effect of increasingly limited options for the retarded person as he or she ages. This limiting factor, combined with the fact that there is powerful age discrimination in our society, regardless of intellectual functioning, leads us to believe that retarded people, once they reach 50 years, are likely to be faced with more and different needs and concerns than a younger group. Since it was clear that group homes for older adults are quite different from other group homes, we have included them as a separate model; how different they, in fact, should be is an important question.

Figure 6-1
Site of a group home for older adults.

Place and People
The 38 group homes for older adults in our sample have been in existence for a little more than 10 years on the average, a significantly longer period of time than other models.* Nearly two-thirds of these residences are large new or old houses, while the others tend to be apartment units, former hospitals, town houses, and farms with equal frequency. They are most often (73 percent) located in towns of less than 30,000 population, and while 27 percent are within walking distance (five blocks) of buses, more than half have no public transportation available.

The typical group home for older adults is staffed by one operator or houseparent who generally owns the facility. He or she is assisted by an average of three other staff members and one relief person. At the time of our survey the operators had functioned in their roles for almost 10 years, nearly as long as the community residences had been in operation. Since operators generally own the facilities, it is likely that most group homes for older adults remain in existence as long as the operators continue to maintain them.

*All the comparisons mentioned here found group homes for older adults to differ from the pool of other models, statistically significant at $p < 0.01$, using a t test.

The average group home for older adults was found to provide a home for 15 residents, averaging 59 years of age. Only 24 percent of these residents previously lived in institutions for the mentally retarded, a lower percentage than in other models. Instead, significantly more residents previously lived in hospitals (19 percent) or in other community residential facilities (17 percent). Two-thirds of the residents were female, a significantly higher proportion than in other models. Unlike in other models, a sizable proportion of residents (29 percent) in group homes for older adults were *not* retarded. Also, the retarded residents were higher functioning than those in other models pooled. To summarize, residents in this model were older, more often female, and less retarded than the typical resident in other community residences studied. They were also more likely to live with nonretarded peers.

Program

Our five residents range from 51 to 83. We provide anything that interest is shown in – one reads, one enjoys puzzles, one has a small transistor radio. The other two want only to sit . . . .

I try to keep a nice home. A Christian home. No drinking. Any drinking, they must leave.

Program descriptions of
group homes for older adults

Residents in group homes for older adults are unlikely to be involved in jobs or other daily activities outside the residence, as indeed would be expected with many elderly nonretarded people. Only 7 percent of residents left the community residence daily for a job, sheltered workshop, or day activity center.

Practically every community residence stated that it provides a permanent home for its residents, and the fact that training for future, more independent living is a low priority was reflected in the extremely low in-house responsibilities score of this model compared to others (Fig. 6-2). Residents were unlikely to be involved in activities like cooking, cleaning, and shopping, although there was no evidence that they were incapable of performing these skills. In the area of responsibilities, as opposed to work, residents *did* differ from elderly nonretarded people, who were usually expected to continue to perform these activities of daily living until they became incapacitated.

The finding that residents in this model also had a low degree of autonomy is even more curious. Fully 100 percent of group homes for older adults provided 24-hour supervision of residents, and most placed restrictions on visitors of the opposite sex. The physical furnishings were further indicative of the quality of life in group homes for older adults. Relative to other models, there was less likelihood for single-toilet bathrooms, residents' own telephones, keys

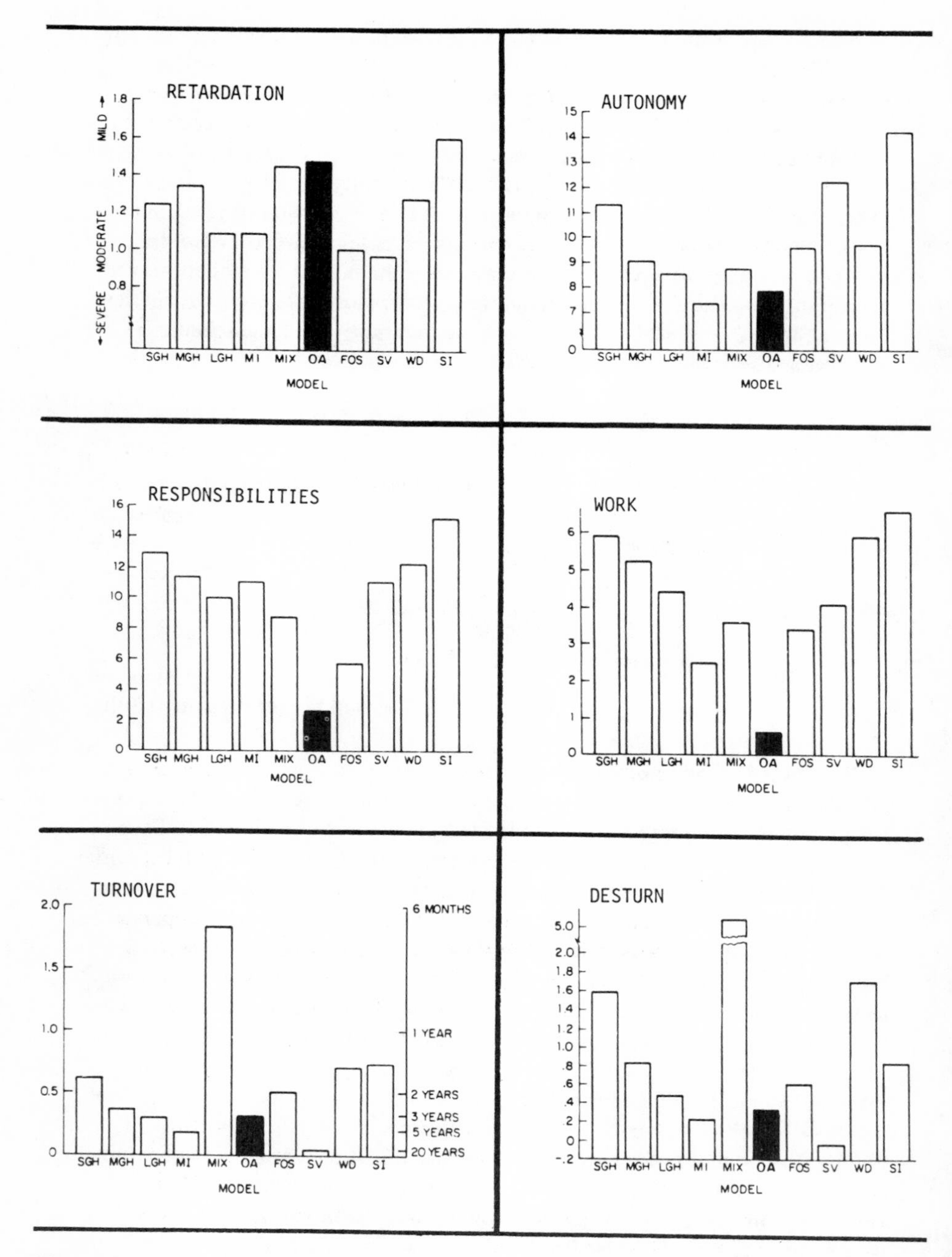

Figure 6-2
Major scales by model.

to the residence, and single bedrooms. Thus the residents' potential for privacy and personal control over their environment was smaller than in other group homes. These restrictions, when viewed in conjunction with low work and responsibility scores, result in an extremely limited program, and we were particularly interested in further exploring the daily program in our on-site visit.

Obviously there is variability among community residences in this model, especially since the physical furnishings and daily programs are so dependent on the owners. There are exceptions that run counter to the composite picture that emerges from the statistical averages. For example, one group home for older adults, obviously an exceptional one, described its program as follows: "We try to help our residents live as normal to regular family activity as possible. If help is needed, we try to help, but our main purpose is to help each person fit back into the community."

Although group homes for older adults are almost always conceived of as permanent homes, a turnover rate of 32 percent was found, which is similar to that of other models which claim to be transitional settings. This discrepancy between stated policy on permanence and turnover rate results partly from the 14 percent of ex-residents who became ill and moved to hospitals and the even higher percentage who, in all probability, died. Even so, a relatively high proportion of ex-residents moved to other community residences (15 percent) or to institutions for the mentally retarded (15 percent). Very few moved to independent living (7.4 percent).

Community

Group homes for older adults are often owned by the operators rather than by outside corporations, and intense efforts to prepare the local community for the opening of the community residence are not seen as necessary. Indeed, operators prepared local constituencies, such as neighbors or city government groups, significantly less often than did staff members of other models. Similarly, the extent of involvement of the community in the community residence itself is less here than in other models. There seems to be little pressure for these community residences to integrate residents more with the community, and operators typically work in a programmatic vacuum, without contact with one another and with little training or supervision from referral agencies.

Sponsorship and Funding

Group homes for older adults were usually owned by the operator; only 19 percent had a board of directors. The community residences in this model derived most of their budgets from resident fees – an average of $245 per month at the time of our survey – which is significantly higher than the average for other models. The average yearly per-resident budget was $3,434, indicating that group homes for older adults were funded almost exclusively by resident fees.

Hickory Manor

Hickory Manor is a home for six retarded women, five of whom are over the age of 60 and one of whom is in her forties. Since its opening in 1959 the house has been owned and operated by Mrs. K., a psychiatric nurse. Impetus to begin the community residence came from Mrs. K.'s desire to care for her elderly mother at home and the need to support herself while doing so. She contacted the area state school's social service department, which arranged for older adults from the institution to move into Hickory Manor. Throughout its years of operation, almost all Hickory Manor's residents have come from the state school. Despite this fact, Hickory Manor was licensed as an old-age home until 1972, when certification was appropriately changed to that of a facility for the mentally retarded.

Setting

Hickory Manor is a two-story house located on a quiet street in a rural area. The nearest shopping center is over 5 miles away (although a state highway is quite accessible), and there is no public transportation. There are three bedrooms for residents (two per bedroom) and one bedroom for staff; all share one bathroom, a sitting room, a kitchen, and an enclosed porch. Mrs. K. has been careful to maintain the familylike atmosphere of Hickory Manor, although she did build a fire escape to conform with state regulations.

Staff

As operator and owner, Mrs. K. is assisted by one part-time worker, Miss B., who also has worked at Hickory Manor since its opening, cooking and cleaning for residents and relieving Mrs. K. In this way, 24-hour supervision of residents is maintained. Mrs. K. is also helped by her daughter and daughter-in-law, who provide transportation when necessary and do all the shopping.

Mrs. K., 63 years old, is in the same age bracket as the residents; she is immediately set apart, however, by the white uniform she wears at Hickory Manor. She reports that she is extremely satisfied with her work, and she finds it helpful that residents are grateful for everything that is done for them. Mrs. K. mentioned that she would prefer to choose the residents herself, since those who make admissions decisions "don't know much about it." She also finds budgeting a problem and would prefer greater compensation for her work; her salary is the amount remaining after expenses, a particularly difficult arrangement.

Mrs. K. would look forward to more residences like hers developing in the area to provide room for more elderly retarded people and to ensure "a little competition for us." She looks forward to improving the grounds of Hickory Manor and perhaps to hiring someone to care for the flowers and shrubs.

Residents

Four of the six women have lived at Hickory Manor since 1963; the two others moved there more recently. All residents were referred by the social worker from the state institution, where each of these women had lived for an average of 20 years. Diagnoses at time of institutionalization ranged from epileptic to alcoholic to emotionally disturbed to retarded, although at the time of our study all residents were functionally retarded as a result of long years of institutionalization. Three women could read and write; two of these women had held jobs in the community before being admitted to the state school. Why these three were ever admitted to the institution in the first place must now remain a mystery. While in the institution, all six women worked at the school's laundry, a job which most of them found enjoyable.

All the residents said that they preferred Hickory Manor to the state school, and most expressed gratitude toward Mrs. K. for giving them a home. Although they were generally satisfied with the living conditions at Hickory Manor, one of the oldest residents said that she had lived there too long and wanted to change her style of life to one less supervised.

Program: A Typical Day

Residents generally awaken at 7:00 A.M., although they remain in their rooms until called to breakfast. Miss B. prepares all meals; residents are not permitted to participate in meal preparation, we were told, because a state regulation "prohibits their using or being near stoves." Menus are posted several weeks in advance, also in supposed compliance with state regulations.

After breakfast, the women clean their bedrooms and spend the rest of the morning involved in activities such as sitting outside, playing cards, drawing, sewing, or watching television. Lunch is served at noon, and the afternoon hours are spent much the same as the morning ones. After supper, served at 5:30 P.M., residents again are free to do as they like until bedtime, which is at 9:00 P.M. Deviations from this typical schedule are infrequent. On occasion, the women go on picnics, give birthday parties, or have guest entertainers. The weekends are indistinguishable from the weekdays except for Sunday mornings, when the women dress up in their best clothes and watch church services on television.

The daily schedule is indicative of the (non) program: protected, benevolent, and for the most part, static. Mrs. K. feels it is futile to teach residents to cook and become more self-sufficient because she sees Hickory Manor as their permanent home. Instead, she emphasizes social skills, such as manners and appearance. She is concerned that the "ladies" are polite and show respect for each other and for the staff. Mrs. K. tries to help them "better themselves, and approach things with a different attitude." She also is anxious to "make the residents feel useful," and therefore sometimes creates unnecessary jobs around the house to meet this goal. The residents at Hickory Manor had less autonomy than at any other community residence we visited.

Some of the women disagreed with Mrs. K. that self-sufficiency is not a meaningful goal. Although most said that they enjoyed working in the house (i.e., cleaning their bedrooms), four expressed a desire to work outside the house. Although it should be easy for one to understand their dissatisfaction, the women expressed hesitation about voicing their complaints to Mrs. K. They also reported that there were not many social activities planned, and that they do not have a role in planning, despite Mrs. K.'s reports to the contrary. Finally, although almost all the 80 other residents that were interviewed in other places agreed that "residents are given a great deal of individual attention in their respective community residences," not one resident at Hickory Manor felt this was true.

Sponsorship and Funding

Hickory Manor is one of 50 residences associated with the state school. There is reportedly much variability among these houses, in part due to the high degree of autonomy given to the operators. A social worker, based at the state school, provides a liaison between Hickory Manor and the institution through monthly visits.

Hickory Manor was exclusively funded by residents' payments. Each woman received $267 per month from Aid to the Permanently and Totally Disabled, which she signed over to Mrs. K., who budgeted according to guidelines from the state's Office of Retardation. Hence the annual per-resident budget was $3,200. Residents were given $5 per month for personal expenses; some personal expenses were paid by the state, and there was no money budgeted for vacations for the residents. Household expenses and the assistant's wages were covered by resident fees, and the remainder each month was Mrs. K.'s salary.

Conclusions and Issues

Hickory Manor is best seen as an isolated and unmonitored community residence for elderly women. Although in some respects life at Hickory Manor is superior to life in the state institution, this is not entirely so. For example, in the state school these women had the opportunity to leave their wards daily and to interact with a variety of people, including men – experiences unavailable at Hickory Manor. They had spent their time off the ward in useful work (laundering), whereas at Hickory Manor they neither had jobs, nor was their work around the house useful. Finally, in the institution, these women had been paid for their work, however poorly. At Hickory Manor, they were given only $5 per month.

This is certainly not to suggest that these women should return to the institution. Rather, it should point out areas for improvement in the programs of group homes for older adults. The move from the institution to the community must represent more than the move from one static environment to another. Philosophically, Hickory Manor is similar to other facilities in this model, emphasizing benevolence and protection rather than growth. Yet there is no reason to assume that a high functioning resident over the age of 50 years could not live in a semi-independent or cooperative apartment, or, if in a group home, one that orients its program less totally to stereotypes of old age. Similarly, day placements should be encouraged: Vocational and recreational programs or involvement of residents as volunteers could add interest and challenge to the lives of elderly retarded people.

The fact that more programming is certainly possible is indicated by other programs that integrate older adults and younger residents. In 33 percent of the small group homes, there was one or more retarded person over the age of 50 years. More dramatic, 50 percent of the sheltered villages, 40 percent of the workshop-dormitories, and 67 percent of the mixed group homes had at least one resident over the age of 50 years. Whether elderly retarded persons are best served when living with younger residents or in separate programs is an unresolved question. If good and, in some ways, specialized residences for the elderly retarded are to be provided, however, the characteristics of this model must be reconsidered by their planners. All involved should try to gain a realistic view of the potentials and desires of elderly retarded people, so that the program can afford some extra help and guidance as needed, while not being so benevolent that the view of the elderly as incapable becomes a self-fulfilling prophecy. Elderly retarded people, like elderly people in general, should be afforded a dignified alternative to institutional living. This alternative should not, by definition, be a permanent setting, although permanence may be desired (or needed) by some. Efforts should be made to integrate retarded and nonretarded elderly people in residential settings and in recreational activities. State regulations must be eased to strike a balance between protection and normalization, thereby allowing the residents to perform more activities of daily living. And, finally, operators of community residences for older adults should receive training and supervision (perhaps through an association that meets regularly), so that their own isolation is decreased and their potential for effective programming can be developed.

7. Foster Family Care

FOSTER family care, more than most of the models presented, is heavily influenced by the idiosyncratic philosophies of the operators. Their views, as expressed in the questionnaires, thus serve as an instructive introduction to the model:

I help them poor children and that's what I'm trying to do because I love them kind of people. They need help and somebody has to do it.

It's strictly a family deal and is run on family lines. The only things expected of residents is truthfulness, honesty, and obedience. They learn as they can, what they can – no more is expected of them.

We are proud and happy to announce that we are living in a 100% Christian home . . . . Our lives are so different since we found the Lord so I would like to pass on this information to other homes and other people.

This home functions as a normal family. Each one has the responsibility of making it a success and a normal home. The residents have literally adopted the operator as a parent figure.

We have tried to keep the boys we care for happy and healthy and we think we have achieved this goal.

A family home for the retarded is no different than any other home in the community in the physical structure. The only difference is the supportive needs of the mentally retarded, personally, are different and their habitational upkeep is greater and more expensive.

We live as a family and feel the children are a part of our family while they are in our house. I have only two now, one is thirty and one is twenty-one . . . . The children are well accepted with both of our sons and even my grandchildren love them.

The model of foster family care, also known as *family care homes* or *board and care homes,* has a long history. "Under ancient Jewish laws and customs, children lacking parental care became members of the household of other relatives, if such there were, who reared them for adult life" (Slingerland, 1919). As early as 1250 A.D., families in the rural Belgian community of Geel fostered mentally ill pilgrims who had come to pray at the shrine of Dymphna for relief from their affliction. Geel is still a foster colony in which "every seventh home has a patient or two" (Fields, 1974b, p. 15). In the United States, foster family care has evolved from a form of indentured service, practiced until the first decade of the twentieth century, to a planned mode of temporary substitute care in child welfare (Kadushin, 1972) and to a more permanently defined form of community care for mentally disturbed and retarded adults. Halfway houses and adult foster family care both represent models developed in response to the philosophical emphasis on keeping the client in the community rather than in hospitals or institutions. The Veterans Administration was instrumental in the development of adult foster family care when it began to sponsor such homes in 1951 (Ullman and Berkman, 1959); and as halfway houses for former mental patients grew along with the community mental health movement (Raush and Raush, 1968), so too did the use of foster family care for adults.

Because of the extensive use of foster family care in child welfare, some generally agreed on components of a good program can be stated. Ideally, foster family care should include (1) training for the family care operators, (2) a placement process that considers the compatibility between the client and the operator, (3) ancillary services, such as casework, provided by the sponsoring agency (e.g., the social service department of a state school), and (4) a periodic monitoring and evaluation of the quality of care. To neglect any of these components is likely to isolate both the operator and the resident and/or to leave successful programming to circumstance. And, unfortunately, we find that in the foster family care homes for retarded adults surveyed, these components have often been neglected.

Foster family care, as used in this report, is the placement of one to six retarded adults into an existing family residence. A goal of foster family care is to integrate the resident into the family constellation, with the expectation that "in a normal family environment, with understanding foster homemakers, he will learn to conduct himself in ways which will make him acceptable to those with whom he must live, and, if feasible, work" (Dorgan, 1958). One might expect that when a retarded person becomes a member of a surrogate family, he or she could assume a dependent, childlike role – and many questionnaire respondents did, in fact, describe their residents as "boys," "girls," or "children." Hence the possibility for this model to become overly protective emerges as an important issue.

Place and People

Eleven states are represented in our sample of 55 foster family care homes. The clear majority come from California (60 percent), followed by North

Carolina (15 percent). Since foster family homes are private residences, it is not surprising that 91 percent occupy old and new private, residential houses. Nearly 45 percent are located in areas with a population of 10,000 or less, significantly smaller municipalities than other models are found in.* Also, supporting the rural character of this model is the finding that fully 50 percent of foster family homes are located more than 1 mile from any public transportation. On the average, foster family care homes have been open for almost 6.4 years, and, as would be expected, there has been almost no staff turnover. The operators of these homes are usually not professionals (and often have very limited formal education). The primary impetus for starting a foster family care home is most often the actions of an individual (66 percent) rather than a voluntary or professional organization.

There are four or five residents living in each family care home. Residents are comparable in age to those in other models, with men and women equally represented. According to the reported level of retardation, 26 percent of the residents are severely retarded, which is a significantly higher percentage than in other models. Thus, the retardation score indicated that foster family care homes have residents that are significantly more retarded than all the other models combined (Fig. 7-1).

The reported larger proportion of severely retarded residents in foster family care may reflect real differences and account for some of the greater protection described in this model. Or operators may have a tendency to rate residents as more retarded than they actually are because of their own limited exposure to the broad range of persons who are labeled retarded. Since structurally and philosophically this model provides more of a sheltered and protected environment in which residents are likely to be treated as adult-aged children, operators, to be internally consistent, may perceive residents as needing shelter and protection and hence as quite retarded. Whether residents have less learning potential to begin with, are simply seen as less capable through the eyes of an isolated and protective model, or, in fact, become less capable as they live in such a model are alternatives not easily sorted out from the available data.

Program

Perhaps the absence of any discernible similarity in programming among community residences is the most outstanding characteristic of the foster family care model. The operators of these homes tend to determine totally the quality of life within the home; and thus residents are dependent on the particular attitudes and skills of their family care operators. Moreover, on both the work and responsibility scales, the foster family care model scored significantly lower than other models. This finding suggests that there is little in-house or out-of-house programming. Foster family care therefore falls short on two fundamental components of normalization: having productive daytime activities

*All comparisons reported were found to be highly statistically significant ($p < 0.001$, by t tests or analysis of variance).

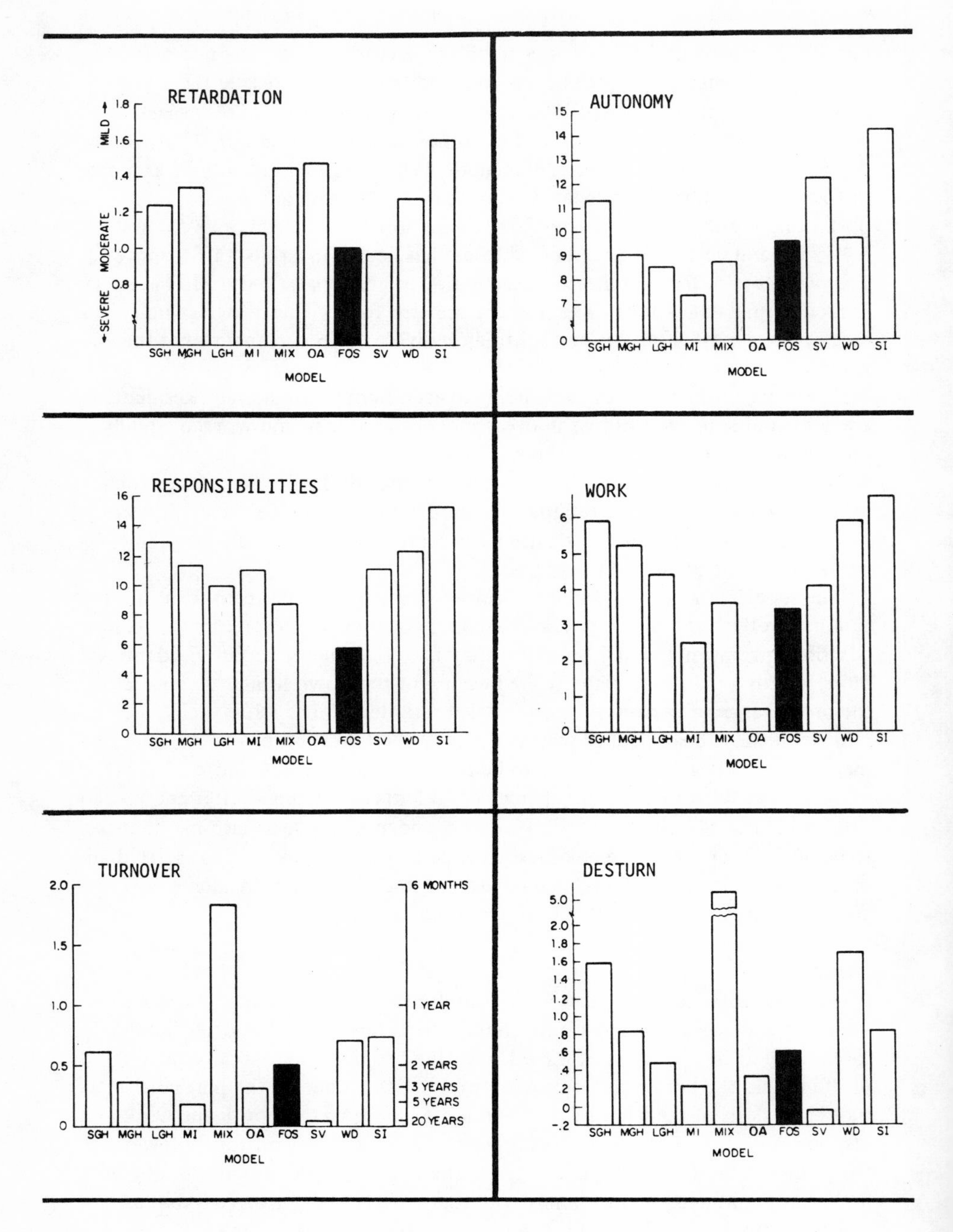

Figure 7-1
Major scales by model.

and allowing residents to participate in the management of their physical environment.

Although foster family care homes did not differ significantly from the other models on the autonomy scale, there is the possibility that rules are subtly and informally enforced, since much behavior in families can be monitored without specific policies. The following responses of operators to questions related to autonomy would lead one to conclude that residents' autonomy is in some measure being restricted.

There are no rules about when I expect the residents in the house, but I don't let them out by themselves unless I take them shopping or to the movies or church.

The house is on five acres . . . . They don't get out of the yard. They are trained not to get out on the road and visit neighbors.

There is no need for a policy on sex in our house. It never comes up in our family.

Thus the composite picture of foster family care homes is one of residential facilities in which a good staff-to-resident ratio has little influence in producing an educational or developmental environment. There are no more stated rules or limitations imposed on the residents' freedom than in other models, but the sheltered family setting does not seem to allow for much risk taking. Given this nondirective, nonrepressive atmosphere, one may conclude that the overriding descriptive characteristic of the foster family care program philosophy is benevolence. That is, the retarded person seems to be treated like a big child/guest – not expected to help much in the daily routine, not encouraged to participate in daily work activity, and not encumbered with strictly stated rules (although probably influenced by implied household practices). Thus benevolence, as seen in this model, may entrap a resident within an impregnable shroud of protection and kindness that deleteriously limits his or her growth potential – a seemingly virtuous philosophy that does not benefit those whom it would help.

Ex-Residents

When considering the length of stay in foster family care, there seem to be contradictions between child foster family care and adult foster family care. In child foster family care, placement is supposed to be temporary, but there are considerable data suggesting the opposite to be true (e.g., Mass and Engler, 1959). In adult foster family care, placement is, in theory, permanent (and reported as such by 76 percent of surveyed operators), but, in fact, our data suggest that persons are constantly moving in and out of such settings. Indeed, 51 percent of the residents move out each year. Fully 34 percent of the ex-residents from homes surveyed went to an institution or hospital, while 23 percent returned to live with their natural families, and 22 percent transferred to a community residence. Only 11 percent of the ex-residents moved into their own apartments. The remaining ex-residents went either to another foster family (7 percent) or some other unknown place (3 percent).

The type of program or nonprogram offered in foster family care does not seem to prepare residents for more independent living; rather, residents either remain in some supervised community setting or return to an institution. The large percentage of residents who return to institutions from a foster family care home is cause for concern. The absence of work placements and the lack of household responsibilities are probably contributing factors in this high recidivism rate. One might even argue that since some residents might be more bored and isolated in some foster family care homes than they were in institutions, returning to institutions is an adaptive move for them. Also, the largest percentage of residents living in foster family care homes came from institutions (56 percent) and therefore probably needed to learn a variety of skills to survive in the community. To expect a family care operator, who has had a minimum of training, if any, to provide the necessary learning environment seems unrealistic. Perhaps a viable option for the operator would be to take advantage of community support services if they exist; however, as will be described, family care homes maintain a low profile in the community.

One operator shared with us what seems to be almost a stream of consciousness about her family care home for severely retarded men. It speaks to many issues involved in this model, among them the need for community support and day placements, the burdens on the family, and the very deliberate choices providers must make for themselves.

Residents are very severely retarded. We find a definite routine is very necessary or they become disturbed and confused. We only accept residents with IQ under thirty. The present residents are two to three in mental age. We find them very eager to please and do what is expected of them; they are very self-centered and selfish. One is very destructive – tears up spreads, sheets, blankets, toys, clothes, and even tore up the carpet. One is toilet-trained, one is trained at home, but has accidents if we go somewhere. They make their own beds and have learned to do it quite well. They are mongoloid and can be extremely stubborn, but this is seldom. They are *not* accepted by the community, and most people don't want them around. I have them well trained – we go shopping often and occasionally out to eat and go visiting often. They dearly cherish their possessions. One is destructive but he doesn't seem to destroy deliberately. They have lots of toys and dolls, teddys, play-school toys, several radios, flashlights, etc., that we purchase for them with their money. They receive enough so that they can be dressed nicely. They like the outdoors, swings, playing ball, and ring-toss. The largest problem we have had is others teasing our own children, ages nine and eleven, at school. The general public is extremely cruel and this creates a very sad situation. The residents keep their room neat, they create an enormous amount of laundry, they eat with bibs on and spoons only. They must be served, as they will continue to eat until they vomit. One is a carrier of serum hepatitis, which leaves our entire family available to contract the disease. We are very clean in our home and so far have escaped this. We buy only the first quality groceries; we all eat the same food; they have their own table. One enjoys coloring with crayons and books, the other eats them. We have made no profit from keeping them, and we are tied down twenty-four hours a day and never have a day off. I think of them as children, not men. The greatest advantages for them to live here instead of the state hospital is they are clean here and they have many personal possessions, which someone else tears up at the state hospital. They must be bathed, shaved, shampooed, and need help getting dressed. I was a state hospital employee for 5½ years and my husband for 16 years, and all these problems are nothing new to us. We knew exactly what we were getting into.

Community

A distinctive feature of foster family care homes is that the operators and their families lived in the home before the arrival of the residents. The need for extensive preparation of the community for the arrival of residents was not perceived by the operators to be important and, as compared with other models, they prepared the community significantly less. Indeed, as many as 39 percent of the operators made no effort to inform members of the community that their previously typical family would now be joined by several retarded adults. Interestingly, community opposition to this change was not marked.

Community participation in the day-to-day operation of the house is minimal, significantly lower than in other models. Similarly, the absence of institutional involvement in the family care home relative to other models raises the question, From where does the family care home receive input? Less involved with either the community or the institution than typical community residences, foster family homes, like group homes for older adults, are isolated and unmonitored. Although a high degree of institutional or community involvement may seem "non-normalized," the opportunities for training, contacts, and experiences that such involvement provides to residents are absent in this model; thus we note again that skills leading to more independent living are often not being developed.

Sponsorship and Funding

A foster family care home, by definition, has no board of directors. Each foster home is a private residence that receives a monthly allowance from the state for each resident to cover the cost of room and board. In most other models, staff members are paid for the services they render, but in foster family care there is no established salary for the operators. They are dependent for a salary on being able to make a profit after budgeting for room and board, and fixed rates are rarely commensurate with rising food and housing costs. This arrangement seems ripe for problems, such as operators spending as little as possible on residents (thereby increasing their profits) or spending so much on residents that they end up with little for themselves.

The average monthly fee per resident was $165 at the time of our survey. In comparison to other models, foster family care had a significantly lower annual per-resident budget, approximately $2,200; and essentially all the budget was met by resident fees.

Issues

Foster family care is a model of community residential service that is highly dependent on the operator, and the data on this model suggest that practices often seem to be antithetical to the development of independent individuals. While there doubtless are some exceptions, in most foster family care placements residents are not often engaged in household duties or day placements outside the home; thus a day in the life of a foster family care resident seems passive at best.

In their research entitled, *Guidelines for Family Care Home Operators* (unique because of their inclusion of the retarded adult), Shrader and Elms (1972, p. 22) stated that:

[Foster family care homes] *are often not designed primarily as re-education in nature, and do not project the end results as being the return of the person to a self-sufficient, independent status in the community. Rather, most care homes are presently operated in a manner that provides long-term extension of the type of care traditionally provided by the state hospital.*

This characterization of foster family care is congruent with our data, except that the turnover rate we found (51 percent annually) casts doubt on the long-term nature of this community placement. Parents, who often have great difficulty in accepting foster family care placement as an alternative to institutionalization also "question the long-term stability of foster care" (*The Right to Choose,* 1973, p. 19). Of particular concern is the large proportion of residents who return to institutions after they leave foster family care.

Given the unanswered questions concerning the turnover and future living arrangements of residents in this model and the other liabilities mentioned previously, some restructuring of this model seems necessary before we can even determine which kinds of residents are best suited for placement. Possibilities for improvement include

1. Training for operators (possibly mandatory)
2. On-going supervision and monitoring of operators, guided by specific program goals
3. Development of associations of operators to share experiences and gain support and leverage with referral agencies (some associations already exist in California)
4. Giving operators a part in the admissions decisions
5. Locating foster family care homes near community supportive services
6. Reorienting foster family care from a permanent to a temporary model of service. Perhaps foster family care can also be utilized as a respite care facility for those living with their natural families.
7. Finding meaningful day placement for residents.
8. Encouraging residents to take part in household responsibilities
9. Changing funding arrangements to ensure that operators will receive a fixed salary and will also have a designated amount for resident programs.

Community Training Home Program

The Regional Center that operates the Community Training Home program is an agency of a midwestern state's Department of Mental Health. Its catchment area encompasses two counties with a population of 1.6 million, bordering a major city. The center's first superintendent was hired in 1971 with the mandate to construct a new and "better" institution. While planning and waiting for the construction of the center's facility, the staff launched an extensive community placement effort. The population to be deinstitutionalized was "hard to place," a phrase used by the staff to describe clientele who have complicating physical and behavioral handicaps and/or who are severely retarded; the Community Placement program, which was begun in October 1972, has since developed a network of foster homes, group homes, apartment units, developmental training homes, and a pediatric nursing home. In July 1973, the Regional Center was awarded a 3-year, federally funded, project grant of nearly $400,000 for the "Deinstitutionalization of the 'Hard to Place' Retarded"; this funding was instrumental in the development of the rapidly expanding comprehensive system of program-oriented, residential facilities.

Many of the suggested program revisions outlined earlier in this chapter are realized in the *Community Training Home program.* For example, in its one-page program description, issues of training, client monitoring, use of community resources, and day placements are addressed.

. . . *all home operators are required to attend an in-service training course consisting of five sessions* . . . .

Regardless of their intellectual or functional ability, all *residents are involved in a full community program through the public school system, vocational programs, or sheltered employment, etc.*

Community resources are utilized as fully as possible for supportive services.

A program contract is written that specifically states the client's needs, the training objectives, and training techniques to be used.

The home operators must complete monthly reports that indicate program development and status of the client in all areas of development, health, and behavior.

Social workers visit their Community Training Homes at least monthly . . . .

With this brief history of the broader administrative aegis within which the Community Training Home program functions, we will consider how the basic foster family care paradigm became transformed into a unique, yet hopefully replicable model for foster family care. It is important to note that the center's objectives, stated in their literature and constantly voiced by staff, are to train, monitor, make accountable, and reimburse fairly both the residents served and the sponsors with whom they contract.

At the core of the Community Training Home program is the *home finding department.* The three full-time employees of this department are responsible for taking part in the screening of residents at the institutions, developing and implementing a variety of recruitment methods to secure homes, and finding a good match between the kind of needs that residents present and what foster parents want. Methods of recruitment employed include

1. Appearances and public service announcements on television and radio
2. A foster care bulletin distributed to schools
3. Speaking engagements with citizen groups
4. Educational (informational) booths at various shopping centers
5. Appeals to existing foster families to identify interested friends and relatives to contact
6. Posters placed in libraries, churches, etc.
7. A well-distributed brochure on the Community Training Home program.

The home finders have found that the most successful recruitment method has been to place advertisements in the classified section of the local newspapers, perhaps because these newspaper advertisements focus on the personal rewards people can enjoy as foster parents and de-emphasize the "exceptional" characteristics of the residents to be placed. The home finders maintain that this approach offers them the opportunity to attract persons who might have been misinformed and thus are otherwise unwilling to consider becoming involved with retarded persons. They are dependent on their preliminary telephone screening of candidates to discern who should be pursued further and to describe accurately the resident population for whom a home is being sought.

Unfortunately, a systematic delineation of characteristics of those who have been most successful foster parents for retarded adults in this program has not been undertaken; such a study would greatly enhance the replicability of this model and suggest some standards that are sorely lacking in the provision of foster family care in general. The home finders report that they do not make initial screening decisions. Instead, they provide extensive information to interested community families and rely on them to use this information to make their own decisions about whether they are interested in pursuing the option of becoming foster parents.

During the month prior to our visit, 94 calls from prospective foster families were received, 36 homes were visited, 12 homes remained under study, and 4 homes had admitted residents.

Once a family has been selected by the home finders, the home must be licensed by the state's Department of Social Services; approval is extended for a maximum of three residents per foster home. Next, the prospective resident moves into the home for a trial visit, lasting up to 3 days. Trial visits are intended to give the family and the resident the opportunity to get to know one another, and there are three possible outcomes: Either party may reject the "match"; both the resident and the family may feel comfortable with each other from the start; or, most likely, the decision may be postponed and additional trial visits completed before a decision is made. The staff of the Regional Center noted that once all parties are agreed, few problems ensue.

During the process of finding a good match between a foster family and a resident, the natural parents are contacted for permission to place their child (even with adults, where such permission is not required). Social workers counsel resisting parents. The intent in gaining the natural parent's permission is to preempt any potential sabotage on their part, since the Regional Center's staff finds that interference from natural families is the most common reasons for having to move a resident from one home to another.

While en route to visit a Community Training Home, the social worker accompanying us related a serious problem she was having with a natural mother who had nagged and interfered with her 38-year-old daughter Nancy's foster parent to the point that 1 year ago the foster parent requested that another home be found. The issue was a difference in religion. The natural mother persisted in trying to change the foster parent's belief system and life-style to accommodate her own religious beliefs. During the intervening year, two trial visits to other homes had been conducted. They had failed, according to the social worker, because the natural mother intervened on the same religious grounds. The social worker, nevertheless, continued to pursue homes for this resident, always outlining the problem with religion for each family.

Nancy's case is illustrative of several common problems in the delivery of foster family care. Confusion usually prevails around the question, What are the rights, responsibilities, and the extent of control that a natural family can or should exercise, and who is responsible for working with the natural parents to clarify and work through these issues? These issues are made even more complex by the mixed feelings that natural parents often hold about another family caring, perhaps successfully, for their child. Obviously, alloting staff members to help understand and mediate the competing demands and needs of residents, natural parents, foster parents, and the agency is an expensive but necessary component of a successful program.

Once a placement has been made, the social work department of the Regional Center is responsible for the continual monitoring, evaluation of the community training homes as well as the provision of supportive services, and the coordination of a day placement for *every* resident. The social worker's role in advising foster parents is facilitated by a Community Training Home packet, which includes information such as emergency procedures, prohibited treatment procedures (e.g., seclusion and restraint), and medical and other agency utilization forms and procedures. Also, the foster parents are required to attend a five-session course structured to teach them general programming techniques and to provide them with other information relevant to working with multiply handicapped individuals. The Regional Center's staff members draw on their experience in conducting these in-service courses. Also, they have developed an excellent and thorough manual that presents a curriculum for the training of foster parents and group home operators.

A social worker carries a case load of about 25 foster families and meets monthly with each foster parent. To enhance the monitoring and social work consultation process, foster parents are required to complete a five-page progress report monthly. This report form is impressive in the specificity and breadth of information sought. Foster parents each month are involved in the following:

1. Developing a series of program objectives and evaluating the progress made during the previous month
2. Describing unusual changes in the resident's behavior
3. Identifying training and informational needs in areas, such as toileting, speech, and hearing
4. Listing the resident's current medications, amounts and frequencies, and the name of any physicians, dentist, or other professional person contacted
5. Documenting the resident's social and recreational contacts
6. Listing any contacts made with the resident's day placement
7. Documenting contacts with the resident's family or guardian
8. Describing those programs developed by the center's consultants
9. Writing a statement describing their satisfaction or dissatisfaction with any or all aspects of the Community Training Home program.

Consultants are available to foster parents on request or when the social worker perceives the need for them. The different specialties represented on the consultant staff are physical therapy, nursing, dentistry, psychology, dental hygiene, and speech and language. If the need arises for a consultant in a different discipline, the center contracts for one.

A Community Training Home Visited

The Brewer family, a couple in their fifties with a teenage daughter, live in a comfortable split-level ranch-style home. Living with the Brewers is Sarah, who is 44 years old and has Down's syndrome. She spent 20 years living in an institution before coming to the Brewer home 16 months ago. Sarah had been placed in the institution when her parents, now deceased, had grown too old to care for her.

Sarah's day seems to have much activity and instruction. Even though she can perform every step of the morning routine of dressing and grooming, she still needs to be told to do each skill, and the Brewers are trying to teach her to get ready more independently. Sarah attends a day activity program from 7:30 A.M. to 4:00 P.M., where activities such as personal hygiene, communication, socialization, and basic academics are taught. The Brewers have visited the program several times and take Sarah there sometimes when the bus fails to pick her up; they get a regular report from the program, which Sarah enjoys very much. In the evening, Sarah eats with the family, which provides an opportunity for them to help her with her developing speech skills, and after dinner she helps to dry the dishes. She is included in all family activities, like going to church every Sunday, and she is encouraged to bring friends home (although she has not done so yet).

Despite a day that apparently promotes acquisition of skills, there is still an element of the benevolent protection here that we have seen in the foster family care model in general. Speaking of Sarah, Mrs. Brewer notes, "You can't wait on her else she'll get dependent." She emphasizes that Sarah is encouraged to do things on her own, "Otherwise she'll sit and not ask for anything until she's told: 'You can get it on your own.'" Yet there are many areas where the Brewers do not consider Sarah ready to learn (e.g., washing dishes and cooking) and, despite Mrs. Brewer's words, much is indeed done for her.

The monitoring from the central agency seems to have had some beneficial effects; it has increased the Brewer's attention to helping Sarah become independent and has promoted a sense of pride in their role. While the monitoring system seems to be a good one, there are the inevitable lapses in program follow-through. For example, when Sarah arrived at the Brewer home, she weighed 108 pounds. She is only 4′8″ tall, and she now weighs 161 pounds; yet she is not on a special weight-reducing program. Mrs. Brewer tries to limit her intake at home, but knows she eats at the activity program during the day. Yet neither the Brewers nor the Regional Center have ever tried to coordinate a weight-reduction program for Sarah with the day program and, in fact, the Brewers have never used any consultant from the center for Sarah.

The Brewers did have, however, occasion to use the center's consultation staff when a previous adult woman placed from the institution became progressively more withdrawn and unhappy. They used many consultants on a crisis basis to help them with specific programming but, according to the Brewers, all the woman did was cry. Toward the end of her stay, the Brewers tried to ease up on the pressure of responsibilities and programming, feeling that the community might be too confusing for her; this relaxation of pressure did not decrease the woman's depression. After 5 months, she was returned to the institution, and the Brewers, who have visited her since, claim that she appears to be much happier there. Sarah, on the other hand, refuses to even visit the institution.

The Brewers feel that they have come a long way since they first read an advertisement in the newspaper about mentally retarded persons being placed in foster care. They knew then, as they still feel now, that they did not want another child in their home; but being interested in people (rather than in additional money), they wanted to share their good fortune in life with another adult. They believe that Sarah has made progress in their home and point to her improved speech as an example of that improvement. Mrs. Brewer summed up their experience of living with Sarah by saying, "We enjoy her. There's been problems, I'm not going to lie about it, but it's really been a joy."

Funding

As we have seen, community training homes are distinct from typical foster family care homes in the attention given to programming and monitoring. Foster parents are paid between $5 and $10 per day *above* the rate for room and board ($7.50 per day). This money is considered salary for the foster parents and, as such, they are responsible for providing intensive training for each resident 2 hours each day.

Since the center requires that the foster family have an outside source of income in addition to the monies they receive as a community training home, being a foster parent does not prevent individuals from continuing in their area of employment. Single persons are not prohibited from becoming foster parents as long as they have an outside source of income. Too, the placement of *one* individual does not interfere with any additional assistance the foster family may now be receiving from the state, such as AFDC.

Conclusions

As of December 1975, the Regional Center had 110 residents in community training homes; about 20 percent were adults. The center projected that the more substantially impaired residents would comprise much of their population in the future, and they anticipated that the proportion of adults in foster care would increase. The Regional Center had the advantage of having developed a range of residential alternatives that allow residents the option to move to different settings within the community, and yet it remained unclear whether a resident in a community training home had a permanent or temporary placement. The center lacked a clearly articulated service plan that projected the different types of residential placements within the system to which a resident might be expected to move. Perhaps with such a strategy in action, more training toward independence for Sarah might have been in evidence in the Brewer home.

One final point about the cost of operating this type of foster family care system is worth noting. Planners and providers of residential care often assume that foster family care is an inexpensive model of service to provide, and indeed for those programs in our survey this was generally true. Although no specific cost figures were available at the time of our visit, the Regional Center's staff assured us that operating these community training homes with a home-finding department, close staff monitoring, consultation services, and the payment of salaries to the foster parents was not a cheaper model of residential service than the group homes they also operate. The Community Training Home program stands as an illustrative example of a well-functioning foster family care system that pays for its quality.

8. Sheltered Villages

THE theme of protection woven through group homes for older adults and foster family care is the raison d'être of the sheltered village. Common to these programs is separation. Sheltered villages are to some degree self-contained, are usually secluded with several buildings on rural acreage, and are typically permanent placements for residents. And yet from one village to another there is much diversity in the extent to which residents are allowed to take risks or are forced to follow strict rules, are responsible for daily living or feel incapable of performing most tasks, or are engaged in meaningful work or sit aimlessly in comfortable lounges or "make-work" shops.

However, common to all sheltered villages is the segregation of the retarded person (and often the live-in staff) from the outside community, and the implicit view that the retarded adult is better off living in an environment that shelters him or her from many of the potential failures and frustrations of life in the outside community – be they coping with landlords, engaging in sexual relationships, buying a Coke, or sitting evenings in a shabby room with only a television's companionship. Sheltered villages have largely been promoted by parents, who find comfort in a placement they feel will be comfortable, protective, and permanent for their children.

Indeed, such programs appear to be quite at odds with the principle of normalization and its expectations for integration. And villages react differently to this. Some, especially religious communities, square off to meet the challenge of this rhetoric by questioning whether coping with the noise, chaos, and loneliness of our cities and the prejudices of our society is really the only "good life." Instead, they argue for bringing a sense of community to the retarded, and this value is a salient guide in program decisions. Others talk of normalization, yet the message is difficult to interpret clearly within a segregated community.

Sheltered villages raise a host of issues and confront some of our most easily held assumptions. Though few in number, they warrant a careful look.

Places and People

The nine sheltered villages surveyed are located in seven states: Massachusetts and California (two each), and Colorado, Iowa, Maryland, Minnesota, and New York (one each). Villages are more likely than other models to be in sparsely populated, rural areas; in fact, all but one of the villages in our sample are in towns with populations of less than 10,000. The locations were chosen for seclusion, for relatively inexpensive land costs, and, in some cases, for farming. The median site has 40 acres (range, 9 to over 500 acres).

Most villages had opened recently (average, around 1968) and had primarily new buildings that were built especially for the village. A typical sheltered village has one or more central buildings (for administration, dining, recreation, etc.), a number of residential houses, and some workshop facilities. On the average, there are 48 rooms, of which 19 are bedrooms for residents.

In the average village at the time of our survey there were 39 residents (range, 12 to 89 residents) with a mean age of 30 years; seven of the nine villages were coeducational. It appears that sheltered villages serve a slightly different population from other models in terms of prior living history and degree of disability. The sheltered village was the only model sampled in which a majority of residents had lived with their own families before moving into the program. Residents in this model were lowest in the reported level of functioning (see "retardation," Fig. 8-1), although due to high variability in the sample, the difference from the pool of other models only approached statistical significance ($t = 1.70$, $p = 0.09$).

The staff-to-resident ratio of 1:1.7 indicates that sheltered villages are the best staffed of any model. Furthermore, staff members in villages are more likely to be involved full time. This high ratio is partly attributable to the unique staffing pattern of some villages; in several church-sponsored villages, the entire staff is unpaid and lives in the village with residents, while in others, a number of paid staff members live in. Consistent with the unique goals of villages, staff members often show commitment to their work as a way of life rather than simply as a short-lived job.

Program

Many programmatic aspects of sheltered villages are predictable consequences of the initial philosophy of separation and protection. The choices of location, facilities, and staff also follow as a consequence of this philosophy. Life at the village emphasizes fulfillment there rather than in the outside community. None of the nine villages surveyed set a limit of under 5 years on resident stay, and six viewed the setting as a permanent home for residents. Indeed, the turnover rate in sheltered villages was by far the lowest of any model (Fig. 8-1).

In some villages residents are employed at the village itself – in a workshop, in a residential house as a cook or cleaner, or on the farm. In others, however, residents do not seem to be involved in any meaningful work program. Virtually no residents are competitively employed in the outside community.

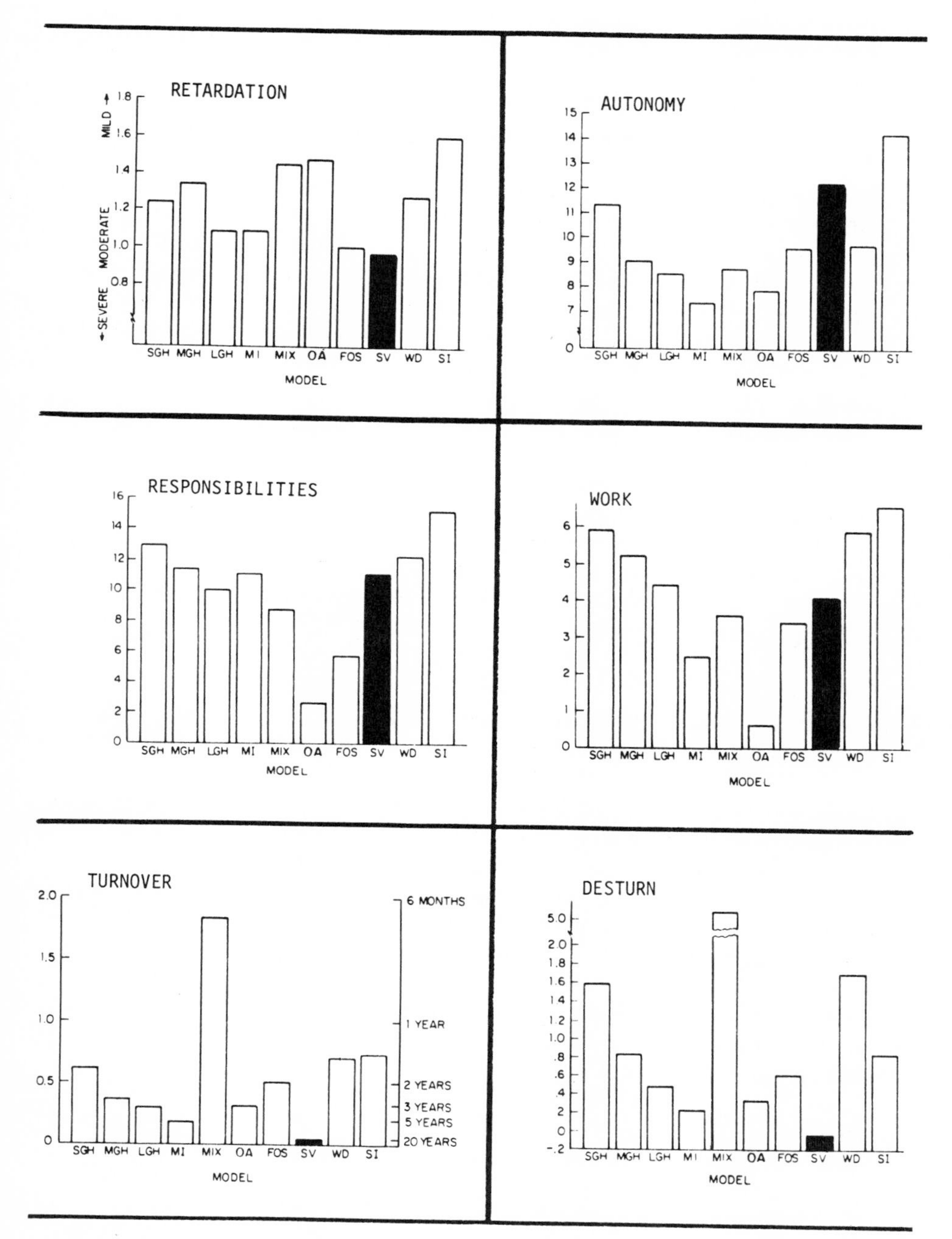

Figure 8-1
Major scales by model.

Residents were reported to have a moderate amount of responsibility for daily routine chores and a relatively high degree of autonomy compared to other models in our sample. The higher autonomy can partly be attributed to the protected environment of the village, in which the safety of residents is easily assured and behavior is more readily monitored. Indeed, policies regarding use of alcohol are as restrictive as in other models, while curfew and bedtime are less so and are more individualized. However, it may be that staff members generally hold the expectation that even without a curfew, residents will stay within the confines of the village. On the question regarding curfew, one village emphatically wrote: "Live here! No permission for leaving grounds to anyone!" While there are fewer prohibitions regarding entertaining the opposite sex, the closed community with a low expected turnover makes unwritten but commonly understood policies more likely.

Leisure activities are mainly generated within the village, and range from the usual television watching, dances, cards, and movies to hiking, topical lectures, gardening, choir singing, and long-range projects such as dramatic productions and crafts exhibits. Outside activities, such as sports events, shopping trips, and trips to local fairs, customarily involve a large group and entail travel by bus. These activities are therefore not frequent. However, many residents in sheltered villages regularly visit their families on weekends or during vacations.

Community

Some villages have their own recreational facilities (e.g., swimming pools), chapel, store, beauty parlor, and barber shop – some even have a dental office and a fire truck! In other villages, residents make use of such facilities in the local community. Generally, though, the sheltered village provides more facilities for its residents than do other models.

Nonetheless, there is some relationship with the community outside the village. Some villages open their facilities for use by the local community and/or volunteer services to the community, and most villages have parent involvement, mainly in their governance. At least five of the villages surveyed were begun through the efforts of parents, and seven have some parents of residents on the board of directors. Five villages involve community volunteers, and the attitude of the outside community is generally seen by the staff as either positive or neutral.

Sponsorship and Funding

All the villages surveyed are private, nonprofit corporations; five are church sponsored. Most villages rely heavily on the monthly fees paid for each villager. The average monthly fee of $334 at the time of our survey was the highest of any model and significantly higher than the $179 for other models pooled.

Payments by parents or guardians were greatest in this model, with 60 percent of residents receiving parental support (versus 7 percent for other models). The remaining residents were supported by Aid to the Disabled, Social Security, or scholarships provided by the sponsoring agency. Only 4 percent of sheltered village residents in our survey contributed toward the monthly fee from earned wages.

State funding seems (with one exception) to take the form of payment for specific residents rather than support for the operation as a whole (e.g., staff and capital improvements). The boards of directors are generally very involved in fund raising and usually have chosen to develop very costly physical plants.

The per-resident yearly budget of $5,200 at the time of our survey probably included more services than more community-based residences. However, this cost would have been higher had it not been for the unpaid live-in staff in some villages. Also, it should be noted that the high capital outlay for facilities did not seem to be included in reported budgets, which were, rather, operating budgets (while mortgages or rents for most other models *were* included in the reported budgets); hence the overall cost of a sheltered village is a good deal greater than the per-resident budget would indicate.

The three villages chosen for visits were quite different; none was really "typical," except that all were segregated communities. Camphill was chosen as an avowedly separate and quite self-contained community, with emphasis on a sense of community and on work roles (especially agrarian). Convent was chosen as a religious retreat, with a sheltered philosophy and a more limited program. Coventry was unique in its attempt to reconcile goals of community integration with sheltered living.

Camphill Village

Nigel . . . long ago accepted the fact of his mental handicap. He is, if anything, rather proud of it. This attitude is noticeable among most of the resident "villagers" of the Camphill Village Trust and at Delrow House, where Nigel and I now live. They say, "This is our *village, because we are handicapped." They handle much of the organization and administration of the villages and are intensely proud of this. One gets the impression from them that to be handicapped is to be especially privileged.*

Hunt, 1967, p. 40

The Camphill movement is international in its scope, yet intensely personal in its spirit. Tracing its philosophical origins to the teachings of Rudolf Steiner (1861–1925), the movement has seen in the retarded person an individual with equal needs for his or her body, soul, and spiritual growth. The school, begun in Scotland in 1939 by Dr. Karl Koenig, became the prototype for others throughout the world. Then, in 1955, a "village community" was begun for young adults on a 280-acre farm in Yorkshire, England. With this community (Botton Village) as a guide, other Camphill villages were established in Scotland, Northern Ireland, Switzerland, Germany, South Africa, and the United States. They are unique in their spiritual core, their unpaid and totally committed staff, and their cultured and purposeful lifestyle, conceived as a viable alternative to the outside community. We visited one of these villages, which we will simply call Camphill (Fig. 8-2).

For any individual who has the true progress of mankind at heart, an increasing awareness of the present sickness of society takes the form of a challenge. It calls for a wrestling with one's own development and a sacrificing of one's personal will in the service of higher aims. The individual who attempts this can find it helpful to live closely with other people in a community.

Camphill Special Schools, Inc.
Beaver Run Children's
Village Report, 1968–1971

Figure 8-2
Fountain Hall, Camphill Village.

Setting

Camphill Village has 175 members living in its community: 90 retarded adults (villagers), 49 staff members (co-workers), and 36 dependents of staff members (children and some parents). No wages are paid, and work and resources are shared according to ability and need.

Camphill opened in 1961 on 200 acres of primarily farmland that was donated by a friend of the movement; additional acquisitions of wooded hills and open fields over the years swelled the property to over 500 acres. There are now 16 cottages at Camphill, each of which is home for a "family" of 9 to 15 persons: villagers, co-workers, and perhaps dependents, of both sexes. Each cottage has single and double bedrooms, a kitchen, dining room, and living room. All buildings were constructed according to anthroposophical principles of architecture:* the use of natural woods, unusual proportions, a great many windows, and the avoidance of right angles. This unusual design is reflected in the main meeting hall, Fountain Hall, shown in Figure 8-2.

We decided to visit Camphill partly because of its farming activities. A walk along Camphill's roads soon leads one to a farmhouse, a food processing and sugar house, a cow barn, an orchard house, vegetable gardens, a greenhouse, and perhaps a few chickens or pigs.

Spring has arrived . . . . Every day offers new surprises, the first daffodils, crocuses, wildflowers . . . . An assortment of chickens has settled down and begun to consider serious egg production.

Newsletter, April 1973
Camphill Village
Kimberton Hills, Pa.

The vegetable garden produces a variety of leaf and root vegetables, tomatoes, beans, squash, and corn . . . . The sugar house substantially increased its output of maple syrup . . . . Pig breeding increased.

Camphill Village U.S.A., Inc.
Fifth Report (1969–1972)

To make meaningful social interaction possible, the Village is divided into four neighborhoods, each with approximately 40 members. Many social events are held within the neighborhoods, and neighborhood meetings function as a type of local government, making full Village assemblies less necessary. Finances from the general fund are allocated to neighborhoods, and it is the neighborhood members who decide how money will be spent. These monies pay for food, household, and entertainment expenses, as well as clothing and personal expenses of co-workers. (Clothing and vacation expenses of villagers are paid by families or by public funds.)

*Anthroposophy is the spiritual philosophy guiding Camphill. Developed by Rudolf Steiner, it is a merging of Eastern philosophical ideas (e.g., reincarnation) with Western Christianity. Steiner's prolific writing embraced many topics, including natural sciences, agriculture, education, art, and architecture. The Anthroposophic Society, 211 Madison Avenue, New York, N.Y. 10016, is a source of information regarding Rudolf Steiner's teachings.

Staff

Work in this community is not of a competitive nature and the absence of the customary fight for advancement, prestige and higher wages allows its members to concentrate with a quiet mind upon their chosen tasks.

Brochure
Camphill Village, Copake, N.Y.

All staff members are unpaid and live at Camphill. The 35 permanent co-workers have made a long-term commitment to the Village movement, while the temporary co-workers are usually students with a time-limited commitment.

Those staff members who function as houseparents are firm believers in anthroposophy. They are usually married couples with families of their own, although in some instances two single people may serve in this role. The houseparents are responsible for the day-to-day operation of the residential cottage and may or may not have other jobs within the Village.

Many of the permanent co-workers have spent much of their lives outside the Camphill community. Often a reevaluation of their lives, sometimes precipitated by illness or another traumatic event, led them to reject their former lifestyles and join the Village movement. There is very little turnover of permanent co-workers, though there is some transfer among Camphill Villages. Temporary co-workers are usually young – college work-study students, or simply people who just want to try this type of life for awhile. In spite of the turnover typical of temporary co-workers, some of these people and some children of co-workers also decide to dedicate their lives to the movement.

Residents

We believe that in every person, be he retarded or not, there is a divine spirit. For the retarded person, it is only the "incarnation" that is handicapped.

Imagine if you will, that you are a very accomplished pianist and a friend asks you to play a Beethoven sonata on his broken down piano which is missing some keys. You sit down to play, but even though you have great talent, what comes out is not beautiful music. Retarded people, similarly, have genius and talented spirits trying to play beautiful music inside them; however, what emerges from them, in many instances, is not beautiful music but cacophonous sounds.

Camphill staff member

The men and women at Camphill are primarily mildly retarded or borderline (15 had measured IQs above 70, 45 in the range of 51 to 70, and 27 had IQs of 20 to 50).

Villagers come from a variety of backgrounds, including institutions, private schools for handicapped children, the anthroposophical school, and their parents' homes. Requirements for admission are that the person be 18 years of age or older, able to take care of basic needs (e.g., dressing and washing), and capable of developing some self-awareness. The Village is seen as most appropriate for those who cannot function in the outside community without undue stress. Prospective residents are interviewed and then spend a number of weeks in the Village for a trial visit. After this, both the prospective villager and current members of the community decide whether the person can fulfill, and be fulfilled by, the community.

The four residents interviewed were split as to whether they had originally wanted to come to Camphill. However, all reported being happy at Camphill now, mainly mentioning satisfaction derived from their work, the peace and quiet, the independence, the availability of activities, and the overall community.

A villager who becomes a member of the community is encouraged and counseled to view Camphill as home, to develop an adult relationship with his or her parents, and to understand that visits home are natural but that his or her primary work, home, and relationships are at Camphill. This pressure for commitment to the group and a giving up of previous ties is a typical characteristic of communal societies (Kanter, 1972). Many villagers told us that they did not visit their parents' homes very often because they were needed for their jobs at the Village. They said that after going to their parents' homes for vacations, they were anxious to get back to their own home at Camphill. Some villagers, though, while feeling Camphill was nice, said they really wished that they were home.

Program: A Typical Day

Each weekday morning, one villager is responsible for waking the other persons in his or her cottage. The housemother usually prepares breakfast with a villager's assistance. After breakfast, all gather around a candle in the living room for a common reading of prayer or a brief passage of scripture. The same portion is read each morning for 1 week. Then the villagers clear the table, do the dishes, make their beds, tidy their bedrooms, and report to work by 9:00 A.M. (or even earlier for those who work on the farm). Villagers and co-workers are given their assignments by the Works Group on the basis of what the community needs; no member of the Village seemed to us to be busy with any job that was not truly needed by the Village, eliminating what one board member called "the make-believe which exists in many sheltered workshops."

There is a variety of workshops throughout Camphill that employ co-workers and villagers alike: a bookbindery, a doll shop, a weavery, a bakery, an enamel shop, and a carpentry shop.* Some co-workers spend their day as workshop directors; others, in administrative or farming roles. One villager, Arthur, whom we interviewed, was the foreman of one of the shops. In the morning he was

*These crafts shops produce products for consumption by villagers and also provide income in excess of $25,000 annually for Camphill (through sales to visitors in a village gift shop as well as a mail-order business and other merchandising strategies). These high-quality products include copper enameled dishes, bowls, candle holders, and key rings (enamel shop); toys and children's furniture (wood workshop); the "Camphill doll" and assorted doll clothing (doll workshop); woven rugs, scarves, and yard goods (weaving shop); and breads, cakes, and cookies (bakery).

responsible for opening the workshop and making sure other workers had jobs for that day. Arthur stated, "It's something I know how to do and I'm good at."

Aside from the workshops, a villager might work in the vegetable garden, on the farm, as a tour guide of the Village, in cottages as a housecleaner and lunch cook (learning to plan and prepare meals), in the laundry or processing plant, or on maintenance or building details. It seemed that the farmers generally enjoyed their work. However, the attitude of those who worked in the crafts shops toward their jobs was more mixed. Some villagers worked well and others seemed uninterested and uncooperative. Nevertheless, low work output from some villagers seemed to be well tolerated by co-workers.

At noon, the community members return to their cottages for lunch; then they have a free period until 2:00 P.M. when work resumes. Supper is held at about 5:30 P.M. The evening includes many optional activities, such as hobby groups (e.g., basketball, candle making, photography, and knitting), music, dramatic productions, folk dancing, or lectures and self-interest groups on topics such as religions of the world, poetry or even bullfighting. All these activities are for villagers and co-workers alike, and co-workers stress that the intellectual level is not lowered unduly to accommodate the villagers. In our experience this was the case, at least for hobby groups; a lute playing group, for example, was co-led by a very skilled villager. Some villagers, of course, are less able to profit from these activities, and many report that their main adjustment difficulty at first is doing without television, a topic on which co-workers are particularly vehement.

By banning the drugging effect of hours spent passively in front of television sets and the indiscriminate day-long outpouring of radio programs, meaning is restored to such active endeavors as learning to play an instrument, choir-singing, or play-acting.

Brochure
Camphill Village, Copake, N.Y.

There are usually no activities planned for Saturday, and Saturday night is "Bible evening," providing members a forum for discussing the scripture that was read each morning during the preceding week. On Sunday morning there is an anthroposophical service for the entire community, although attendance is not required and temporary co-workers often choose not to attend. On Sunday afternoon members generally visit with their friends from other cottages.

There is no apparent curfew or bedtime. Regarding other rules and policies, there is always, as in the case of watching television, a strong philosophical rationale.

Community

We see our challenge not to bring the retarded to the community but rather to bring a sense of community to the retarded.

Camphill staff member

Camphill's relation to the outside community is very much guided by the vision of creating, within Camphill Village, a community that is more humane than the larger society. A co-worker talked of how life in the cities has reached a pitch where it is unnatural and abnormal for everyone, and several other co-workers followed with questions such as "Why train a retarded person to fit into an abnormal outside community where he will feel stress and run a high probability of being exploited? Why force a retarded person to live like that because many 'normal' people live like that?"

Outside involvements, then, are often for the purpose of educating the wider community. Visitors are always welcome at Camphill, and a local Friends of Camphill Village organization seeks to foster a better understanding in the community through activities such as talks to local service organizations or occasional visits by villagers to private homes. Camphill Village also serves the wider community in some limited ways. Co-workers at the Village presently serve as volunteer firemen for the local community, and the Village has made a monthly fund-raising pledge to Futures for Children, an international aid organization that provides funds for tools and technical assistance in developing areas. A committee of 14 villagers and 2 co-workers is responsible for fund-raising projects within Camphill.

Despite some organized trips into surrounding towns, it seems that the Camphill villagers and co-workers alike leave the Village infrequently, and there is no emphasis on helping the villager to cope with the outside community. Local shopkeepers seemed to have had very little personal contact with villagers. Hence while the integration of Camphill into the community at large is fostered, the eventual integration of villagers is not. Camphill, in fact, reports virtually no resident turnover; we did receive reports of individuals leaving after several months, but apparently these were viewed as being still in the trial period.

Sponsorship and Funding

As noted, Camphill is a private, nonprofit corporation with a board of directors. At the time of our survey, the total annual operating cost per villager was about $3,600, almost 90 percent of which was covered by fees ($300 per month). Approximately half the villagers received public funds, Aid to the Disabled or Social Security, while the others were supported by parents. The remaining operating costs were met by income from Camphill crafts shops and farm, as well as by contributions.

This relatively low operating budget, particularly given the larger number of staff members and services, is largely made possible by unpaid staff, economically productive Village enterprises, and the provision of a good deal of needed food from the Village's own farm. However, the support for the building of Camphill's very expensive physical plant has been privately contributed and is not included in the operating expenses.

Conclusions

Camphill, as we experienced it, is a purposeful community that is clear about its philosophical underpinnings. It epitomizes separation, not primarily for the protection of the residents but as a searching on the part of residents and staff alike for an alternative lifestyle, one that emphasizes religious commitment, mutual interdependence, and sharing of work and resources. Such a total community may only be possible within a religious or otherwise spiritually oriented framework.

Of particular note was the attention given to meaningful work and leisure activities. The retarded adult's right to be different was well respected, with high tolerance for uncooperative, bizarre, or withdrawn behaviors. Yet mature adult options, such as useful jobs or nonpatronizing activities, were available and encouraged.

Convent

The second sheltered village we visited, which we call Convent, might just as well be called a large group home, since it is housed in one large building. However, because of its similarity to other villages in its philosophy and its live-in staff, we included it in this category. We chose to visit this setting because it represented an example of a church-affiliated and church-administered community residence and because it did not aspire to integrate the resident into the community but, rather, to provide a healthy, self-contained environment in which the values of the religious order could be expressed. Much about Convent spoke to the protective and benevolent aspects of sheltered villages, beginning, certainly, with the choice to build a facility where all would live under one roof.

Why do people consider young people who go off to the country to join a commune more normal than us? The only major difference between us and the young people nowadays is that we have retarded women living with us.

Convent staff member

Setting

Convent is a unique community, including 40 retarded women, 15 retired nuns who had served the sponsoring order, and 16 working nuns who perform staff functions. The religious order has operated 11 facilities throughout the world, from the United States to China. At present some of these facilities are closing, and Convent serves partly as a nursing home for elderly nuns, some of whom are bed-ridden.

Convent opened in 1970 in a specially constructed building on 33 acres of woodland in a wealthy suburb of a major city; no neighbors' houses are visible. The major impetus for the facility came from parents of the present residents. These parents, concerned about the future of their handicapped children after their own death or debilitation, and frustrated by attempts to gain suitable services in the community, sought a life-long home that would provide security and protection for their daughters. In the first year, 200 applications were received.

During the 1½ years before opening, the staff directed its attention toward facilitating community acceptance; staff worked closely with the board of selectmen, the planning board, and the board of health. They spoke with parent groups, professionals, local business people, and clergy, and they made house calls in the neighborhood. In previous years, two other towns had refused the order permission to open a program, but this time Convent seemed to be well received.

Much careful planning went into selecting a site and choosing an architect to design a setting that would enhance the order's philosophy of serving the retarded. A single facility, costing $1.5 million, was erected, merging the two goals of providing opportunities for communal life and privacy for both staff members and residents. Long, carpeted hallways, off which are resident and housemothers' bedrooms, funnel into expansive discussion halls, dining halls, and classrooms. There is a private bedroom for each resident; those who so choose have roommates. A bathroom is shared by two residents on the average. The effect is of a very pleasant, comfortable dormitory. The retired nuns live in a separate portion of this same building.

Staff

The Convent staff members are predominantly Episcopal nuns, who are unsalaried, although there are several paid laymen and laywomen on the staff. The nuns live at the residence and serve a dual role – as staff for the residence (called *housemothers*) and as helpers to the retired sisters. The nuns, who are hard-working and committed, feel, with justification, the burden of their work and would appreciate more staff. However, the order is diminishing in size and has a policy not to transfer a nun from one facility to another unless she genuinely wants to move.

The current staff members come from diverse backgrounds – from the local area, from the Philippines, and from a former home operated by the order in a nearby state. Most of the sisters have experience in working with retarded people and remain well informed about the field by reading and taking courses at local universities. There seems to be some deficiency, however, in the staff members' programming abilities, and the professional backup consultants have been primarily medical. Many of the activities are carried out by volunteers, recruited from churches and community organizations and under the supervision of the program's director. There seem to be mixed feelings among the sisters toward the volunteers, some appreciating their work and feeling it is good for residents to interact with outsiders, others having reservations about the volunteers' reliability and the discontent they are apt to stir up.

Residents

The sisters generally feel that Convent is "not for everyone," but that it is a good placement for residents who need long-term care and want to live there.

Acceptance criteria for residents include that they be at least 19 years old, be able to take care of themselves, and not be overly disruptive.

The 40 women are 18 to 65 years old, although 78 percent are between the ages of 31 and 50 years. The majority (78 percent) are considered moderately retarded; the remainder are equally divided – more and less handicapped. A number of residents have medical problems, such as epilepsy or diabetes, and a third of the residents take medication regularly.

Before moving to Convent, 55 percent of the women lived at home with their families, while 38 percent lived in a state school or hospital. It seems that apprehension about sexuality and fear of abuse of their daughters can account for at least some of the parents' motivation to seek the safe environment of Convent. Fully 50 percent of the residents had been sterilized, most before the age of 11 years and some before the age of 6 years; no woman had been sterilized since becoming a resident of Convent.

There was an especially childlike quality to the residents. They seemed to be docile and easily directed, and competed for attention from visitors. They also tended to gossip about, and sometimes pick on, one another. Many of these behaviors seemed characteristic of a very interdependent and isolated family, a model that Convent encourages. This was the only setting in which residents were not interviewed. The nuns expressed concern about interviews, saying that the residents' feelings might be hurt by this process. In the one interview that was carried out, the woman broke down and became very upset about "gossip behind my back." No other interviews were attempted since there was much concern about who would be interviewed and fear that those who were *not* interviewed would be hurt.

Generally, the level of emotional maturity was not high. This seemed to be largely fostered by the expectations the staff held for the residents. For example, the ambivalence about the residents' maturity is reflected in the following choice of words of one staff person: "Residents are adult women, with the same problems as ordinary women. The *girls* sometimes question why they can't marry, have closer relations with men, etc." (Emphasis ours.)

Program: A Typical Day

The daily program at Convent is rather low key, providing some activities, although certainly not a full schedule, and some training, although not with planned regularity. While the aim of decreasing dependence is voiced by the staff, the daily routine, in fact, prescribes much of what is expected of residents. Throughout the program, there appears to be a respectful benevolence and an acceptance of the residents' behavior; comfort and communal living in a large simulated family emerges as a higher priority than growth toward independence.

The home part is what Convent is for. We're all in agreement about this. Living together happily – not activities – is the focus.

Convent staff member

One sister expressed the view that a very activity-oriented day had proved to be "too much" for the residents.

But even the young ones – it's easy to overestimate their strength. They get tired more easily than we realize.

Residents are awakened in the morning by a bell and someone going around to their rooms. Most have adequate self-care skills, and the more able residents help others who have difficulty. Appropriate grooming is definitely encouraged, and volunteers give lessons in these skills. Breakfast, like other meals, is planned by the cook, but meals are prepared with the help of residents, who are given increased responsibility as they are able. Residents must attend meals and sit at assigned seats. They wait on the tables, but housemothers serve the food since "having the girls serve themselves did not work out." Grace is said both at the beginning and the end of meals.

During the morning, most of the women attend a sheltered workshop in the building or do chores at the residence. The workshop reports some difficulty in obtaining contracts and is not really oriented toward providing income. Following work, the women tend to congregate in the lounge to relax and talk. Two residents are allowed to smoke, but housemothers keep the cigarettes.

Afternoons are generally free, with some classroom teaching and scheduled activities available. Teaching mainly relates to academics and living skills; there is no formal teaching about sex, health, legal rights, or time and money skills – knowledge that would be useful in moving into the community. There is a daily optional chapel service that most residents attend and a required service on Sunday.

A Typical Weekly Schedule

(This schedule is illustrative of the rather thin and nonindividual programming.)

Monday:	Morning – bowling or workshop and sewing
	Afternoon – arts and crafts
	Every other Monday evening – square dance at a local church
Tuesday:	Afternoon – music program
Wednesday:	Afternoon – swimming class or music class (modern)
Thursday:	Afternoon – walking, drama, and cooking
Friday:	Art program
Saturday:	Varied
Sunday:	Afternoon – visitors

There is no evening curfew as such; however, because the nearest public transportation is 3 miles away, residents do not leave unescorted. All residents have their own radios and half own their own television sets and record players. No alcoholic beverages are allowed, and residents do not date. Even in organized social activities, they have very limited contact with men.

The dual purpose of Convent as a home for both retired nuns and retarded women seems to have some repercussions for the retarded residents. One sister noted, "There is a great strain upon the housemothers. They must be constantly quieting things down for the other sisters on the other side of the wall in the dining room; the need for the residents to make noise and that of the retired nuns to have quiet, conflicts."

Community

Convent's physical isolation from neighbors, shops, and transportation means that contacts with the community are limited. Our interviews with neighbors and the operator of a bowling alley used by Convent revealed that while their feelings toward the program are quite positive, they do not really know the residents. Some of the sisters, however, said they feel isolated at the residence – for example, they miss being able to walk to the grocery store. The residents, while spending almost all their time at Convent, are encouraged to take vacations of up to 30 days at home once or twice a year. There are few ex-residents of Convent.

There are many unresolved questions about the program's aims. In our interviews with staff members, many expressed reservations about the normalization movement, feeling that in principle it does not make sufficient allowance for alternative (e.g., communal) lifestyles, and in practice it does not ensure long-term and sufficiently comprehensive aid, where needed. Yet some sisters mentioned certain residents who should move toward more independent living; they felt their places should be taken by more severely retarded women.

As noted, although a number of community persons volunteer at Convent, feelings about their value are mixed. One sister expressed justified disdain for the patronizing involvement of charity groups' activities, such as Christmas parties with Santa Claus. Yet, while verbally expressing that the residents need to be regarded as mature women, the staff has not comfortably reconciled these words with the benevolent maternalism of their setting and has not clearly articulated what forms meaningful involvement with the community would take.

Sponsorship and Funding

The average monthly fee was $400, and the primary source of income was from the residents' families. Roughly 25 percent of residents came from families with incomes less than $12,000, and for these residents fees were supplemented by scholarship support. The cost of the building was raised from the church, the order, and private donations. The sisters work without salaries. The program, as it now operates, depends on the dedication of these unpaid nuns, and the diminishing number of women entering the order is a potential source of concern.

Convent, then, shares a philosophy of separation in a self-contained community with other sheltered villages. The emphasis is more on life within the communal residence than on preparation for leaving it. In this relatively new facility, some issues remained unresolved, such as questions of *activities* and opportunities for independence. Unlike some villages that have a fully planned day of work and recreation, Convent presently offers a less intentional and less intense program. There is also a potential contradiction between the parents' aim of seeking protection and security for their daughters and the feelings of some staff members that residents should become less dependent.

The net result may be a program that provides opportunities for the residents to take risks that are within such narrow and protected limits they will really be "just pretend."

Coventry Village

There must be a continual conscious effort to recognize and allow for the norm in all instances and not permit administrative convenience, unconscious following of traditional approaches, or an unwarranted concern for protection to circumvent the goals of normalization.

From Coventry Village literature

Our third visit was to a setting that we will call Coventry Village, a new, semirural community where 25 retarded adults and a number of staff members live and work. Coventry differs from Camphill and Convent in its subscription to the philosophy of normalization and therefore its view of separatism, not as a long-term situation but rather as a means of short-term training toward community integration. We visited Coventry Village to determine whether these aims were compatible with a segregated community and the aims of the residents' parents who were funding the program.

Setting

Three couples, all parents of retarded children, began meeting in 1965 to discuss the problem of providing a meaningful life for their children and others once they reached adulthood. Soon the meetings became more regular, a fourth couple became involved, and the group decided that it would try to devise a program that would cost less than state institutional care and would provide a higher quality of life. Coventry Village was incorporated in 1966; the board of directors included the original parents, other parents of retarded persons, and professionals. After studying different resources and visiting a number of existing alternatives to institutions, the board chose a village as their model. They sought property that was relatively inexpensive and within 50 miles of the metropolitan area, where most of the parents lived, and found a 75-acre plot with a stable in a semirural area for $68,000. A $216,000 federal grant paid for the land, administrative costs for the initial period, and some construction.

After an extensive search for architectural plans that captured the board's conception of the Village, construction was begun on three cottages (each costing about $80,000) and a workshop-administrative building. The resulting village is quite attractive; it has a modern design with picture windows and skylights looking out on the greens and browns of clearings and pine woods. In each cottage there are two wings – one for women and one for men. There are three double bedrooms, four single bedrooms, and one bathroom for every two persons. A large, nicely furnished living room with a fireplace opens into a dining room and a modern kitchen with a separate laundry room. Although each cottage is decorated differently, they all have modern conveniences, such as dishwashers and color television sets. The workshop-administrative building is one large room with a high ceiling and skylights; off the main work area are a snack bar and several offices. The executive director lives in a converted barn adjacent to Coventry's land.

Staff

Coventry admitted its first residents in September 1972. The program is well staffed with 14 full-time and 2 part-time persons. The cottages are staffed much like small group homes, with two live-in employees and others for their relief. The Village also has administrative, vocational, and recreational staff not customarily available in separate group homes.

Consistent with the careful planning that went into Coventry, the executive director was hired a full year before any residents were admitted; he was responsible for developing the philosophy of the Village and now oversees its staffing and daily operation. The assistant director, a social worker, has, among her responsibilities, meetings three times each week with the live-in cottage staff. The workshop director supervises the sheltered workshop, obtains contracts, and is responsible for arranging work placements in the local community.

In contrast to most group homes, only single people are employed as live-in staff members; this policy facilitates the staff members' ability to take time off. Still, Coventry views the house staff member's role as a full-time commitment and acknowledges that outside ties will be difficult to maintain. One house staff member told us that he was hired with the agreement that he would be totally committed to the Village while he was there, and when he was "burnt out" and could not give any more, he would leave.

The staff seemed quite committed to Coventry and to the village concept. To paraphrase the executive director, this is less a job and more a way of life. "It's a nice way to work with people." But the isolation and totality of the "way of life" means that the commitment of live-in staff is usually time-limited.

Residents

The Village will accept mentally retarded adults . . .
1. *Above the age of 18*
2. *Who have no physical or behavioral disabilities which would prevent them from participating as members of the village*
3. *Who at the time of admission cannot be expected to live independently*

From Coventry Village literature

At the time of our visit, there were 25 residents at Coventry, 13 men and 12 women. These men and women (the terms preferred by the Village) are primarily mildly (16) and moderately (7) retarded and young; 15 are aged 18 to 21 years and an additional 6, aged 22 to 30 years.

In the cottage in which we interviewed residents, there were five women and three men, mainly in their early twenties. Before coming to Coventry, three had lived at private residential facilities (one at Camphill, one at Convent), one had lived at a state institution, and four had lived at home. Four of the eight persons we spoke with had close relatives on the board of directors.

All these men and women seemed to take care of their personal needs quite competently. Most could read and write, and several were able to shop and handle money. Four persons reported that they had wanted to come to the Village, and four said they had not – two of these persons felt that they were put there because their parents did not want them anymore. Three residents said they would be happier if they could live more independently now. It was not immediately apparent, given the high skill level of these men and women, why more independent living could not be expected at this time.

Program: A Typical Day

Adults living at the Village must be given every opportunity to develop independent skills. They must also have the privilege of making an occasional mistake or to be wrong. (Coventry Village) will provide supervised living, not a sheltered life.

From Coventry Village literature

Sally crystallized for us the issue of shelter versus independence. She had recently "graduated" from the special education class of a suburban high school and possessed some minimal reading and writing skills. Her parents were on the Coventry board of directors, and Sally's move there after high school had been assumed and was quite natural, as if she were "off to college." This enthusiastic 18-year-old, with a bedroom full of records, contemporary posters on the door, and constant chatter about boy friends and rock stars, was very much the boarding school teenager. But as her talk, still incessant, turned more serious, Sally spoke of her future, of living in an apartment with other women, when she is ready, when she grows up. Coventry to Sally is transitional, but she is not clear about what she must learn to do – in the cottage, in the workshop, in her part-time job with a community newspaper – to be ready. She is really looking forward to moving to the planned quarter-way cottage, still on the Coventry grounds. But we, and no doubt Sally, could not help wondering when, and by what criteria, her parents and the Coventry staff will feel she is "ready" for independent living.

The weekly schedule at Coventry is characterized by an emphasis on work and a reasonable degree of autonomy for the men and women. On a typical day, residents wake themselves and prepare their own breakfast. They clean their own rooms, clean parts of the cottage, pack their lunch, and arrive at the workshop by 9:00 A.M. If their job for that day is in the community, one of the staff members drives them to work. During the workshop hours, some residents return to their cottage to receive instruction in living skills from the house staff. Otherwise, they are encouraged not to return to their cottages during the day in an attempt to simulate normal working conditions. The workshop, which serves retarded people from the community as well (eight at the time of our visit), is run with regular coffee and lunch breaks. The workers receive wages according to the regulations of the Department of Labor and are paid by check every Friday. All workers have savings accounts.

All the eight men and women interviewed worked at the workshop on the Village grounds. (Each person was required to start at the workshop until it seemed he or she was ready to work in the community.) At the time of our visits, contracts included stuffing advertising brochures and packaging dog biscuits for local companies, and, as is often the case, contracts were difficult to find. Five of the eight persons interviewed stated that they would not be happy working for very long at the Village workshop, due, in some instances, to boredom. Several reported specific occupations they would rather pursue: taking care of children, working in a pet store, drugstore, or library, or washing floors (but not at the Village). Six of the men and women interviewed already held part-time jobs on some days in the community – collating newspapers or cleaning offices and doing gardening as part of a Village work crew.

The men and women return from their jobs at 4:00 P.M. A daily rotating, assigned schedule is posted for setting the table and preparing dinner. Some of the men and women plan and prepare the meal by themselves, while others require assistance from the house staff. Dinner is the only meal that staff members and residents eat together. Following the meal and shared cleanup responsibilities, the men and women are free to do as they wish. On some evenings, optional activities in the workshop are held, such as arts and crafts taught by a community volunteer or a drop-in center where residents get together to socialize. Snacks are available as desired. The most frequently mentioned leisure activities are watching television and taking trips to the movies.

A series of forced-choice questions was asked of the executive director, the house staff, and the residents. There was good agreement that the men and women were proud of the Village, helped each other often, and received individual attention. However, there was disagreement about their respective perceptions of Coventry's rules. While the staff maintained that there were no formal rules, the residents felt that there were (e.g., "everyone must be in their bedrooms by 10:00 P.M." and "men and women cannot go into each other's bedrooms"). Also, the staff felt that activities in the Village were spontaneous, while residents reported that activities were carefully planned.

Generally, however, in keeping with its outspoken adherence to normalization, Coventry grants considerably more autonomy than most of the other programs visited. Personal grooming is not regulated and dress is informal. The use of alcoholic beverages is permitted in houses on occasion. Residents take care of their own money, are allowed to smoke, and may choose whether and where to worship. Also, residents are assisted and encouraged to vote. Teaching is offered relating to health, sex education, and money skills, all useful in making an adjustment to the community. One could question whether retarded persons who are able to function within these normalized guidelines might not also be able to function outside a sheltered village, although, of course, the implicit protection and supervision within the village may minimize the risks in granting such autonomy.

Community

Coventry is some distance from the center of town, and since there is no public transportation, the men and women must rely on the Village's staff for rides. Yet the Village has purposely not duplicated services available in the community, thereby encouraging use of medical and dental services, theaters, barber shops, banks, and stores that exist in the town. There are plans, however, to build a recreation hall at Coventry. There are also plans for constructing semi-independent apartments on the Village grounds for residents who are able to graduate from the cottages but are not perceived as ready to live on their own.

The neighbors were originally quite leery of this village being established, expressing concern for their children. Yet at the time of our visit they were quite satisfied with Coventry as a neighbor, both because their contact with the Village had been minimal and because *the residents were seen as well supervised.* One wonders, though, what this acceptance, based on supervision, bodes for the ultimate goal of residents living independently in the community. When we visited there were no ex-residents.

Sponsorship and Funding

There's no reason why anyone has to live in a state institution when it costs less to run a nice place like this.

Coventry resident

Coventry Village is a private, nonprofit corporation. The annual fee of $5,500 ($458 per month) was paid by parents, with no public assistance support at the time of our visit. Although the resident's statement previously quoted about relative costs may well be true, several points are not considered. First, many costs are not covered by tuition, including medical, dental, and clothing expenses, and the cost of therapy programs and individual recreation, as well as personal spending. Second, while tuition covers daily operations, the very sizable costs of building a setting as luxurious as this one are met by the fund-raising activities of the board of directors. Because of good organization, they have been able to raise a considerable amount of capital. Yet it should be noted that there is criticism leveled by some outside professionals, who are displeased that a program serving a small number of advantaged persons obtains such a large portion of private donations – monies that citizens might otherwise contribute to programs for retarded persons who are less financially advantaged.

In sum, Coventry leaves us with some favorable impressions and some questions that can be more easily posed than answered at this early stage in the Village's development. *Regarding normalization,* What is that fine line between persons who can now function with the high autonomy afforded by the Village but supposedly could not live in community-based group homes or semi-independent apartments? *Regarding future placement,* Is a rural community the best location for a program that aims for community integration and meaningful work roles? *Regarding goals,* Does the aim of parents to find safety and permanence in a placement mesh well with the normalization philosophy voiced by the Village?, and Which perspective is more likely to be compromised as individual decisions about a resident's staying or leaving are confronted? Moreover, To what extent does the resident have a choice (or voice) regarding placement? *Regarding permanence,* Are parents' aims for a permanent placement really met in principle at all, since there is no current provision for funding when parents can no longer provide tuition?

Issues Related to Sheltered Villages

The main issue raised by the sheltered village model is that of *separation and protection,* for while these characteristics typify those of many of the other community residences surveyed, they are the defining characteristics of the sheltered village. Casting a backward glance at institutions, many persons cannot help being skeptical about the rebirth of the "sheltered" notion. Yet others, among them many parents, remind us that the rush to "integrate" with the community has sometimes left the retarded as unprotected pawns of enlightened rhetoric. In any event, the villages visited gave humane expression to the aim of separation, and obligate us to consider its redeeming values.

Separation might be, in part, for protection and security, as at Convent, or for a richer life, as at Camphill, or for the first steps in training, as at Coventry. And separation therefore may have differing effects on residents. For example, we have seen that the autonomy and risk-taking potential varies greatly, depending on the reasons for separation. It is noteworthy that in the most protected settings (e.g., Convent) residents were somewhat immature, docile, and vulnerable, with limited views of themselves as agents in their own futures. In Coventry's relatively less protected setting, residents openly criticized and expressed future hopes for living or working as integral members of the community. High staff expectations for normalized behavior, and the experience of autonomy and risk taking within the security of a setting that still affords some protection, may together help the resident to build confidence in his or her abilities and ideas and create some desire for even greater independence.

A related issue is the provision of *work and leisure.* One rationale for the rural location of sheltered villages would be an emphasis on farming, yet we were surprised to find in our entire survey almost no agricultural programs wherein retarded adults staffed a working farm. Camphill approaches this, although its program is more differentiated. It seems that a group home with a farm or sheltered village that is agriculturally productive, though partially subsidized, might be a viable working and living model, suited well to some retarded adults and to the future economic needs of our society. But if a sheltered village seeks eventually to move residents toward greater independence, a sparsely populated area will have clear disadvantages, such as limited future work opportunities. If a program is permanent and rural, then it faces the difficult choice either of becoming a total community that provides work, leisure, and health facilities (and thereby secludes the resident from the outside, as at Camphill) or of making use of community facilities that are usually not accessible except by car (thereby making the resident quite dependent on staff and limiting individual recreation, as at Coventry).

Regarding *staffing,* it seems to us that sheltered villages that are permanent should have a live-in staff (probably with some cohesive philosophy, religious or otherwise). There is a savings in cost and a better likelihood that a genuine alternative community will develop. A sheltered village where the staff does not live seems particularly hypocritical, an unreal village, actually oriented toward the segregation of the retarded citizen.

Clearly the sheltered village is a model in which the quest for a psychological sense of community overrides themes of independence and training. However, there is a certain paradox here. Sarason (1974, p. 8), writing of special classes and residential institutions, stated: "Nothing is as destructive of the psychological sense of community as segregation." Sarason went on to discuss the ways in which removal from family and community to an institution accentuates feelings of difference and rejection and weakens the sense of community with one's family. Further, professional staff in such settings feel apart from and unvalued by the community, and indeed the institution itself has "little or no relationship to the community in which it is physically embedded" (p. 178).

Perhaps this seeming paradox cannot really be resolved without further study of how individuals indeed *experience* different settings. However, it is worth noting that Sarason was speaking of the traditional institution, which not only separated individuals from their home community but also segregated them from nonhandicapped peers. The prospects for a psychological sense of community *within* institutional walls are not explored, and with good reason. However, the sheltered village with a live-in staff separates but does not segregate, and while it assuredly weakens ties with the family and home community, it intentionally strives to build a sense of commitment and belonging, an alternative psychological sense of community within its boundaries.

It is difficult to summarize the impressions from a model in which the philosophy is so debatable and the implementation so variable. The residents in the settings visited seemed as happy as any other residents interviewed. At Camphill and at Coventry residents seemed to be more productively engaged than in many other facilities we visited and seemed to have at least as much satisfaction with and pride in their jobs. All three settings had attractive facilities, privacy, concerned staff, and some interesting activities; by many measures, the quality of life was high. Also, parents and the neighboring communities seemed pleased with the villages, although mainly because of their separation and supervision of residents. Whether the "safe" sheltered village serves as a first step toward broader acceptance of the retarded by the community or, conversely, further strengthens attitudes of segregation, remains unclear. The latter, however, would seem more likely.

A case may be made for providing this environment for severely retarded individuals who will never move to complete independence, and who might find within the protective boundaries of the village more dignity than within the symbolically higher walls of supervision and rules of an urban residence. The resident moving from an institution may also benefit from a time-limited transitional experience in a setting such as one of those visited. More generally, we could argue that in an ideal system of alternatives, the choice of life in a sheltered village should be open to any retarded adult who has had ample opportunity to learn about the options.

Section 3. Training Programs

Littleton House is a place where people believe in you . . . and are willing to explain your budget book to you every day, if necessary, because they know that some day it will all make sense.

Community Center's Annual
Newsletter Report

PEOPLE who are truly committed to "making available to the mentally retarded patterns and conditions of everyday life which are as close as possible to the norms and patterns of mainstream society" (Nirje, 1969, p. 181) should not expect this condition to occur spontaneously. This is an arduous process of equipping people with the behaviors necessary to strike an appropriate balance between themselves and that amorphous construct we call the community.

Thus there is a need for intentional training programs, especially for persons who are moderately or severely retarded and for those mildly retarded individuals with a long history of institutionalization, an isolated family upbringing, or behaviors that are likely to interfere with adaptive performance in the community. Planners must be mindful of the 22 percent of residents in our sample whose return to institutions from their community placements partly reflected unmet training needs. Also there are many others whose lives are still characterized by underdeveloped abilities and unfulfilled aspirations. Thus the need for carefully conceived training programs will increase over time. As is commonly recognized, many of the first residents of community-based facilities were those higher functioning individuals who obviously "did not belong" in institutions and for whom simply the provision of a more normalized environment could lead to more normalized behavior. Yet many staff members have already reported to us that residents were more retarded than they expected and that their own quickly acquired and embraced philosophy of normalization was, by itself, too lacking in substance to be of much help.

The focus of this section, then, is on programs in which training is a primary value. These programs are typically transitional and oriented toward preparation for life elsewhere; they commonly employ a behavior modification approach.

Behavior modification refers to training that aims at changing behavior by systematic programming of environmental antecedents and consequences. Many programs with this orientation have been successful in enhancing the functioning of retarded (and other) persons (Bandura, 1969; Gardner, 1971; Baker, Brightman, Heifetz, and Murphy, 1976). Specific behavioral objectives are established; skills to be learned are broken down into finely graded steps and taught gradually. Reinforcement is provided for successively better performance, and progress is continually monitored. Many training programs for retarded adults are either based on behavior modification or contain some components of this approach (such as pay being made contingent on work done).

Most of these training facilities are short term. Individualized training plans are developed, incentive programs are used, and residents move through stages of skill acquisition to more independent levels of functioning. However, two factors are crucial for these programs to succeed. First, the staff must be well trained in the teaching approaches to be used and should have backup, specialist supervision; professional degrees or formal education are often not deemed important, but the program itself must provide both a model and a staff training program that is adequate for its purpose. Second, the staff must make systematic and intense efforts to establish community ties with potential residential and work placements for individuals in the training program, so that training can be directed toward realistic placement goals and so the training staff can provide continuity in following up ex-residents.

Training programs can be located anywhere along the deinstitutionalization route. They are often located within large institutions (Lent, 1968; Martin, 1972, 1974), where a highly structured skill teaching program, specialist supervision, and a progressively more normalized routine are engineered to ease the transition to the greater autonomy and increased responsibility of noninstitutional life. Or, regional assessment and training facilities of a short-term nature can be made available for the placement of some individuals coming from either an institution or a home, but requiring additional development of living skills. Two such community preparation programs are considered in Chapter 9.

Alternatively, the community-based residence itself can provide an intentional training program. Programs vary widely, ranging from Achievement Place, a small family-training-group home begun in Kansas (which has now been duplicated in several other states) (Timbers et al, 1973) to Laradon Hall in Colorado, where residents are trained in simulated work situations (e.g., cafeteria, warehouse) and in independent living skills. Chapter 10 will consider this model of a workshop-dormitory.

9. Community Preparation Programs

BY community preparation programs we mean short-term, residential training programs, often located on institutional grounds, that have some specialized staff and are intentionally designed to teach requisite skills for daily living in community residences. The primary goal of these programs is to provide structured environments in which residents can be taught skills in areas such as time and money, recreation, work, use of public transportation, domestic routines, shopping, peer relationships, and legal rights and responsibilities. If a resident has behaviors that interfere with his or her ability to learn new skills or use present skills adaptively, then the modification of these behaviors becomes a part of the program.

As a rule, community preparation programs are not listed by state agencies or associations for retarded citizens as community residences, nor is the unique nature of these programs congruent with the design of our survey. Therefore no attempt was made to collect survey data about this model; instead, we visited two community preparation programs.

Quarter-Way Cottage Program

In June 1971, two employees' cottages on the grounds of an old state school were converted into living quarters for residents who were slated to leave the institution. Two dynamic rehabilitation counselors, Bob and Nancy, became responsible for developing a program to teach residents the necessary skills for their move to the community. They were also instrumental in selecting residents who were appropriate for the program. When the state school was unitized in December 1971, Nancy became the director of the Rehabilitation Unit, and the Quarter-Way Cottage program officially began operation. Nancy, who had been employed at the state school for many years, was familiar with the institutional system and with community resources. Being a strong individual, she knew how to battle for services. Also, her reputation as a fair and capable administrator helped her attract a staff that was well suited for the task of training residents to live in the community.

Setting

Operating on the edge of the state school's grounds, the Quarter-Way Cottage program's physical facilities consisted, at the time of our visit, of four and a half cottages, all physically alike, each with a capacity for 20 residents. These cottages, formerly for employees, were renovated and furnished before the residents moved in. They are large, each including a reception room, 20 bedrooms, two bathrooms, and a basement.

The cottage we visited is a study in contrasts. In front of the cottage is a neatly arranged flower garden, planted and tended by one of the residents, but there is no front lawn as such, and the area behind the house looks relatively unkempt and unused. The cottage is made of stucco and cement, with a large screened-in porch in need of paint.

The cottage has a coffee percolator, a large refrigerator, and a toaster, but lacks a kitchen or a dining room for the residents to use. Each resident has his or her own bedroom and a key that locks the bedroom door from the outside; however, staff members have duplicates of all keys. Residents may, if they wish, purchase their own bedspreads, curtains, and other personal articles, but the furniture and linens are provided by the state school. There is a doorbell on the front door, but no names by it. The reception room is furnished as a living room but also contains a bureau, a doctor's weighing scale, and a large soft drink vending machine. There is a phone in the cottage, but it is connected to the state school's central switchboard. Each bathroom has one enclosed shower stall and a bathtub but has two sinks and two toilets. Also, there is a sign on the outside bathroom door instructing residents not to use too much toilet paper, a sign over the sink requesting them not to wash their clothes in the bathroom sinks (there are utility sinks in the basement), and a sign on the tub requesting them to clean it after they use it.

Hence the physical facilities reflect the program's placement in between the institution and community residences. The physical plant deviates considerably from the other buildings in the institution in that there is an attempt to ensure privacy and to instill a sense of pride in the acquisition and display of personal possessions. Still the facilities do not provide many of the homelike qualities that characterize most residences in the community.

Staff

The staffing pattern is more specialized than in other models; staff positions include a medical doctor, licensed practical nurses, attendants (called *housemothers*), a unit director, two social workers, two rehabilitation counselors, a psychologist, and several student interns. Consultant services, such as speech, hearing, and vocational training are also available. Although a staffing hierarchy is specified on paper, staff members talked about the team approach, which they said meant that every issue was dealt with in as democratic a way as possible.

We have egalitarian working conditions – everyone is working together.

We work in teams, everyone helps one another work together. Titles don't matter, unlike the rest of the units at the state school. I have worked at most of them and know.

It was our observation that, although team members maintained their professional roles, there was a spirit of cooperation and a sharing of responsibilities among them.

Housemothers in each cottage work 8-hour shifts and some rotate among the cottages. The housemothers have many responsibilities outside of those normally expected of ward attendants, such as teaching community survival skills and personal hygiene and monitoring targeted behaviors. One might be skeptical about the ability of those previously in custodial roles to change their focus and become programming and teaching personnel. However, the housemothers we interviewed and observed do function as teachers now and express great satisfaction with their roles.

I applied for the job because I wanted to work with those going out into the world. I like to see something I have accomplished. I love my work.

I like knowing that I am accomplishing things, which is much different than before – before there were too many people to take care of, had to follow schedules, had no time to teach, and no motivation because there was no program or plan.

All but one of the staff members interviewed indicated their intention to continue working in the program for at least another year. Some mentioned their desire to eventually phase out the necessity of their present jobs in anticipation of finally closing down the state school. Then, as residents continue to be placed in the community, these staff members hope to move to more community-based work.

The following is an abridged list of programming responsibilities that are supposed to be carried out by housemothers:

1. Taking residents shopping; making sure they know their own sizes and measurements; helping them pick out their own clothes, matching colors and materials; helping them to handle their own money, pay for their purchases, and count their change.
2. Teaching residents to do their laundry – showing them how to sort laundry; teaching the use of coin machines; teaching how to put clothes, soap, and bleach into the machines; teaching how to use the dryer.
3. Taking residents on field trips – teaching behavior in a group and social interaction.
4. Teaching self-medication – teaching simple first aid, use of medication, ointments, douches, and enemas.

5. Teaching residents to sew and knit – teaching how to mend clothes, sew on buttons, hem, and knit.
6. Taking residents out for a meal – helping them save money for the meal, teaching table manners, helping them choose a well-balanced meal, and helping them pay the check and tip the waiter or waitress.

Residents

All the residents in the Quarter-Way Cottage program had previously lived on wards at the state school. There are two cottages for men and two for women, housing a total of 80 residents. One additional cottage is shared by seven older male residents and male employees. The age of the residents in the Quarter-Way Cottages is in the range of 18 to 55 years. Residents of the Quarter-Way Cottages feel that they have a higher status than others in the institution, and being sent back to a ward is viewed as a serious punishment.

Residents are quite vocal about the increased autonomy and privacy afforded them in the Quarter-Way Cottages.

Here you have your own room, can smoke, can have a boyfriend, and have more privacy. You can go uptown when you like.

We can go to bed late. You can go whenever you want to. Sometimes I watch late movies.

I have my own clothes and my own cigarettes and matches. Before I had to ask to smoke and had to do it in the bathroom.

Catching the late show, having a smoke, wearing one's own clothes – givens for most people – are a newly discovered experience to these residents.

Yet, despite these gains, the majority of residents expressed a desire to move into a community residence ("It's all right here, but I would rather be out"), although a few residents noted some fears about leaving ("I don't know if I can live out there"). Quite a few of the residents in the cottages had already had a community placement and had subsequently returned to the state school. The pattern of leaving, returning, and then leaving again appeared to be relatively common. Many of the staff members attributed this pattern to the inability of residents to cope emotionally, particularly with their feelings of loneliness rather than to a lack of skills.

At the time of our visits, the pattern of loneliness was not well addressed in the Quarter-Way program. In evaluating prospective residents, criteria such as IQ and performance levels were considered to be important, whereas emotional stability was less of a consideration. One staff member said that it was difficult to encourage residents to interact with one another, and several of the residents said that they had no close friends. Indeed, many people did seem isolated. Perhaps placement success would be enhanced if emphasis were placed on increasing social interaction within the program and if people were moved out of the institution in friendship groups.

Program
The cottage program is intentionally structured to simulate conditions that exist in the community. On admission to the Quarter-Way Cottages, each new resident signs a "Lease for Independent Living," which is an agreement between the resident and the unit team – an attempt to accustom the resident to the tenant-landlord relationship that he or she might face in the community (Fig. 9-1). The economy program teaches both budgeting and money skills by including community tasks in the curriculum, such as paying for room and board and banking one's money.

The economy system is a means of providing a training experience of working, receiving pay, and paying living expenses here at the state school to make the transition to community living easier for the resident. Each resident is required to have a work situation and work a full 40-hour week. The resident is paid in "Rehab. Unit Currency" at $1.75 per hour. Every other week, the resident receives a bill for room, board, heat, telephone, etc. After paying the bills, the resident will receive his spending money in real currency. A bank account has been established for each resident in one of the local banks. As a part of the program, the resident is required to bank a portion of his spending money. The majority of the residents go to the bank themselves to deposit their money.

Annual Report, 1972

The Progress Assessment Chart (PAC: SEFA Publication, Ltd., 1963) is employed to evaluate and monitor the residents' skill level and progress. The PAC goes with the resident when he or she moves to a community residence. This system offers a compact means of assessing and specifying an individual's progress in the areas of self-help, communication, socialization, personality, and occupation. Housemothers at the cottage review the PAC with the resident and integrate any differences of opinion that may arise between the resident's perception of his or her skill level and what is recorded in the chart.

On approving their PAC profiles, residents enter into a system of contingent privileges whereby the learning of skills (such as addressing an envelope or using the correct amount of postage) earns personally chosen rewards, and the skills accrued advance a resident to a higher privilege level. Most rules and policies in the Quarter-Way Cottages tend to be individualized according to this privilege-level system. For example, when one has earned a certain privilege level, he or she might be allowed to have dinner guests or extended curfew hours.

Skills are taught in several different programs. Cooking, shopping, money budgeting, and time skills along with reading, writing, arithmetic, and current events are taught at night school in the adult education department of the state school. A special course, Community Living and the Law, was added to the adult education curriculum to teach the residents about their human and legal rights. Housemothers instruct residents in such areas as housekeeping, laundry, mealtime skills, and shopping. Work skills are taught only in the workshop.

Lease for Independent Living

Cottage ____________________ Room Number ____________________

Participants:

____________________ Tenant (Resident Member)

____________________ Landlord (Unit Team Members)

Agreement

Tenant:

Upon becoming a member of the Rehab. Unit and, therefore, living independently in a cottage, I, ____________________, agree to live, act, and behave to the best of my ability according to the rules and regulations set up by the Resident members and the Unit team.

All Unit Team members agree to help the above named Resident member in adjusting to Unit living. The Unit Team will support the resident in his or her efforts to follow their individual programs, the rules and regulations, and to improve behavior and attitudes. The Unit Team members agree to work individually and in groups with any and all residents to improve their social, emotional, and intellectual abilities.

Signed ____________________ Tenant

____________________ Landlords

____________________ Superintendent Approval

Date ____________________

Figure 9-1
Lease signed by new residents of the Quarter-Way Cottage program.

There is a formal program of sex education attended by the residents and the staff. Last, but of no less importance, residents are encouraged to teach skills to each other.

Community

The staff of the Quarter-Way Cottage program is acutely aware of the need to maintain and further cultivate community contacts. Thus all the professional staff members spend at least 50 percent of their time in the community. In conjunction with a few community residences affiliated with the state school, a council has been formed consisting of two of the program's staff members, two persons from a local association for retarded citizens, two persons from the regional office of the Department of Mental Health, and two staff members from each participating community residence. This council meets monthly and attempts to coordinate the Quarter-Way Cottage's services and the community services, much as a board of directors might function. According to the annual report, selected members of the staff attend all community residence council meetings and are available to community residence houseparents for consultation.

Finally, the staff of the Quarter-Way Cottage program provides follow-up services for discharged residents who are living in the community. These services include assistance in job procurement, finding new living situations, and solving any emotional problems that may arise. According to the annual report in 1972, 40 of the 87 residents were successfully placed in the community, and, of these, 16 were discharged from the state school. Discharge, the ultimate criterion of successful community placement, is dependent on successful adaptation to community life.

The older men, who share the cottage with the employees, used to work on the state school's farm colony before it was closed. These men are now minimally under the supervision of the program staff, receiving a visit from a housemother about once a day. They are quite competent, but they are very close to retirement age and have lived nearly all their lives under the aegis of the state school; they say they are "comfortable" living in an institutional environment. Since they are all good friends and dependent on one another, they do not want to separate. Even if a community residence were willing to accept them as a group, which is unlikely, they would not be anxious to move to the community.

Three issues are highlighted by this example. First, how much choice should retarded adults be afforded as to where they will live? To the extent to which these seven men are competent to make such major decisions, should they be permitted to remain in the institutional setting when they may be capable of more independent living? Certainly, one would not want to force these men to move to a community residence against their will, yet one might well argue that they do not belong in an institution.

A second and related consideration is the possibly unrealistic demand placed on aging retarded people to begin new lives in the community. As we have shown in Chapter 6, elderly retarded people in the community are unlikely to find a work placement or accessible leisure activities, so perhaps a typical community setting as it now exists offers few incentives.

Finally, the possibility of friendship groups of residents moving from the institution to the community together should be entertained seriously. Although there are currently numerous bureaucratic impediments to this arrangement and the argument might be advanced that moving ex-institutionalized residents out together might maintain "institutional behavior," it seems equally likely that placement success would be maximized if a peer group were provided for a retarded adult to ease the transition to a new and potentially hostile environment. This approach has been demonstrated to work well with former psychiatric hospital patients.

Fortunately for the men in question, the staff of the community preparatory program were exploring the possibility of moving them out together to live with an older couple on a farm. The farm is close enough to the state school so that the men could continue to work and obtain services from the institution.

Epilogue

A look at the Quarter-Way Cottage program 1 year later revealed several interesting changes, influenced in part by the increased number of lower functioning residents entering the program. To accommodate this new population, the number of residents had been reduced to about seventy with plans for a further reduction to fifty. Also, programs described earlier had been altered to better meet the new residents' needs. This restructuring was usually in the direction of simplification. For example, the bills residents receive for room, board, and heat, which used to be printed in words, were presented as pictures of the items to be paid for.

There were changes in program offerings as well.

1. *Day Placement Program.* The Quarter-Way Cottage program now utilized the services of three community-based vocational training programs, placing about 70 percent of the residents in these settings during the day.
2. *Language Stimulation Program.* A speech and language consultant provided in-service training for staff and individual instruction for some residents in the basics of functional sign language.
3. *Social Activities Program.* Recognizing the need to program more for the appropriate use of leisure time, the unit team now planned supervised community exposure, such as shopping trips and dining out; large group activities, such as dances; small group activities, such as arts and crafts workshops; and individual hobbies.
4. *Respite Care.* A program of respite care for retarded adults living with their families was offered for 1 to 30 days. Actually, for the 10 admitted at the time of our survey, the need had been more for crisis intervention. In any case, one could question the advisability of locating such a program on institutional grounds rather than in the community.

The number of residents served by this Quarter-Way Cottage program had increased considerably over the year. The program had placed over 150 residents into some type of community setting. Yet even with this large number of persons placed out of the institution, the Rehabilitation Unit staff adamantly stressed the need to open more group homes to accommodate residents who have more difficulty adjusting to community life.

Young Adults Program

To explore a second example of a community preparation program, we visited the Young Adults program. Our visit to this program was shorter than to the Quarter-Way Cottage program and is included only to highlight several programmatic issues.

Setting and Residents

Located in an urban residential neighborhood of a large metropolitan area, the residential treatment facility that houses the Young Adults program is licensed as a mental health center, a hospital, a private school, and a rehabilitation center. Several other programs, primarily serving severely physically handicapped children, are also operated by the facility. The Young Adults program is housed in one wing of a modern brick building. Although much of the training conducted by the Young Adults program occurs in this wing, residents spend significant portions of their day elsewhere: in school in another part of the building, at an outside competitive or sheltered job, or at a specialized service unit in the area (e.g., a counseling center for the deaf).

The Young Adults program provides services for about fifty residents between the ages of 14 and 24 years. They are a mixed disability group, including mentally retarded, mentally disturbed, blind, deaf, delinquent, learning disabled, epileptic, physically handicapped, and cerebral palsied residents. The mixing of disabilities is one of the most unique aspects of the program and apparently results from historical, philosophical, and practical considerations. The facility has been serving severely handicapped children and youths for more than 70 years, a tradition that has been carried over to the Young Adults program. Also, the staff members continually express their determination to overcome the stigmatizing labels affixed to different disabilities. At the same time, however, they recognize that different treatment and teaching materials are needed by people with different problems. By virtue of the size of the Young Adults program and a specialized professional staff, a great variety of treatment and training experiences can be provided. Thus a multi-disability group can be well served.

Approximately seventy percent of the residents lived with their families before entering the Young Adults program. The remaining thirty percent came from a variety of community-based or institutional settings. A resident's tenure in the program can range from a 6-day evaluation to a 2-year treatment period.

Program

The Young Adults program seems to help significantly those who need a structured and individualized program for a limited period of time. The residents' behavior modification program begins before admission. Parents or the referring agency are helped to fill out a form listing the prospective resident's strengths and weaknesses in behavioral terms. During the first 2 weeks in the Young Adults program, the staff observes the new resident to determine specific behavioral objectives. At the end of this time, the staff's observations are reconciled with the parents' list, and a treatment plan is devised.

All residents are in the "general program," in which the resident earns points by completing certain tasks and attending certain activities. Residents are responsible for collecting their points on a payroll slip, and they may exchange them for a variety of desired activities and items. Certain maladaptive behaviors result in the deduction of points, for example, hitting, under-age drinking, taking illegal drugs, carrying weapons, smoking in unauthorized areas, or not taking medication. Point values for positive and negative behaviors, as well as point costs for purchasing favorite backup activities, are negotiated between residents and staff members.

If the general program does not adequately address all the resident's target goals, short-term individual programs are planned. (At the time of our visit, 40 percent of the residents were on individualized programs, developed by all the staff members who were working with the resident.) Individualized programs often require the cooperation of staff members from the workshops and day activity centers and employers of the residents. As the targeted behavior is increasingly maintained by social reinforcement, the individualized program is phased out. Over time, residents often request that their individual programs be discontinued, since they feel they can perform the desired, targeted behaviors without additional contingencies.

There are many residents who do not fit into one of the day programs offered in the community, and recently the Young Adults program set up a Work Adjustment program for them. This program is conducted daily within the residential facility by two staff persons and nine foster grandparents. The program concentrates on teaching the 18 participants the basic skills necessary to navigate and work in the community. Target goals are to increase attention span and memory; to teach money skills; to improve prevocational abilities (e.g., sorting colors and shapes); to increase awareness of current events; to teach basic survival-word recognition (Walk, Don't Walk, etc.); and to facilitate community integration. The schedule of the program is designed to simulate a normal schedule at a job or a workshop. Several workshops have made an agreement with the Work Adjustment program to allow graduates to attend the workshops on a half-day basis until they are ready to make the adjustment to a full day schedule.

Issues

One critical problem noted in the Quarter-Way Cottages was the partial deficit in programming for the emotional and social growth of the residents. Although the program excels in its ability to teach new skills, it appears to fall short of creating contingencies that promote behaviors necessary for interpersonal growth. One might conjecture that learning new skills should lead to more positive feelings of self-worth; but, given retarded persons' long history of failure, any new skill learning must be accompanied by a surfeit of social reinforcement to help the residents come to perceive themselves as successful. It is important to note that insufficient communication of success as a resident masters skills is not a shortcoming of the behavioral orientation per se, but of its incomplete application in this program. Also, what was lacking in this environment was the development of programs that promote successful cooperative behaviors among peers. In contrast, the Young Adults program was more successful in providing residents with a rich variety of social activities. (This was perhaps possible because the residents had already mastered many other basic skills.) Evening activities are a required part of the Young Adults program and include a considerable array, such as the following:

1. Vocational "rap session" (required of all who are working)
2. Sex education (offered at four levels of sophistication)
3. Counseling
4. Movement group (for lower-level residents; this group deals with body imagery, dancing, touching, etc.)
5. Weight-watchers group
6. Woodworking group
7. Model group (airplanes, ships, cars, etc., led by a resident)
8. Driver's education group
9. Outside recreational activities (residents go on an individual basis and must earn enough points to buy a ticket, fare, etc.).

Hopefully more normal social relationships evolve from learning leisure time activities, becoming more aware of one's appearance, and having structured opportunities to come together with others to talk or enjoy recreation. By now it should be apparent, however, that neither the teaching nor the learning happens without careful planning and skilled instructors. Although most typical residences cannot be expected to offer the array and depth of learning opportunities outlined here, certainly every region should have some kind of community preparation program available as an adjunct to group homes and other models.

In terms of community involvement, the Young Adults program contrasts sharply with Quarter-Way Cottages. While the Quarter-Way Cottage program staff members were frequent visitors to outside communities, the residents for whom they sought placement had been, and still were, in a state institution. Ties to families in many cases had been severed long ago, and other potential placement settings all too often sought the less handicapped person to minimize the inevitable adjustment pains. The Young Adults program is physically *in* the community, is short term, serves a generally younger clientele, and takes most residents directly from their families. On completing the program, residents, by either returning to their families or moving to more independent residential facilities, typically have smoother access to a place to live than do the Quarter-Way Cottage residents.

Another important factor affecting placements from these two programs is the state and regional service system to which they relate. The Quarter-Way Cottage staff, in speaking of difficulties in placing residents, noted the array of competing agencies, state and local, that presented innumerable bureaucratic snags and funding delays but offered limited variation in programs. By contrast, the Young Adults program is in a state with generally better organized and more facilitative services. Also, it is in a community where one large placement organization provides a series of living options for residents and works closely with the Young Adults program to match persons with an appropriate placement.

In sum, both the Young Adults' and the Quarter-Way Cottages' contributions lie in their commitment to creating environments in which learning needs are systematically met by consistent individualized and group programs. This programming process gathers its strength by using a behavioral approach to effect change in the residents. Since the residents of these programs are ultimately learning the skills and behaviors necessary for their eventual integration into the community, no theoretical or functional contradiction exists between the principle of normalization and the end goals of these programs.

10. Workshop-Dormitories

COMMUNITY residences that are programmatically and administratively (although not necessarily physically) associated with vocational training programs have been classified as workshop-dormitories.* Typically, the workshops have been operating prior to the opening of the dormitories, which, in general, provide a home for only a small proportion of the workshop's clientele. Residents remain in workshop-dormitories for an average of only one and a half years before moving on to other models of community residential facilities and, it is hoped, more challenging jobs.

Workshop-dormitories are oriented toward vocational and community living skill training for residents at all levels of retardation. The close association between the work and residential settings has caused some professionals to be wary of this model. Nirje (1969) and others have argued that a separation in these two spheres of life is necessary to approximate a normalized experience. Yet workshop-dormitories are quite concerned with normalization, as experienced by the emphasis placed on functional community living skills, and staff members feel that the coordination of residence with employment sometimes enhances the learning process.

Places and People

The workshop-dormitory model is relatively new. Open on the average for 3 years at the time of our survey, these programs are most often located in large old houses in residential neighborhoods. More than half the workshop-dormitories in our sample of 16 are situated in towns with populations of less than 30,000. In small towns there are fewer groups concerned with the provision of

*Even though the Quarter-Way Cottages and Young Adults programs described in Chapter 9 operate workshops for some residents, most of their residents are placed in nonaffiliated day programs. In those programs, training in activities of daily living assumed highest priority, while in workshop-dormitory programs, vocational training is given strong emphasis.

services for retarded people, and thus a single organization is more likely to sponsor both a residence and a workshop program. The following description of one workshop-dormitory exemplifies this mode of sponsorship:

Our residence is an outgrowth of a nonprofit charitable corporation which provides a sheltered workshop, a prevocational shop, nursery and early child development programs, a summer recreational program, parent education . . . .

Workshop-dormitories were found to serve an average of 21.9 residents each, with the dormitory staffed by approximately nine workers. Staff members fill the functions of administrators, houseparents, relief persons, and counselors. Residents are typically young (average age, 28.6 years) and most likely moderately (48 percent) or mildly (38 percent) retarded. Previous to moving to the workshop-dormitory many have lived in institutions (40 percent), although a higher proportion than in other models have lived with their families (44 percent versus 27 percent; $t = 1.91$, $p = 0.06$).

Program

The program of workshop-dormitories is oriented primarily toward training residents for employment. The vast majority of residents (81 percent) spend their days in vocational training programs or sheltered workshops, significantly more than in other models ($t = 4.54$, $p < 0.001$). Among the remaining, some are new residents not yet placed, some are temporarily in day activity centers, and some have begun competitive employment.

Within the dormitories, residents are involved to a considerable extent in house maintenance responsibilities, ranking second highest in this category among all the models surveyed (Fig. 10-1).

Motivation begins on the most basic level, with immediate rewards for any improvement . . . . As the mentally retarded adult improves, the forms of the reward are upgraded to tokens, money paid in cash, and then finally a paycheck, all carefully accompanied with praise, the best motivator of all . . . . The relationship between doing a job well and its rewards is stressed . . . with the end result being the preparation for more independent living.

Residents work in the kitchen or elsewhere in the residence as part of their training . . . . They are paid for all work performed around the property, and in everything they do are helped to prepare for a time when they may be more independent.

Program description of
The Chimes, Maryland

Residents' autonomy is somewhat limited in the areas of alcohol consumption, entertaining visitors of the opposite sex, bedtime, and curfew. The residences are geared not as much toward training for independent living as toward providing a place for people to live, and learn, while attending a work program. In some ways, workshop-dormitories are similar to boarding schools in which

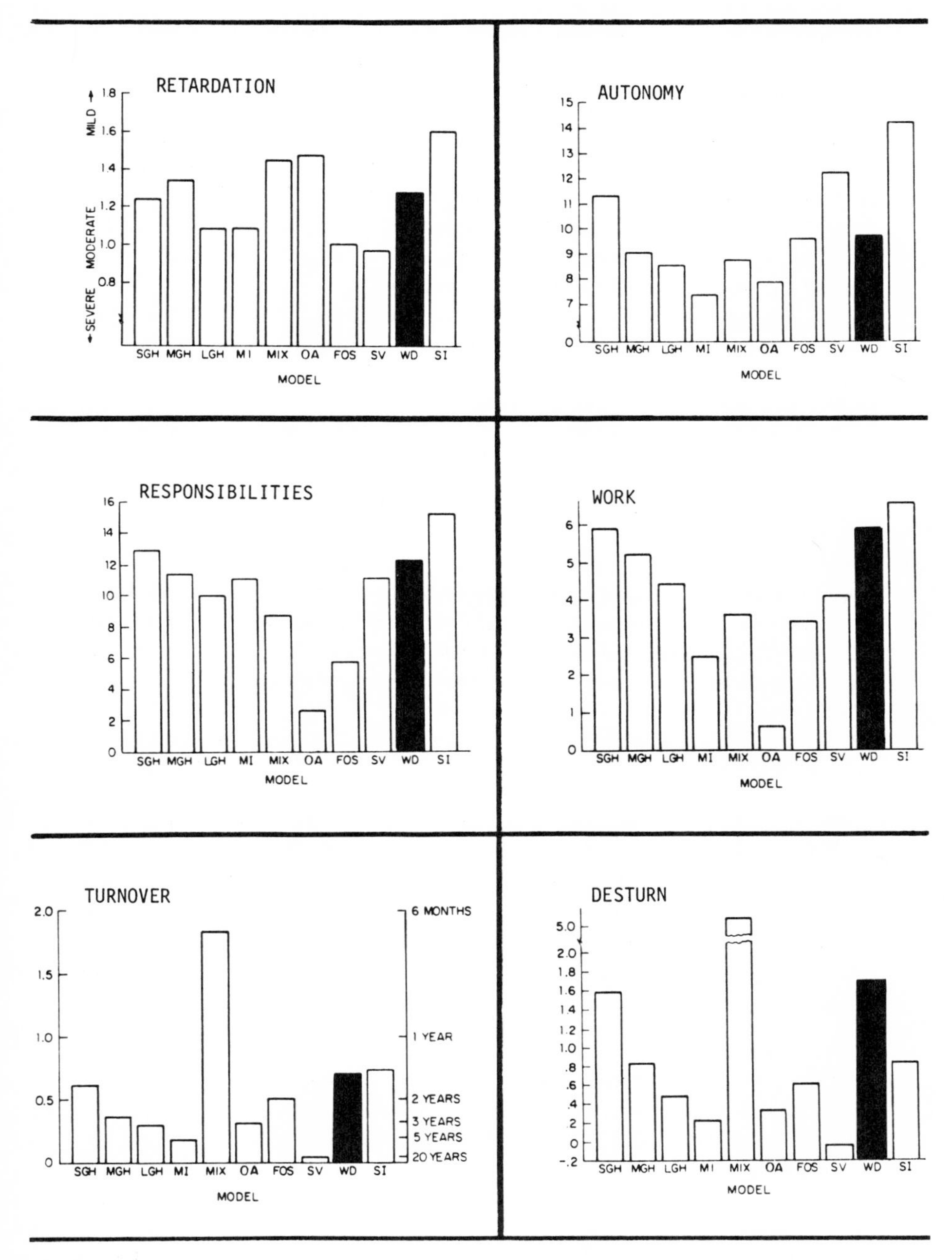

Figure 10-1
Major scales by model.

restrictions are common and are determined on the basis of the school's schedule. Similarly, limitations on residents' autonomy are often in keeping with the schedule of the work program.

Our program is designed to allow you as much independence in your living situation as you are capable of handling. At the same time, any group living situation requires some general guidelines to operate to the benefit of all concerned . . . . You are encouraged to use community recreation facilities both with and without supervision. If you are not participating in any program at that time, you may leave the dormitory . . . .

Vocational Rehabilitation Center
Handbook, Pittsburgh, Pa.

Also in keeping with the boarding school atmosphere is the tendency of the workshop-dormitory staff to encourage residents to return to their parents' homes on holidays and for vacations.

Work

There are more than two million retarded persons of working age in the United States, and more are added to this group every year. Vocational services for the retarded therefore grow increasingly important to the national economy . . . . The federal government has employed more than 7,000 retarded workers in the past decade with a high degree of success in several hundred kinds of jobs.

Laradon Hall Brochure,
Denver, Colorado

The main program emphasis in workshop-dormitories is on vocational training with attention to related living skills. Beyond a simple administrative connection between work and residence, workshop-dormitories should ideally ensure program coordination. If staff members from both spheres fail to work together to set goals and carry out programs for residents, the true potential of this model will not be realized (as we will see later when we discuss the Town House program).

Our residence is a sheltered living facility for our sheltered workshop. It helps us to have a more effective program in that we can work on a twenty-four hour basis. It is easier to attend to those needs that might have a detrimental effect on the client being placed into gainful employment.

Staff member in
a workshop-dormitory

The workshop-dormitories in our sample provide an encouraging variety of work and community-living training programs. Typically, a newly admitted resident begins this training with an 8- to 12-week *evaluation,* or *assessment period,* during which time data are collected on his or her abilities, skill deficiencies, and work habits. Often, job samples (a variety of tasks from different kinds of jobs) provide the means for a behavioral assessment.

Once the evaluation is completed, clients are assigned to a work training program. The wide variety of these programs, reflected in our sample, is striking. Some examples follow.

Community Survival and Basic Education Programs. These are often provided to teach residents skills such as budgeting and traveling, how to complete job applications, reading and writing, activities of daily living, and familiarity with community resources.

Work Activities Programs. These programs are typically for residents who are not yet ready for competitive employment or for specific job training. They generally emphasize the development of good work habits and social and communication skills. Residents are expected to learn to follow directions, accept supervision, work with others, build physical tolerance, obey rules, and develop satisfactory work habits.

Sheltered Employment. These programs provide extended employment for those clients whom the staff members assess as being unable to work competitively now or in the near future. Yet the possibility for work skill building still exists, as evidenced by the following list of contracts reported by respondents:

1. Polishing
2. Packaging silverware
3. Making and packaging candles
4. Processing stereo and television headsets for airlines
5. Answering fan mail for baseball teams (e.g., sending pictures)
6. Assembling door locks
7. Stuffing toy animals
8. Packaging fish hooks.

This list, abbreviated for reasons of space, does not reflect the wide range of contracts. For example, one workshop-dormitory noted that they complete contracts for over 300 firms yearly! An often noted criticism of sheltered employment is an overconcentration on meeting contracts while the clients' needs for vocational training take second priority; however, within a large program with many contracts there is a greater possibility of matching the client's training needs with the task.

Vocational Training. Training is provided for specific occupations, such as food service, janitorial service, landscaping, maid work, furniture refinishing, carpentry, commercial cleaning, doing laundry, and warehousing among others. In some workshop-dormitories, vocational training is conducted at work stations in actual industrial or business settings to approximate as closely as possible the competitive employment situation.

Work-Study Programs. These programs allow mentally retarded high school students, on a part-time basis, to both attend school and participate in the workshop.

Competitive Business. There are some programs in which residents operate a retail business and live in nearby facilities or actually on the premises of the business. This variety of the model has been successfully used in the Scandinavian countries and has great potential for use in this country. For example, in Denmark a group of retarded people operate a gas station and live in an apartment building above it. In our sample, residents of one workshop-dormitory operate a boutique and sell items produced in their workshop. In this way there is the opportunity for retailing as well as manufacturing experience.

The Activities Center is divided into work areas where the clients can learn silk screening, to produce greeting cards and stationery; weaving, rug making; ceramics; sewing and stitchery, in order to make pillows, pocketbooks, and wall hangings; paper and cloth flower making and arranging; photography; and lawn and ground care . . . .

There is also . . . a boutique on the grounds, featuring articles produced by the clients, and made available to the public. This provides the public with a chance to become acquainted with the many talents of mentally retarded children and adults, and gives the clients further experience in retailing.

Brochure, The Chimes, Maryland

The concept of competitive businesses or work crews deserves further consideration, because these are recently developed alternatives to both the solitary placement of a retarded adult into a competitive setting and to extended employment in a sheltered workshop. Although the use of the work crew to promote vocational success has been reported with mildly retarded adults, it has been especially effective with more severely retarded persons (Hansen, 1969; Chigier, 1972). When working in the midst of a peer group, the retarded adult has the benefit of being able to model others' skills and work habits and of competing with equals rather than with much more competent co-workers. Competitive jobs and the resulting community exposure are provided to those who would otherwise be restricted to sheltered workshops. The most successful work crews have been those that have concentrated in farming or parks maintenance projects. Perhaps most important, the work crew allows the retarded person the chance to find in work a supporting and integrating atmosphere that is not alienating a problem which was often reported by residents interviewed in the present study.

One illustrative program, located in a major urban area, is presently planning to use a retail business as a sheltered training setting for more severely retarded persons. The program will open a mini-mall, with several businesses in one location, such as a thrift shop, grocery store, and plant store. Each business will be staffed with two mildly retarded adults, two more severely retarded adults, and one supervisor. Tasks will be divided so that each worker will have responsibilities that are appropriate to his or her functional level. The group will form a supportive team; all will have daily interactions with shoppers; and the possibility for profit sharing will be explored. This plan has several implications worth highlighting: More severely retarded persons will have the unusual opportunity for sheltered employment in a setting that does not stress factory simulation; the workers will have public exposure; and the program will utilize the work-crew concept of having a group of retarded persons work together, support each other, and divide job functions by ability.

While the business model has considerable promise, the majority of workshop-dormitories provide residence for people involved in more traditional vocational training or extended sheltered employment. One philosophical theme common to workshop-dormitories is the recognition that residents should be paid for their work and that earning money is an important component of work training. Some workshop-dormitories pay residents by the hour, others by piece work, and some use a combination of both. One respondent mentioned that he makes an effort to assign clients "to a variety of work situations where the difficulty and complexity of the situation is proportional to the individual's ability," so that she or he can earn the maximum amount of money possible. Often, specific jobs are broken down into their component steps and clients move from one step to another as their skills increase.

Finally, most workshop-dormitories provide *placement services* for clients who are ready for competitive employment, and follow-up staff often monitor the quality of these placements. Usually, placement in a competitive job means that the resident will move out of the dormitory. Most ex-residents move to another supervised setting, such as foster care homes or another community residence (23 percent), their family home (26 percent), or back to an institution (21 percent). Less frequently residents move to their own apartments (12 percent). The rate of turnover is high (71 percent per year), and workshop-dormitories had the best desturn score (amount of turnover and quality of new placement) of any model except mixed group homes.

Community

Workshop-dormitories are significantly more involved with their surrounding communities than other models. For example, an average of 14 people volunteer at a typical workshop-dormitory. Also, in 69 percent of the settings the evaluation of community attitudes toward the community residence was "concerned and interested." One could speculate about the reasons for these positive relations. Certainly, the involvement of local businesses, either through providing contracts or job stations for residents, must heighten their awareness of and appreciation for the needs of retarded people. Similarly, support is gained from parents of retarded adults who live at home and participate in one of the workshop's programs. In addition, as residents move to competitive jobs, they interact with employers and with co-workers who are not necessarily retarded and thereby improve community attitudes. Finally, the workshops give interested community people the opportunity to volunteer and become involved with the clients, whereas it is more difficult to do so, for example, in a small group home where few activities are structured and the residents form a more self-contained group.

Sponsorship and Funding

Almost all (94 percent) of the workshop-dormitories surveyed are sponsored by nonprofit corporations. Residents pay an average monthly fee of $183 for room and board. The average annual budget of workshop-dormitories is fairly low, equivalent to $3,450 per resident for the dormitory component alone (Table 10-1).

Table 10-1
Comparison of Workshop-Dormitory (WD) and Small Group Home (SGH)

	WD	*SGH*
Number of residents	22	8
Staff-to-resident ratio	1:2.1	1:1.7
Level of retardation		
Mild	36%	35%
Moderate	45%	48%
Severe	12%	13%
Work setting of residents		
Competitive employment	4%	20%
Sheltered workshop or training program	81%	46%
Turnover per year	71%	62%
Ex-residents in own apartments	12%	24%
Ex-residents in another community residence	15%	9%
Ex-residents in institutions	21%	19%
Resident monthly fee	$183.00	$170.00
Annual budget per resident place	$3,450.00	$5,690.00

Note: With residents of essentially the same abilities and having the same staff-to-resident ratio as small group homes, workshop-dormitories spend at least $2,000 less per resident place and ensure about 20 percent more of their residents a work placement, though few are in competitive employment. Turnover in workshop-dormitories is higher, though residents in small group homes are more likely to move to their own apartments when they leave the program.

Our visit to a workshop-dormitory, Town House, will be discussed only briefly, because this program proved to be somewhat unrepresentative of the model (e.g., smaller and less focused on work). Town House is not a positive example of this model's potential, but it is an illustration of its possible problems. We include it for what can be learned from its shortcomings.

Town House

Town House is an attractive facility, situated in a residential neighborhood in a town of 18,000 and sponsored by the local Association for Retarded Citizens (ARC), which also sponsors a large sheltered workshop and other programs.

At the time of our visit, Town House served three women and eight men, who were 19 to 46 years old; eight were employed at the association's workshop, two were in competitive jobs, and one was unemployed.

The staff consisted of a director, a housemother, a counselor, and a relief person. Also, the housemother's husband lived at Town House, and despite his annual salary of $3,000, he was not at all involved with any of the residents. Staff roles were similar to those in a small group home except that the counselor was responsible for the development of goal-oriented resident programs and the conduct of weekly sensitivity group sessions.

The atmosphere at Town House seemed generally tense. The housemother felt that she would prefer to leave her job; her husband wanted to stay, but not to work. Town House had been unable to attract a more qualified and enthusiastic staff, perhaps because of the lack of university resources in the surrounding area; consequently, the present staff was retained.

The situation of the residents was similarly unsatisfactory. The staff, expressing the opinion that many of the residents were emotionally disturbed, did not feel competent to deal with the severe behavior problems displayed by the residents. Indeed, residents were poorly screened before moving to Town House for two reasons: First, the state institution system did not differentiate between the mentally retarded and the emotionally disturbed, and therefore community programs were presented with a less-than-clear understanding of the specific disabilities of any given applicant. Second, and more important, the director of Town House had not delineated any acceptance criteria, and he was hesitant to refuse admission to applicants even if they were quite likely to be unsuccessful in the community residence. Therefore the staff had virtually no opportunity to select residents on the basis of program goals and capabilities, and dissatisfaction of both staff members and residents was the consequence.

All but three residents said they were not happy living at Town House, and residents had not formed close relationships with one another. Several noted that being in the community residence was not an improvement over institutional living ("No better, no worse, just different") and specific complaints included being "bossed around," being forced to assume responsibilities of cooking meals and doing laundry, and feeling "stuck" in the workshop placement. Among the possible reasons for this discontent were three problems with this workshop-dormitory: (1) inappropriate training procedures in the workshop program, (2) inconsistency between the workshop and the dormitory, and (3) poorly articulated program objectives.

The workshop program and the residential program had different vocational goals for residents. The workshop was initially begun to provide a daytime activity for retarded adults living at home. The emphasis was on work activities and contracts such as assembling kits and sorting screws that were repetitive and uninteresting to most of the residents of Town House. There were limited competitive job opportunities in the area, and consequently the workshop did not maintain a strong vocational orientation. In direct conflict with the objectives of the workshop, however, was the view of the Town House staff that residents should find competitive jobs before moving out of the house. The pressures to be vocationally competent were high, yet residents were not offered the training they needed to become employed. Many residents expressed a reluctance to attend the workshop much longer, but they had not developed any independent work skills to provide an alternative.

This inconsistency between workshop and residence goals is directly attributable to each program's having its own separate advisory board, although the Association for Retarded Citizens is the sponsoring agency for both. Program guidelines are developed independently without coordination. As a result, the most important advantage of having a workshop-dormitory model – that the two programs be programmatically integrated – is unrealized. Even a competent, motivated, and satisfied staff would find it difficult to coordinate de facto administratively separate programs.

Program objectives in both the residence and the workshop were ill defined at the time of our visit. The workshop asserted that their program was a behavior modification program, yet two of the most basic tenets of this teaching approach were violated: Reinforcement was not contingent on performance, and no individualized programs were developed. In the residence, there were no clear sanctions: Residents learned that they would be tolerated no matter what disruptive behavior they displayed, while at the same time staff verbally demanded that they perform well and develop independent, socially appropriate skills. New residents were not even given a tour of the neighborhood, much less guidelines as to what would be expected of them in Town House. Residents experiencing crises were attended to by staff members, while those who did not present extreme problems were virtually ignored; this crisis orientation seemed to breed additional crises. That resident confusion was high was easy to understand.

However, resident discontent should also be considered in relation to factors raised elsewhere in this book. Town House residents were mostly young and high functioning; a number of them had come directly from their families (the average resident had been in the program only 6 months), and the autonomy granted at Town House was quite *high.* One is reminded of the discontent of young, high functioning residents from families in the highly autonomous environment of Coventry. As we noted earlier, living in a small group no doubt brings stresses both for those who have lived in anonymous institutional wards and for those without peers in their own families, and the early adjustment is difficult. Adjustment also seems particularly difficult for the resident with the intelligence and inclination to question program restrictions and staff control, however reasonable or minimal they are. Expression of such discontent is as much an expression of a newly realized sense of self as the adolescent's rebellion against parental restrictions, however slight. Indeed, the parallel with typical adolescent behavior was drawn by a number of staff members we visited. Finally, at Town House the sensitivity training sessions may well have encouraged nonconstructive expressions of discontent.

Before we leave resident discontent, however, it is interesting to look at the rate of turnover at Town House. Many residents expressed a strong desire to live on their own, and perhaps the unsatisfying atmosphere at the house was an impetus to their moving out. Town House in its brief 2½-year history already had 15 ex-residents. Of these, 13 had moved either to informally supervised apartments (not a part of the Town House program but supervised by the counselor) or to independent apartments. One ex-resident joined the Job Corps and one returned to an institution. This highly successful placement of residents from Town House raises some questions about the discontent and criticism residents expressed. It may well be, as we hypothesized in our discussion of Coventry, that programs allowing autonomy and providing for some expression of discontent will, in fact, help the resident to gain the self-confidence to break out on his or her own. This is, of course, not to advocate a program's fostering discontent through poor programming, which seemed to be partly the case at Town House. It does mean, however, that expressions of discontent as one copes with autonomy in a well-planned program may be, ironically, a good prognostic sign.

Further Issues

A common criticism of the workshop-dormitory model in principle pertains to its structural characteristic of having the residence and the work setting either physically under one roof or in very close proximity to one another. The argument that is often presented emphasizes the fact that "normal" people have a separation in these spheres of life and that the same separation of work and residence should be afforded retarded people.

In response to this objection, others have noted that a separation of residence and employment is not always normal or advisable, citing farmers, physicians, and architects as examples of persons who often live and work in the same place. Ironically, one state that refused to fund workshop-dormitories, advancing the argument about separation of work and residence, only funded small group homes whose staff lived there. Clearly, for retarded people consistency in expectations, contingencies, skill teaching, and reinforcement between the residence and place of work can sometimes result in more rapid and thorough learning. Workshop-dormitories provide only a short-term integrative experience, and when goals are met, residents can move into settings that are more normal in their separation of work and residence.

Workshop-dormitories are not optimal settings for all retarded adults, as evidenced by the 21 percent rate of return to the institution which, while not higher than that of other models, is nevertheless a concern. However, for some, the model could be used very effectively. Residents who are severely retarded and/or multiply handicapped, for example, would benefit from having a placement that minimizes the extent to which they have to cope with traveling;

such a model would free them to spend as much of their time as possible in intensive skill-building programs, with travel possibly planned later as other skills develop.

Mildly retarded persons can also be well served in workshop-dormitories, entering the program to receive short-term intensive vocational training to gain those skills necessary for specific competitive jobs. Also, workshop-dormitories could integrate mildly retarded adults well with other clients who are not mentally retarded but whose disabilities necessitate some type of work training. Finally, workshop-dormitories may be a good living and training model for persons whose family home is too distant from a workshop for daily commuting; such persons could live in the dormitory five days a week and return home on weekends.

We conclude this section on training-oriented programs by again raising the point made in its introduction: These programs are only effective when staff members are competent in teaching residents new skills and preparing them for additional community integration. Teaching cannot simply be added to the job description of a well-intentioned but untrained houseparent in the expectation that it will somehow happen, and residents cannot simply be released into the labor market in the hope that they will find work. A guiding technology, such as behavior modification, must be more than convenient words voiced to secure funding; it must be understood and implemented in all its complexity by a specially trained staff for it to be both fair and effective. Workshop programs must also be diverse and individualized as well as oriented toward possible competitive employment opportunities in the local community. The degree of intentional planning and staffing, necessitated by programs derived from a training philosophy, is greater than in other models, and the better programs have taken this responsibility seriously.

Section 4. Semi-Independent Apartments

11. Semi-Independent Apartments

A prominent characteristic of institutions is 24-hour supervision of residents, with staffing patterns and programs force-fit into various shifts. It was expected that in viewing the movement away from institutions and toward supposedly more normalized community residences, we would also see a decreased need for constant staff supervision, a practice that fosters dependence in residents. Surprisingly, the project identified only 19 community residences, or 5 percent of our sample, that did not have 24-hour supervision of residents. Because constant supervision had been so strongly maintained in the new community-based facilities, it seemed important to analyze as a separate model the 19 facilities that deviated from this practice. As it developed, the semi-independent model, based on the single variable, *amount of supervision,* differs from other models in several other important ways, such as level of retardation, autonomy, in-house responsibilities, and employment of residents.

While all semi-independent community residences have less than total supervision, the pattern varies. In some group home programs staff members live with the group but work directly with the residents for only a specified number of hours; in others staff members live elsewhere and come into the house for certain periods of time. Several staffing options also emerge when residents live in apartment units. Fritz, Wolfensberger, and Knowlton (1971) delineated three variations of apartment living, with differing amounts of independence and integration as follows:

1. *The apartment cluster,* composed of several apartments in relative physical proximity, functioning to some extent as a unit, and supervised by staff members who reside in one of these apartments

2. *The single co-residence apartment,* for one or two adult staff members (often college students) and two or three retarded persons, living together as roommates and friends
3. *The single "maximum independence apartment,"* occupied by two to four retarded adults, with all supervision and assistance supplied by a citizen advocate or by a case worker who would be employed as a staff member of the residential services division of the regional services system.

Regardless of the staffing variation among semi-independent community residences, the pervasive program theme is normalization, characterized most dramatically by a greater degree of risk taking on the part of staff and a greater amount of independence given to residents. The high-potential, high-risk nature of this program is evident from the large percentage (24 percent) of ex-residents who have moved on to independent living and the equally high percentage (23 percent) who have returned to an institution.

Place and People

The 19 semi-independent community residences in our sample are from 11 states, with the highest number coming from Nebraska and Pennsylvania (four each). At the time of the survey the average semi-independent community residence had been open for only 3 years. The majority are located in urban centers; 63 percent are in population areas of over 50,000, which is greater than the other models.* Also, fully 53 percent of semi-independent community residences occupy apartment units or entire apartment buildings, while no other model even approximates this typical urban housing arrangement.†

The average semi-independent community residence provides a home for nine residents, which is similar to the size of a small group home. However, sizes range from 2 to 30 residents, a spread that reflects the program variability within this model. Residents on the average are younger and less retarded than those living in other models; in fact, there are significantly more residents judged to be mildly retarded (56 percent) and virtually none are severely retarded (less than 1 percent).

Although we would expect to find fewer staff members in a model fostering independence, the data indicate that there are as many staff members in this model as there are, for example, in small group homes. These ratios are not comparable, however, in that staff members are present for less time in the semi-independent community residence, and also some of these relatively new programs are not as yet filled to resident capacity.

Program

More than other models, semi-independent community residences subscribe to the principle of normalization, as evidenced by Figure 11-1 (autonomy,

*$\chi^2 = 4.17; p < 0.05$.
†$\chi^2 = 39.9; p < 0.001$. All subsequent comparisons reported were significant at $p < 0.01$ by analysis of variance or t tests.

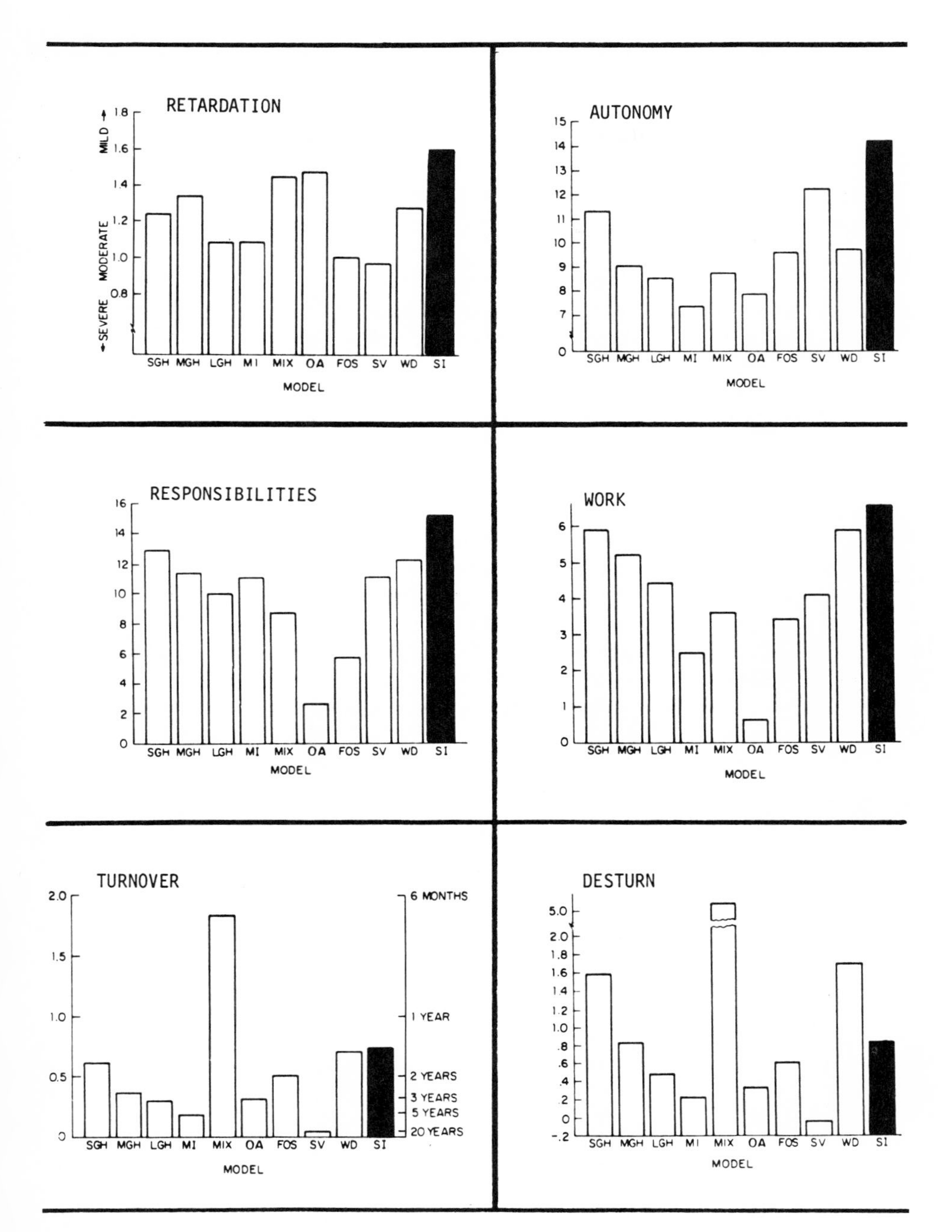

Figure 11-1
Major scales by model.

responsibility, and work). On each of these scales, semi-independent community residences score higher (i.e., are more normalized) than any other model. Using these scales and other data, a composite picture can be developed to depict the quality of daily life within a semi-independent program. A typical tenant is likely to be living in an apartment unit and sharing with other tenants the household responsibilities of shopping, cooking, and cleaning. A certain degree of privacy is assured, this resident being likely to have his or her own bedroom.

In the morning, the typical tenant prepares breakfast and then leaves the apartment for a day at work, often taking public transportation to work, since 79 percent of these community residences are within a half mile of public transportation. Being younger and less retarded than residents in other models, these residents have a greater opportunity to be competitively employed, and, in fact, a significantly greater proportion (29 percent) of tenants are employed on the open labor market than in other models. Other tenants most likely attend sheltered workshops (56 percent) or participate in training programs (only 7 percent have no day placement).

When payday arrives, the tenant can decide how to allocate earnings (in 90 percent of community residences) and, coupled with the greater degree of autonomy, likely finds more latitude to spend leisure time as he or she wishes. Thus after work, the tenant is likely to be able to decide for himself or herself whether to stay out late, entertain visitors of the opposite sex, drink a beer, or spend money on such items as records.

Last, a tenant's stay in a semi-independent community residence is relatively short, an average of 1.36 years (a turnover rate higher than other models except mixed group homes). Once discharged, a person is likely to receive follow-up from the staff and is welcome to visit his or her former residence.

Community

Semi-independent community residences were less likely than other models to prepare local communities for their presence; 47 percent made no effort to prepare the community. This model was the next to least likely to receive community opposition; 76 percent reported none. One wonders what the impact of moving into an *integrated* apartment complex might be on the "normal" neighbors. In our sample, not one of this type of facility consulted the neighbors before moving in, yet none received opposition; hence this low profile in relation to neighbors seems to have been a good strategy. The prevailing community attitude toward these facilities was assessed by staff as "neutral" in 45 percent of the sample and "interested and concerned" in 31 percent.

Although a high proportion of residents came from institutions, semi-independent community residences did not typically maintain an on-going relationship with an institution. Possibly the high staff-to-resident ratio, a high professional-to-resident ratio, and the high functional level of the residents account for this model's ability to effectively sever institutional ties.

Sponsorship and Funding
Fully 84 percent of the semi-independent community residences have boards of directors, usually representing nonprofit organizations. As for funding resources, almost all receive state funding (89 percent) and resident payments (95 percent). Often residents contribute some from their own earnings to the upkeep of their apartments, since the percentage of residents receiving wages in the semi-independent model is significantly higher than in all other models combined.

The average monthly fee in 1973 of $101 was significantly lower than the average of $187 for other models, which only made up a small portion of the average annual per-resident cost of $5,440. Much of the budget was supported by direct government funding to the program.

These survey findings suggest an intriguing model of a program that takes risks through lessened supervision and more flexible rules; the potentials for growth and failure alike lie just beneath this statistical surface and invite a closer look. Hence we chose to visit a program that had been utilizing semi-independent apartments for 3 years as its only residential model.

First, though, a brief digression to hear the recollections and hopes of a resident in this program, as related in our interview. In a sense, these words could have introduced most of our community-based programs and could have been spoken by many of their residents.

Susanna, a young, very pretty woman, talked with us about many facets of her life. Having a speech impediment, she has difficulty saying the word "retarded," but she has no difficulty relating the connotative impact the word has for her. She vociferously hates the word and resents being looked at strangely and regularly hearing, "Look at that girl, she's retarded." She explains, "Maybe I am a little slow, and have some trouble learning things and can't read and write and things like that, but I do try hard."

Susanna talked excitedly about her "new life" in the Apartment Project, at her job, and with her many friends in the program. Her new life is in marked contrast to her former life at the state school, where she had been placed as an infant.

She remembers the state school as a terrible place and said that many people had tried to run away from it, although most were eventually brought back. She told of the different times she had run away. Once she was pulled into a car by a strange man and raped. Another time she was literally running away from the school and accidentally fell into an open sewer and broke her leg. She was found only after several hours by another, older resident of the school. Susanna now lives with this older woman and describes her as being more like a mother to her than anyone else ever had been.

She remembers often being locked up in the "blue room" of the state school for misbehaving. She remembers being forced to work as an attendant on the wards of more severely and profoundly retarded children and adults, cleaning up after those who were not toilet trained and couldn't dress, feed, or bathe themselves. She remembers her work in the school laundry. She remembers being harshly reprimanded once, and falling asleep crying on the older resident's lap.

She remembers the pains in her side for quite a while before she left the state school, so severe that they caused her to double over and sometimes faint.

She remembers the doctors at the school telling her she shouldn't worry, that it would go away, and giving her some pills.

When Susanna came to the Apartment Project, the coordinator recommended that she see a doctor in the community, who diagnosed an ovarian cyst that required an operation. She is now fully recovered.

She remembers when she was about 15 years old discovering through a social worker that her parents were alive but had put her in the school because they didn't want her. "The tears were running down my face." And she began to understand why she never had any visitors.

She remembers the four foster homes she lived in before coming to the Apartment Project. At the last place, she was expected to do all the housework and take care of the family's five children. She was then blamed for the youngest child's running in front of a car, and was beaten by the foster parents. She spoke of being "black and blue" when she came to the Apartment Project.

Susanna's two hopes now are to settle down and have one nice place to live, and to find a man she can love and eventually marry.

Apartment Project

In July 1970, wishing to create an alternative to the state institution, an urban regional center began its semi-independent living project. The project staff decided to rent several apartments scattered throughout the community, where retarded adults could reside without live-in staff. This model was chosen, in part, to avoid the stringent fire and zoning laws that had impeded the development of group homes within this state. In August 1970, the first apartment for four men opened, followed in October by an apartment for four women. At the time of our visit, seven apartments were occupied by a total of 30 residents.

The direct service staff work with the residents from about 3:30 P.M. to 10:00 P.M. daily. The primary population served are men and women who moved in directly from the state school, although some residents had been living with their families but needed temporary housing, and others had been living independently in the community but had had bad experiences.

Setting

The seven apartments are located in a metropolitan area with a population of about 190,000. Three of these apartments, all for men, are located in one house that previously was a rectory. In the most independent of these apartments, three tenants pay rent directly to the landlord; they have furnished the apartment themselves and have no set time for staff supervision (although staff members are available to consult). The other two supervised apartments, for four and five men, are oriented toward training. Two additional apartments, one for four men and one for four women, are located in a new low-income housing development. Another apartment for four women is located on the upper floor of a large house. Finally, there is a ranch-style, three-bedroom house for six women. The two living units primarily studied were the house for women and one of the staffed men's apartments in the former rectory.

The women's house is located on a suburban residential street, which has minimal traffic and is safe for walking at night. The house is a brick ranch design with a spacious lawn and shrubs. Every resident's name is on the front door, and the one-car garage houses their bicycles. Inside is a living–dining room with a large fireplace, a kitchen, three bedrooms, a bathroom, and a semifurnished basement. The house is comfortable, with warm furnishings, wall-to-wall carpeting in some rooms, and several pet cats and kittens. The landlord owns a small grocery store just across the street and lives over it.

The men's apartment is located in an urban residential area, described as a "rough" neighborhood by the staff. An abandoned church is adjacent to the apartment house. There is a large, partly fenced-in back yard with a sprawling grape arbor and a small flower garden, planted and tended by one resident. The apartment we visited is at the rear of the building, on the second and third floors; it includes two bedrooms, a living room, kitchen, dining room, and two bathrooms. The furniture is new and chosen for its attractiveness, sturdiness, and moderate price. In this apartment unit, as in the other six, there are no fire extinguishers, sprinklers, alarms, or exit signs.

Staff

The Apartment Project's staff overlaps with the Regional Center's staff. The executive director of the center (who is also responsible for the center's workshop, job placement program, adult education program, various recreation and therapy programs, and child development programs) is the administrative head of the Apartment Project. The assistant executive director is responsible for helping to design individualized programs for all clients of the center. He interviews all potential apartment residents.

The Apartment Project coordinator, two full-time homemakers, and two part-time homemakers comprise the direct service staff. The Apartment Project coordinator is responsible for the day-to-day operation of the project and hires and trains the homemakers. She initiates and supervises any new programming for residents of the apartments and acts as a liaison between community facilities, resources, and the residents.

There is one full-time and one part-time homemaker for the three women's apartments, and one full-time and one part-time homemaker for the three men's apartments. These homemakers are responsible for direct supervision and training of residents. As one homemaker said, "We teach the residents how normal people live, including all basic survival skills, such as cooking, laundry, household repairs, budgeting, use of public transportation, and shopping." There is a minimum education requirement of a high school diploma for a homemaker; beyond that much less emphasis is placed on formal education and training than on proved competency. Homemakers are hired on a 3-month trial basis to determine how well they can work with the residents.

The assistant executive director believes that a staffing pattern that includes a live-in married couple as the houseparents is definitely not normalizing, because it may perpetuate a childish form of dependence on the part of many residents. Also, he feels that such a staffing pattern places unwarranted pressure on the staff. As contrasted with the usual houseparent role in group homes, the homemakers in this project have a clear and delimited job description, which includes teaching of community survival skills, housekeeping skills, and adjustment skills. Their job description does *not* include learning to live with the residents and developing a cohabitational relationship. Although they are acutely aware of their influence on the residents' value system, they honestly believe that they are not acting in loco parentis. The staff feels that defining their relationship with the residents as a job to which they go and from which they return home to their own families prevents them from being entrapped as surrogate parents.

The most striking feature of all the staff members is their degree of commitment and enthusiasm about their work. They all see themselves continuing to work for the center in their present capacities as far into the future as they can predict. Often mentioned was the satisfaction of seeing the residents progress and succeed in learning to become independent and competent individuals, and the desire to see more institutionalized adults be given the same opportunity.

Residents

During its 3 years in operation, 44 persons have been admitted to the Apartment Project, all but five from the state institution. Prospective residents must have basic self-help skills and must express a desire to live in the apartments. The Apartment Project staff has depended on referral agencies to make the initial judgment on new residents, and they are admitted for a 1-month probationary period. According to a paper prepared by the Apartment Project staff, "The most recent testing before intake for those from an institution indicated a measured intellectual range from 32 to a high of 78. We have found, however, no relationship between these test scores and the possibility of success in semi-independent living. Emotional stability appears to be a more important factor."

In the men's apartment, three of the four residents had recently moved to the project from the state school. The fourth, who had previously lived with his family, had been part of the program for 2 years and was moved into this apartment to act as a helper to the new residents. The two newest residents seemed ambivalent about living in an apartment, since they missed their friends from the institution and were unsure of what advantage life in the apartment might have. In an overzealous manner, Larry, the senior resident, was dominating the newer residents, and their distaste for his behavior contributed to their hesitations about community living. All the men were working at the Regional Center's workshop but said they would like to be competitively employed. Larry thought that he would be working in a competitive job and living independently soon.

The six residents of the women's house ranged in age from 28 to 45 years. Four of the women could read, write, and do elementary arithmetic. Five had been institutionalized before coming to the apartment, but only three had come directly from the state school. Most of the women who had been at the state school had known each other and were able to form and maintain close friendships among themselves. In a maternal manner, Muriel, the oldest resident, spoke often of watching one of the youngest residents grow up at the institution. Muriel, as the senior resident in the women's residence, also tended to dominate, but she was often effectively countered by other residents who had been in the program nearly as long as she. All the women worked at the center's workshop; however, the newest and most capable resident had already been hired for a competitive job and two other women were actively seeking competitive jobs.

Program

The project coordinator summarized the goal of the program as "on an individual basis, to teach each resident as much as he or she can learn in order to live as independently as he or she possibly can." The attitude of the whole staff toward achieving this goal was well put by a homemaker in the oft-quoted words, "Every journey begins with one step." The steps, however, have been slower in coming than originally anticipated, and the notion of the apartments as only a short-term transitional facility has been modified. Not only are residents allowed to stay for a prolonged period of time, but also the possibility of utilizing some apartments as permanent homes for those persons not capable of totally unsupervised living is now being entertained. Actually, one of the men's apartments in the former rectory has informally become a minimally supervised permanent facility that is still structurally and programmatically a part of the Apartment Project. Thus the program has been flexible enough to be shaped by the developing needs of its residents.

Although there is no rule that a resident must be employed, residents are encouraged to work at some day activity. Six residents are competitively employed, and the other nineteen attend a workshop program. Almost all residents have savings accounts, control their own finances, and are learning to budget, although the staff reserves the right to place controls on specific residents if they deem it necessary. It is hoped that some residents soon will be able to have checking accounts.

The use of leisure time is the province of the residents, although the homemakers have found it necessary to make suggestions about ways residents might use their free time. The Regional Center conducts grooming classes, dances, bowling, and an Adults Club (a social activities organization for retarded adults). Even though no explicit efforts are made to encourage dating, several residents are dating seriously, and the relationships seem to be encouraged with constructive concern and counseling by the staff. Also, the apartment tenants have organized themselves and meet monthly to plan a range of social activities. A number of residents attend adult basic education courses for slow learners and the foreign-born, sponsored by the local school department.

Evening meals are an important event, since they provide a forum for learning. The homemakers structure meal preparation and serving, eating, and cleaning up as learning experiences but are available more for consultation than for direct help. Staff members eat with the residents only when invited. The apartments have developed different means for distributing the mealtime responsibilities; for example, in one men's apartment, each resident is designated "housefather" for 2 weeks and does all the kitchen work during that time. During meals there are resident-imposed verbal sanctions against disruptive behavior and bad table manners.

Health needs of residents in the Apartment Project are met through a variety of community resources.

Health education is done informally by the homemakers, especially in the area of personal hygiene. Each resident has a private physician; the resident calls to make his or her own appointment, if possible. Emergency services are obtained from hospital emergency rooms and the community's rescue squad. Dental services are provided by community dentists. Counseling is provided to some former state school residents by a part-time consulting psychologist affiliated with the school. Other residents are served by the community's mental health clinic. Every resident has a physical examination and dental checkup at least once a year. The women see a gynecologist at least once a year for PAP tests. Every resident has had hearing and vision tests since entering the program.

One person is on medication for chronic heart disease, two are on medication for epilepsy, one takes a mild tranquilizer, and two women use birth control pills. Residents are responsible for taking their own medication and are checked regularly by their private physicians. Several women have had hysterectomies and three have had tubal ligations at their own request; none of the men have been sterilized.

Residents are encouraged to go alone to doctors and dentists, although they are sometimes accompanied by another resident or a staff member more familiar with the bus routes. Most residents receive total medical coverage through state Aid to Disabled Persons, others are covered by Blue Cross through their place of employment, and a few who have savings pay cash for these services.

Rules and policies do not seem very restrictive and staff members have, over time, tried to be less protective to encourage more self-reliance. Residents may awaken and go to bed when they choose, although there is a 10:00 P.M. curfew that is enforced. They may leave the house whenever they wish as long as the homemaker knows that they are leaving and they have completed their household duties. There are no rules concerning personal grooming. There are restrictions regarding guests of the opposite sex in bedrooms, but residents may have dinner and evening guests if they want. Alcohol and smoking are permitted. The firm rule against drug use is quite consistent with resident values; most residents seem openly opposed to and afraid of drugs. A sign on one bedroom door reads "Peanut butter is better than pot."

The residents monitor one another's behavior a good deal, partly as a result of being less supervised by staff members than are residents in group homes and partly because the staff members encourage peer group teaching. For instance, residents who need to learn the use of public transportation are sometimes taught by other, more skilled residents who are paid for the teaching they do.

Ex-Residents

During the time between our two visits, two residents had left the program. One had been returned to the state institution because of an attempted suicide and general inability to cope, and another had left to live with her boyfriend and his mother, a move of which the staff disapproved for a variety of seemingly sensible reasons.

Over its 3 years, 14 persons have left the Project. Six were returned to the state school where they had formally resided because of various crises. Of these six, three have now returned to community living in more supervised facilities. Two persons were placed directly into group homes with 24-hour supervision. The remaining six made the decision to leave on their own: Four are now living independently; one decided to return to the institution; and one is now living with a family (not her own). Thus of the 14 ex-residents at the time of our visit, four were again living in the institution, six were living in more supervised settings in the community, and four were living independently.

Some apparent contradictions are posed by responses of residents and staff to our inventory about house climate. Although staff members in the Apartment Project are only present part-time, both residents and staff rated *staff control* very high, and both rated residents as less free "to complain about things to staff" than in any other program visited except Hickory Manor. And although resident autonomy in the Apartment Project was reasonably high, both residents and staff strongly agreed that rules are clearly understood and important to follow, and that consequences are clear, including transfer or discharge for breaking the rules.

It seems that as residents indeed become more on their own, they and staff alike must depend more on a clear expression of what contingencies there are. Also, with increased independence, residents may become more cognizant of those aspects of staff control that remain, and they may not feel as close to the staff as they would with live-in houseparents.

Further Variations: Toward a Comprehensive System

As we have seen, there is a variety of ways a residence can be semi-independent, and a program with several such variations could make better placements. The possible variations are many: The Apartment Project has one unit that is almost independent. It has others with greater, but still not continuous, supervision. Other programs have nonretarded co-residents or informal assistance from a citizen advocate. A group home could move toward independence by having staff live in for a period of time (e.g., 1 year) and gradually detach themselves from the home.

Also, a type of partially supervised program we have not considered elsewhere in this report is the vacation resort/camp, providing varying degrees of supervision for recreational activities. For retarded persons living either in supervised settings or independently, who lack the skills or inclination to take vacations on their own, such a 1- or 2-week vacation program could not only be enjoyable but could provide a "safe" way to try out new activities and meet new people.

Table 11-1
A Proposed Comprehensive System

Facility	*Maximum capacity*	*Anticipated length of stay*	*Kind of structures*	*Residents served*	*Program emphasis*	*Staff function*
1. Extended care in lieu of institutional care	50	Terminal	Nursing home	Combined M and F. Profoundly retarded, unable to care for self	T.L.C.	Usual institutional staff
2. Intermediate care	35	Long term, may be several years	Nursing home	Combined M and F. Severely limited	Custodial care, some program emphasis on self-help skills	Nursing and rehabilitation-oriented staff
3. Intermediate care	8–10	1–3 years	Small group living home	Combined M and F. Low functioning client, potential for work activities center	Self-help skills, personal and interpersonal relationships, readiness for work activities center	Skilled professional houseparents
4a. Residential hostels	8–10	2 years	Small group living homes	Separate M and F. Moderately retarded client in work activities center	Community skills, learning for living, personal and interpersonal relationships, housekeeping and work skills	Professional houseparents

4b. Residential hostels	8–10	6 months		Separate M and F. Moderately retarded client working in competitive employment		
5. Beginning independent apartments	20	6 months–1 year	Motel-like apartment units	May be combined M and F. Moderately retarded, fairly independent living skills	Independent living skills	Consistent supervision, central kitchen, laundry, housekeeping
6. Semi-independent apartments	10	1 year	Self-contained living units	Combined M and F. Functioning independently, working in stable full-time employment	Counseling to help sustain and/or increase skills	Resident counselor
7. Independent apartments	Not limited	Permanent	Apartment house or units close to one another	Combined M and F. Well-adjusted independent adults	Reassurance for emergency or special needs. Integration with the nonretarded adult	Counselor available on request

Perhaps, too, the semi-independent model should not be oriented exclusively toward moving people from less independence to more independence. There are certainly retarded persons living independent but very isolated lives in shabby room-and-board facilities and/or experiencing other serious adjustment problems. If some form of semi-independent living arrangements were offered, this alternative might prevent their admission or readmission into an institution or simply make their daily lives more fulfilling.

Throughout this book, the issue of independence versus dependence of residents has arisen. The prevailing ethos in the community residence movement is to help residents become as independent as possible, but the question still remains, Independent toward what end? We should recognize the psychosocial benefits of belonging to a network of social relationships, especially for persons whose social marginality is likely to isolate them further if they are to live completely independently. To avoid this potential isolation and alienation from a community, semi-independent group living arrangements should be considered. Whatever the particular design chosen, by conceptualizing the semi-independent unit as a long-term and possibly permanent home for residents, the recidivism rate found in this model might be reduced; independence then becomes the possibility of risk taking with the support of a peer group and consulting professionals on whom the residents can depend.

There are obviously many variations within the semi-independent model that could coexist in a full-service system. Also, a closely related model is the more supervised group home. Indeed, many group homes studied were planning to add semi-independent apartments to their program, and the Apartment Project, during our visit, was opening a group home for less skilled residents with 24-hour (although not live-in) staff. A number of residents who had "failed" in the Apartment Project seemed to require, at least for a while, more supervision. Hence by incorporating the group home into this system, the Regional Center could possibly reduce the rate of return to institutions without enforcing unnecessary supervision for residents who do not need it (Table 11-1).

Section 5. Comprehensive Systems

Photograph by Thomas Szabo

12. Comprehensive Systems

IN previous chapters we considered a number of community-based residential alternatives that are currently operating in the United States. Clearly, no single type of program can provide an appropriate setting for all retarded citizens, given the heterogeneous nature of the population. Thus it has been our assumption throughout that to facilitate each individual's living as close as possible to mainstream society, every region must make a thorough assessment of the present and future needs of retarded persons within that region and then provide a network of different residential models.

However, only a few programs identified by the project simultaneously included a variety of models for residents with different levels of ability and needs, although many single-model programs indicated a desire to expand in the future. Perhaps the best known comprehensive system is ENCOR, the Eastern Nebraska Community Office of Retardation, which operates 10 models, graded developmentally, for retarded children and adults.

Each program is designed to ready the retarded citizen for the next step of his developmental program, whether it be in a developmental center, public school program, vocational program, employment, training residence, or independent living. There is always a goal or next step . . . .

Preface, ENCOR Brochure, 1973

The 10 models included in ENCOR's system at this time were the following:

1. Children's hostels
2. Adolescent hostels
3. Adult training hostels

4. Adult board and room homes
5. Apartment clusters
6. Supervised living units
7. Co-resident apartments
8. Independent living
9. Behavioral development residential hostels
10. Development maximization units.

The six comprehensive residential systems in our sample share many common characteristics. All are sponsored by nonprofit corporations and had been operating for an average of 6 years at the time of our survey. By definition, each system provides more than one model of community residential living, most often including group homes, and semi-independent apartment units. All the systems provide residential services for a large number of retarded people, ranging from 33 to 450 persons per program. Often children and adolescents as well as adults are served. Every comprehensive residential system noted that it accepts residents whose functional levels range from severely to mildly retarded. In addition, there is a marked emphasis on employment; some comprehensive residential systems operate vocational training programs for residents capable of competitive employment in the future and sheltered workshops for more limited individuals. None of these programs provides permanent homes; all are oriented toward moving residents to more independent settings in the future. Table 12-1 depicts salient characteristics of four comprehensive systems; the remaining two in our sample were visited and are described next.

The two programs we will describe provide comprehensive systems of community residences; one is an attempted replication of the other, located in a different state. Although several of the community residential models described in preceding chapters are not included in these multimodel programs, these systems also represent a definite move toward multimodel programming (see Fig. 12-1).

Transitional Services – Pittsburgh

Transitional Services is an agency in Pittsburgh, Pennsylvania, which moves large numbers of men and women out of state institutions. It was started in 1966 as a demonstration project by United Mental Health of Pittsburgh, a private, nonprofit corporation. After a fairly turbulent but successful start, it separated from United Mental Health and became an independent agency. Although Transitional Services originally served former mental hospital patients exclusively, there are now approximately equal numbers of mentally retarded and mentally disturbed residents integrated into all residential facilities. At the time of our visit, the agency provided residential services for about 450 adults.

Philosophically and programmatically Transitional Services holds that no person should be denied the opportunity to live normally in society. Hence

Table 12-1
Comparison of Four Comprehensive Systems

	Comprehensive System 1	*Comprehensive System 2*	*Comprehensive System 3*	*Comprehensive System 4*
Number of residents	172	78	33	63
Level of retardation	Severely retarded to borderline	Severely retarded to mildly retarded, multihandicapped	Severely retarded to mildly retarded, multihandicapped	Profoundly retarded to mildly retarded, multihandicapped
Age	16 to 40 years	12 to 50 years	Birth to 30 years	4 to 30 years
Models	Dormitory Semi-independent apartments Co-resident apartments	Group homes Boarding homes Apartments	Specialized developmental foster care Supervised apartments	Cottages graded according to level of retardation
Monthly fee	$250	$200	None	$45
Sources of funds for the program	Fees Charitable contributions Federal and state grants Workshop contracts	Fees Charitable contributions Church funds State funds	County funds	State and county funds Fees

the goal of the program is to reduce the individual's dependency on institutional supports and to increase those skills necessary for independent living. Three graduated models of residential facilities are provided by the program: assessment centers, supervised apartment buildings, and independent apartment units.

Physical Facilities

In general, Transitional Services has selected buildings that meet the following criteria:

1. The neighborhoods in which they are situated must provide learning experiences and easy accessibility to services and shopping areas.
2. The neighborhoods must be sufficiently crime-free so that the residents' personal safety is not threatened.

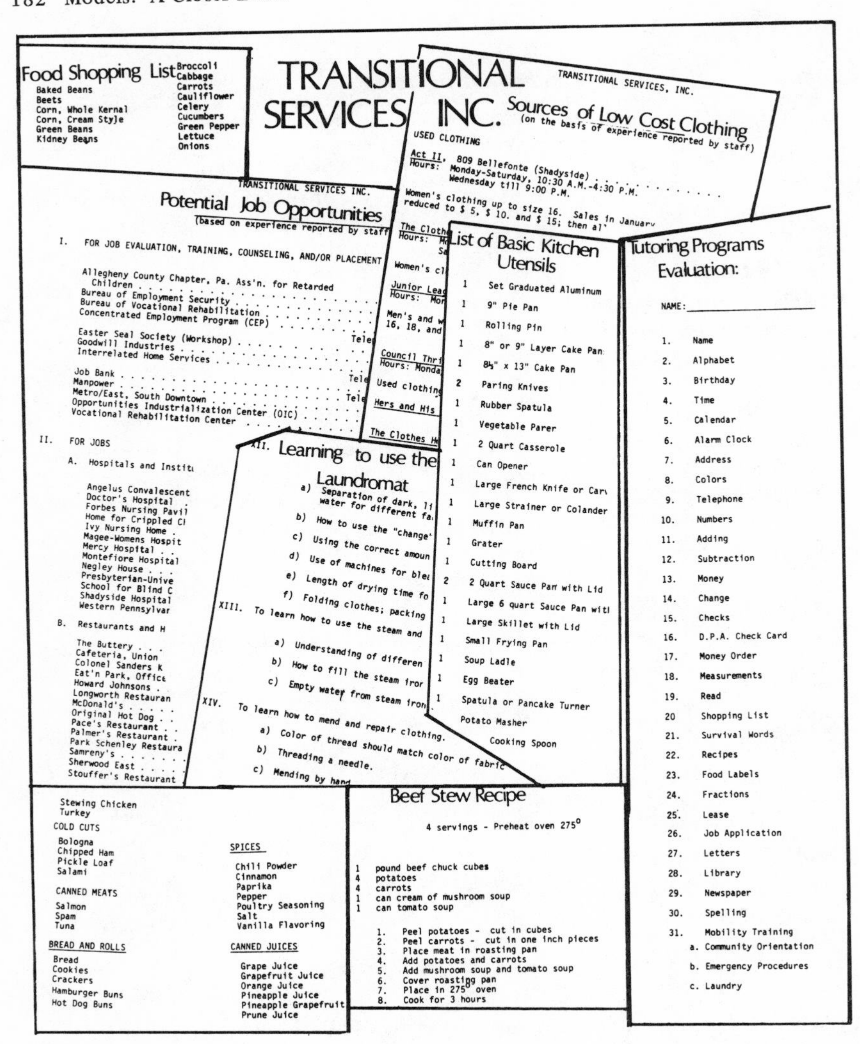

Food Shopping List

Baked Beans
Beets
Corn, Whole Kernal
Corn, Cream Style
Green Beans
Kidney Beans
Broccoli
Cabbage
Carrots
Cauliflower
Celery
Cucumbers
Green Pepper
Lettuce
Onions

TRANSITIONAL SERVICES INC.

TRANSITIONAL SERVICES, INC.

Sources of Low Cost Clothing
(on the basis of experience reported by staff)

USED CLOTHING

Act II, 809 Bellefonte (Shadyside) . . . .
Hours: Monday-Saturday, 10:30 A.M.-4:30 P.M.
Wednesday till 9:00 P.M.

Women's clothing up to size 16. Sales in January
reduced to $ 5, $ 10. and $ 15; then al

The Cloth
Hours:

Women's cl

Junior Lea
Hours: Mon

Men's and w
16, 18, and

Council Thri
Hours: Monda

Used clothing

Hers and His

The Clothes H

TRANSITIONAL SERVICES INC.

Potential Job Opportunities
(based on experience reported by staff)

I. FOR JOB EVALUATION, TRAINING, COUNSELING, AND/OR PLACEMENT

Allegheny County Chapter, Pa. Ass'n. for Retarded Children . . . .
Bureau of Employment Security . . . .
Bureau of Vocational Rehabilitation . . . .
Concentrated Employment Program (CEP) . . . .

Easter Seal Society (Workshop) . . . . Tele
Goodwill Industries . . . .
Interrelated Home Services . . . .

Job Bank . . . .
Manpower . . . . Tele
Metro/East, South Downtown . . . . Tele
Opportunities Industrialization Center (OIC) . . . . .
Vocational Rehabilitation Center . . . .

II. FOR JOBS

A. Hospitals and Instit

Angelus Convalescent
Doctor's Hospital
Forbes Nursing Pavil
Home for Crippled Cl
Ivy Nursing Home
Magee-Womens Hospit
Mercy Hospital
Montefiore Hospital
Negley House
Presbyterian-Unive
School for Blind C
Shadyside Hospital
Western Pennsylvar

B. Restaurants and H

The Buttery
Cafeteria, Union
Colonel Sanders K
Eat'n Park, Office
Howard Johnsons
Longworth Restauran
McDonald's
Original Hot Dog
Pace's Restaurant
Palmer's Restaurant
Park Schenley Restaura
Samreny's
Sherwood East
Stouffer's Restaurant

XII. Learning to use the Laundromat

a) Separation of dark, li
water for different fa
b) How to use the "change"
c) Using the correct amoun
d) Use of machines for blea
e) Length of drying time fo
f) Folding clothes; packing

XIII. To learn how to use the steam and

a) Understanding of differen
b) How to fill the steam iror
c) Empty water from steam iron

XIV. To learn how to mend and repair clothing.

a) Color of thread should match color of fabric
b) Threading a needle.
c) Mending by hand

List of Basic Kitchen Utensils

1 Set Graduated Aluminum
1 9" Pie Pan
1 Rolling Pin
1 8" or 9" Layer Cake Pan
1 8½" x 13" Cake Pan
2 Paring Knives
1 Rubber Spatula
1 Vegetable Parer
1 2 Quart Casserole
1 Can Opener
1 Large French Knife or Carv
1 Large Strainer or Colander
1 Muffin Pan
1 Grater
1 Cutting Board
2 2 Quart Sauce Pan with Lid
1 Large 6 quart Sauce Pan witl
1 Large Skillet with Lid
1 Small Frying Pan
1 Soup Ladle
1 Egg Beater
1 Spatula or Pancake Turner
Potato Masher
Cooking Spoon

Tutoring Programs Evaluation:

NAME: ____________________

1. Name
2. Alphabet
3. Birthday
4. Time
5. Calendar
6. Alarm Clock
7. Address
8. Colors
9. Telephone
10. Numbers
11. Adding
12. Subtraction
13. Money
14. Change
15. Checks
16. D.P.A. Check Card
17. Money Order
18. Measurements
19. Read
20 Shopping List
21. Survival Words
22. Recipes
23. Food Labels
24. Fractions
25. Lease
26. Job Application
27. Letters
28. Library
29. Newspaper
30. Spelling
31. Mobility Training
a. Community Orientation
b. Emergency Procedures
c. Laundry

Stewing Chicken
Turkey

COLD CUTS
Bologna
Chipped Ham
Pickle Loaf
Salami

CANNED MEATS
Salmon
Spam
Tuna

BREAD AND ROLLS
Bread
Cookies
Crackers
Hamburger Buns
Hot Dog Buns

SPICES
Chili Powder
Cinnamon
Paprika
Pepper
Poultry Seasoning
Salt
Vanilla Flavoring

CANNED JUICES
Grape Juice
Grapefruit Juice
Orange Juice
Pineapple Juice
Pineapple Grapefruit
Prune Juice

Beef Stew Recipe

4 servings - Preheat oven 275°

1 pound beef chuck cubes
4 potatoes
4 carrots
1 can cream of mushroom soup
1 can tomato soup

1. Peel potatoes - cut in cubes
2. Peel carrots - cut in one inch pieces
3. Place meat in roasting pan
4. Add potatoes and carrots
5. Add mushroom soup and tomato soup
6. Cover roasting pan
7. Place in 275° oven
8. Cook for 3 hours

Figure 12-1
The goal of Transitional Services is to prepare residents for independent living by teaching them the necessary skills.

3. The neighborhoods must have a mixed and somewhat transient population so that the residents' anonymity is maximized.
4. The buildings must be able to meet zoning, safety, and health standards.

Even in a city as large as Pittsburgh, it is difficult to find very many neighborhoods that fulfill these requirements. Therefore Transitional Services has concentrated its 450 residents in primarily two urban residential neighborhoods; the effects of the resulting saturation of neighborhoods will be considered later in this chapter.

Program

The main emphasis of Transitional Services' program is training the residents to live independently and, at the time of our visit, 18 home management and academic tutors and 56 program counselors provided this training.

Assessment Centers. Four assessment centers, serving approximately 60 residents, provide the most supervised and sheltered living situations within Transitional Services. Residents living here need the most intensive resocialization into the community. Two of the centers are group homes with common living and eating areas for all residents. A cook prepares all lunches and dinners; however, residents are responsible for preparing their own breakfasts. The other two centers each have several self-contained apartments for residents and one apartment for staff; these residents live in groups of four or five and do their own cooking. The atmosphere of these latter two assessment centers is much less institutional than the group homes in that more privacy and autonomy are afforded in apartment living.

Staff members in all four assessment centers concentrate on determining those areas in which residents need training and then begin the teaching process. Tutors in assessment centers focus primarily on mobility training. They start with a general orientation to the community: They show the residents where significant services and resources are located and how to find their way around the neighborhood. Tutors teach residents how to go to stores, to shop, to ride buses, to cross streets, to recognize "Walk" and "Don't walk" signs, and to do laundry. In the two apartment-unit assessment centers, tutors begin teaching the basics of food preparation. In general, however, tutors primarily concentrate on assessing the skills that need to be learned by each resident. It is at this point that extensive record keeping on residents' learning and performance is begun. A resident may remain in the assessment center for as long as the staff determines is necessary for him or her to become accustomed to the often bewildering demands of city life, although typically, the stay is for a few months.

Supervised Apartment Buildings. The next step in this graduated system is the supervised apartment building, where there is less staff supervision than in the assessment centers. There are seven supervised apartment buildings, with a total of about 250 spaces for residents. In each building there are 7 to 11 apartments for residents and one apartment for staff. Transitional Services chose to rent buildings that approximate the quality of apartments that residents can expect to rent when they live on their own; therefore the units are not luxurious but are in good condition and well maintained.

Because this level of residential living represents the core of Transitional Services' program, one particular apartment building – Damon House – was studied in depth. The agency had totally remodeled the building at a cost of approximately $2,500 for each four-person apartment, and 48 persons were in residence.

The staff members of Damon House (and of the other six supervised apartment buildings) are charged with the responsibility of training the residents for future unsupervised living. Tutors teach housekeeping skills, food preparation, shopping, budgeting, and some academic skills. Teaching of housekeeping skills occurs daily with the help of a manual published by the Soap and Detergent Association. Food preparation is also taught by practice, and staff members have developed a series of simple recipes for the residents to use. Shopping and budgeting are taught weekly; a tutor and the residents of an apartment decide on the week's menus before going shopping. Special consideration is given to nutrition, costs, and simplicity in menu planning, and a shopping list is prepared using these guidelines. For those residents who are unable to read, tutors have designed pictorial shopping lists that can be reorganized for each shopping trip. Then the tutors accompany the residents to the supermarket until they are capable of going alone.

Budgeting is emphasized constantly in Transitional Services. At the time of our visit residents received $136 each month from Public Assistance. Of this, $71 was paid for rent, $36 ($9 per week) was alloted for food, $5 for paper products and toilet articles, and $24 for spending money. There is very little room for error here. If one lends a friend some money and he doesn't pay him back, he may have to take out a loan from the corporation, but this, too, must eventually be repaid. If one buys unwisely or plans poorly, it is very easy to run out of money by the third week of each month. Or, if one should suddenly decide to buy a radio for himself, his food money can disappear (he may then have only government surplus food). For example, when one resident was without funds because she had just bought her third radio, not much sympathy was offered.

Some academic skills are clearly necessary for success in the areas mentioned thus far. Emphasis is placed on functional learning. Residents are taught to sign their names and memorize their addresses and birthdates. They learn to make change and to recognize the value of coins and bills. Telling time and recognizing such simple "survival" words as *men, women, in,* and *out* are also stressed. In general, tutors try to teach the residents in intensive individual and small group sessions that last for about a half hour. On the average, there is one tutor for every 20 residents. Residents may spend only a few months or as long as 2 years at the supervised apartment level.

Independent Apartment Units. As residents approach the level of competence required for independent living in the general community, they are provided with a trial run experience in an independent apartment unit. The 40 independent apartment units are scattered in numerous buildings throughout the neighborhood and can accommodate about 150 residents. Three to five residents share an apartment, with staff available to them on a nonresidential consulting basis. Skills previously learned at the supervised apartment level are reviewed and refined; however, the tutor attempts to fade out assistance gradually to prepare the residents for totally independent living.

However, the progression from assessment center to supervised apartment to independent apartment is not mandatory for all residents. An individual is placed at the level and in the setting most appropriate to his or her abilities and background and may move ahead or drop back to previous levels if necessary.

Counseling Program

On all residential levels tutors share many of their duties with the 56 program counselors. However, whereas counselors attend to the psychosocial needs of residents, responding to emotional crises and everyday problems, tutors concentrate on teaching community survival skills. Counselors also assist residents in securing community resources. They help residents apply for Public Assistance, Social Security, and other disability allowances and actively seek out and secure services for residents in the areas of vocational training and placement, recreation, psychiatric and socialization groups, medical care, and special disability services. Residents with serious emotional problems are referred by counselors to the local mental health–mental retardation units.

Placement of Residents

Because Transitional Services provides services for such a large population, residents' entrance into the system is facilitated by a placement staff of one supervisor and 10 placement counselors. Their functions within the agency are threefold: (1) to seek out referrals to the program; (2) to begin to construct a "life plan" for the resident by assessing his or her need for training and education; and (3) to place the resident into the appropriate facility within the agency.

The placement staff stated that from the beginning of the Transitional Services program the need for an aggressive outreach program was recognized; thus they put a high priority on working with a referral staff from other agencies. Ninety percent of the referrals to Transitional Services come from state schools and hospitals. After the referring agency completes a referral form and the applicant is given a physical examination, a placement counselor meets with the client to discuss his or her application. Ideally, this meeting is held at Transitional Services, so that the applicant is able to see the facilities. The applicant is informed of some of the expectations of residents and then fills out a resident application and contract. Assistance is given to the applicant as necessary. Then all applications are reviewed by the staff psychiatrist. Grounds for rejection include the following: a history of arson, homicide, suicide attempts, or indiscriminate sexual behavior (such as child molesting); uncontrolled epilepsy; or a lack of basic self-care skills. Fewer than 20 persons of over 2,000 applicants have been permanently rejected from the program on the basis of these restrictions. In addition, the applicant must have an income of not less than $136 per month, which was the local Public Assistance rate at the time we interviewed them.

After an application is accepted, the placement staff assigns the applicant to an assessment center, a supervised apartment, or an independent apartment unit, whereupon he or she signs a lease, pays 2 weeks' rent in advance, makes a $5 key deposit, and moves into the new residence.

Staff

Transitional Services has a highly organized staffing pattern.

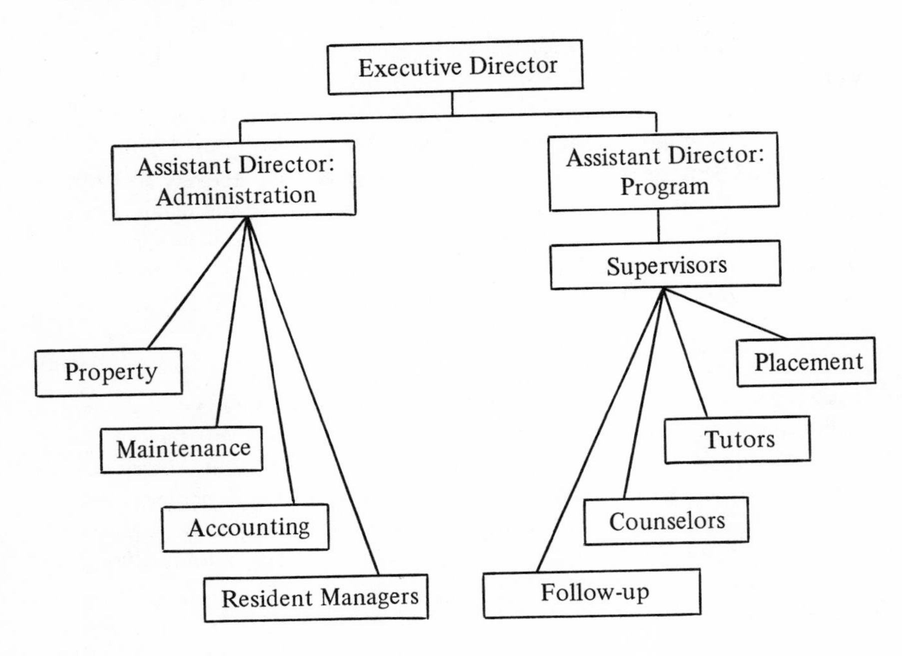

Figure 12-2
Staffing pattern of Transitional Services.

We have already considered the responsibilities of the program staff. The resident manager's role largely depends on the type of facility. Resident managers in assessment centers work in husband-wife teams (each receiving a separate salary) for 5 days at a time, 24 hours a day. They are involved in some of the counseling and home management and provide part of the supervision of residents that is necessary in these highly structured settings. The resident managers in the supervised apartment buildings are usually single people who work only in the evenings; they sleep in the apartment 5 days each week to provide some supervision and to be available in cases of emergency. All 15 members of the resident management staff are expected to maintain separate residences for their days off, when they are replaced by relief resident managers. The administration feels that it is important for resident managers, as well as for other staff members, to treat their work at the agency as a job and to maintain a life outside of work; the administration tries to avoid creating a situation in which the staff members' work becomes their total lives. If this happened, they feel, the staff would "burn out" quickly because of the extremely demanding nature of such a life. However, at times staff members find this separation a difficult goal to achieve, since they still may be frequently called to the house after hours for emergencies.

The agency has divided the residential facilities into units, each headed by a supervisor. Supervisors are responsible for all the tutoring and counseling staff within their units. They consult these staff members and take an active role in the planning of programs for individual residents. Also, supervisors act formally as liaisons between the administration and staff; however, the rapport and exchange of information between the direct service staff and the administration seemed quite fluid.

All staff hiring and firing procedures are controlled by the executive director who notes his preference for people with "commitment, energy, vitality, openness, and honesty." When presented with the observation that his staff's enthusiasm was almost religious in nature, the executive director replied that creating this atmosphere was deliberate. He observed that what keeps the agency going is a "super-confidence that you can do it," and this type of climate draws to the agency a certain type of personnel. He avoids hiring people who have worked in institutional settings for long periods of time.

Another staffing pattern characteristic of Transitional Services involves the movement of staff within the agency. Every 6 months counselors and tutors are moved from one residential facility to another; they remain in the same functional position but in a different locale. The rationale for these moves is twofold: to familiarize staff with the entire agency, and to prevent staff members and individual residents from becoming too interdependent. One benefit of moving the staff is that it enhances the agency's ability to promote people from within. When a counselor or tutor has moved several times and is familiar with all facets of the program, he or she will then have had much of the preliminary training necessary to become a supervisor. Indeed, all management staff, except the executive director and a program consultant, began as counselors or tutors and were promoted after several such moves. It is noteworthy, however, that this policy of movement has caused some confusion among the residents, and one wonders if it is clear to them that the staff members are just as transitional as they are.

Each person is employed subject to a probationary period of 6 months. At the end of 3 months and again at 6 months the supervisor writes an evaluation of every employee's performance and discusses it individually with the employees. After the probationary period, evaluations are conducted yearly. Thus record keeping and evaluation are instrumental parts of the agency's policies for staff and residents alike. From our observation, records are concise and kept to a functional minimum.

In general, our observations left us with the impression that the staff at this agency had regular opportunities to develop their own programs creatively, were consistently enthusiastic, and had a sincere commitment to their work with the residents. In contrast to most other models, the staffing pattern of Transitional Services promotes intensive training of the residents. Consistent supervision of direct service personnel results in a competent staff. The well-defined division of labor permits the staff to provide specialized training to residents; and staff members who have different areas of expertise can meet the broad range of residents needs. In Transitional Services, there are people who have worked in the agency for as long as 5 years and who remain enthusiastic and creative, perhaps because they have taken advantage of the possibility for upward mobility.

Ellen, a counselor at Damon House, believes her role is that of a "counselor and friend." When asked if she would take the job again, there was no hesitation: "Yes, I like working with people, and they help me, too. Once I get involved with them, I forget my own problems. I have learned to be more patient with people and it makes me less self-centered. I do less thinking about myself, spend less time at home than before, and consequently use what time there is more effectively." Ellen was in complete accord with Transitional Services' policy on deinstitutionalization. "They should be able to live in the community and still get the services they need without being institutionalized." In fact, the staff expressed the desire to get residents to the point where they would demand services themselves.

Several aspects of the staffing situation at Damon House and throughout the agency seem important to us. First, there is a constant *positive* emphasis on what one *can* do rather than what one cannot do; this follows from the teaching focus of the daily program. Second, staff members are expected to be effective for a certain amount of time each day, and no guilt-inspiring messages are given to them, such as "always be available" or "this is really a 24-hour job." Thus staff members can, and do, maintain their own lives apart from Transitional Services.

Residents

We don't dwell on labels. And the mixing of people with different diagnoses is a policy. They teach each other.

Residents recently discharged from institutions for the mentally retarded and mentally disturbed live together, and staff members believe that labels are not important, especially after years of institutionalization; more important are the strengths and potentialities of each person. Yet the staff members have noticed behavioral differences between people who are primarily diagnosed as retarded and those who are primarily diagnosed as mentally disturbed. They feel there is an advantage to the differences as they perceive them: that is, generally retarded people tend to be less moody and maintain a positive attitude, and former mental hospital patients have less difficulty coping with daily tasks. Thus each one complements the other.

In this model there is a place for almost everyone, from the multiply handicapped individual just beginning to be mobile and learning to cook to the resident who holds a job and has no easily discernible signs of handicaps, yet who has been institutionalized for many years. Most residents spend much of their time in individual or group tutoring sessions; relatively few hold outside jobs. The agency sees itself as providing an intensive training experience for residents and prefers to use the short time they have in the program to quickly increase their community survival skills. Furthermore, staff members mentioned that they have no objection to some residents *never* working in community jobs; after a lifetime of living in institutions, they feel that residents should have the option to choose whether or not they want to work. After all, they argue in defense of their controversial position, millions of Americans are unemployed. Ex-institutionalized people, who often have few marketable skills, should not be stigmatized further by choosing not to work. However, as residents become more capable and move to independent apartment units, staff members begin to help those who are interested in working.

Catherine is an ex-resident of Transitional Services. She had been a resident of a state institution all her life, and when she was 72 years old had applied for admission to Transitional Services. The placement counselor determined that Catherine was qualified for the program but was curious about why she would want to leave the institution at her age. After all, he reasoned, all her friends were there and it would be difficult to start anew. When he expressed these thoughts to Catherine, she replied, "You probably don't understand this, but I've got to see what it's like on the outside before I die."

Catherine was admitted to the program and spent the next 5 months intensively learning those skills necessary for survival in the community. At the end of this period she moved to an apartment with three other women and began her life on the "outside." Catherine is physically handicapped and has difficulty carrying heavy bundles. Therefore she arranged with her roommates that she would do all the cooking and light cleaning in exchange for their being responsible for the shopping and laundry. This arrangement has worked out admirably, and when we interviewed Catherine, we found that she had indeed become self-sufficient and thus had met the extremely challenging goal she had set for herself.

Program

The program philosophy of this agency can be discerned from the flexibility of its rules and policies – a flexibility ensured by having most regulations formalized at the local level, unit by unit. The few agency-wide rules are as follows: Residents wake up, go to sleep, leave their apartment, and return as they please, except in group homes, where residents must let someone (resident or staff) know where they are going. Residents are encouraged to carry a business card from Transitional Services that indicates their name and the address of the facility where they presently live to be used in case of emergency. No restrictions are placed on dress, grooming, smoking, or dating. However, no guests may visit a resident in his or her bedroom, and visitors must pay for meals when they eat in any of the facilities. Residents are not permitted to have pets in their rooms or apartments.

Damon House articulated some specific standards and regulations for the 48 residents who were living there at the time of our survey. Only if someone is gone for 72 hours is the missing persons bureau contacted. Behaviors such as stealing and fighting are dealt with by the counselors; however, as one counselor said, "the program is not set up for anyone to be policed 24 hours." Residents are aware of the fact that if no improvement is shown in their behavior, termination is a possibility. But as one staff member noted, residents are free agents; they are not under the strict control of the house. On our autonomy scale, Transitional Services ranks quite high relative to other models, with a score of 22 out of a maximum of 24.

A second aspect of the program philosophy involves the transfer of residents within the agency. There is constant pressure, exerted by the administration on counselors and tutors, to keep residents moving toward greater independence and to avoid stagnation. The director of the agency feels that if high expectations are set, residents will be more likely to become independent and competent in the shortest period of time. A major criticism raised by outside agencies about the program concerns this frequent transfer of residents (and even of staff) within the system. These agencies feel that as a result of this constant movement interagency communication is less consistent and meaningful than it could be. Perhaps a more serious criticism of this policy concerns the effect of this movement on the residents themselves. One agency specifically disagreed with the attitude that staff and residents should not become too attached to each other, arguing for the importance of attachment in developing confidence and trust and noting that residents are likely to have several counselors each year. In general, the policy of movement seems to be very poorly accepted by outside agencies.

It can be said that practicality is central to the philosophy of Transitional Services. At every level frills are systematically eliminated so that concentration can be given to useful endeavors. This is evident in the academic tutoring program, in the physical nature of the buildings, and in the emphasis placed on teaching budgeting. In the same vein, staff members continually point out that every experience is a teaching situation, that the world is a laboratory for learning, and that the residents' improvement is based on this constant pressure to become independent.

Outside Agencies

Transitional Services shares the responsibility for meeting many of the residents' needs with local mental health and mental retardation agencies (base service units). Although these units are understaffed and do not have as much time to spend with Transitional Services residents as they would like, Transitional Services refused to duplicate the services the units are mandated to provide since (1) if Transitional Services provided all services required by residents, it would quickly become indistinguishable from a total institution;

(2) residents need to learn how to integrate into the community, and their utilization of outside agencies encourages them to do so; (3) residents may continue to need such services after they leave Transitional Services; therefore they must learn how to use outside facilities while they are still residents; and (4) duplication of services is wasteful.

Transitional Services' residential facilities are located in two of the mental health and mental retardation catchment areas. Both these base service units have increased the scope of their services, partly as a result of the influx of Transitional Services residents into their areas. Thus Transitional Services residents are registered with a catchment area unit that is responsible for providing medical care. Also, both base service units provide a variety of groups for residents of Transitional Services, including prevocational training, arts and crafts, discussion, medication, psychotherapy, resocialization, and sex education groups, and most residents participate in one of these groups on a regular basis. These groups give the residents an opportunity to vent some of their feelings about problems they are having at Transitional Services to outsiders. In addition to the base service units, residents of Transitional Services are clients of a number of other agencies in the local community, such as sheltered workshops, a vocational training center, a counseling center for the deaf, and some church-sponsored recreational groups.

In general, the outside agencies that we visited or contacted were very enthusiastic about Transitional Services. They agreed that Transitional Services is the only residential program in the area that is making a large impact on reducing the state school's population; and most agencies were comfortable with the fact that Transitional Services will not provide psychiatric treatment or vocational services for the residents, leaving them with the responsibility of meeting these needs.

One of several questions we asked staff members of outside agencies was, Is there anything unique or especially effective about the Transitional Services program that you would like to comment on? The response of the director of one base service unit is instructive:

In spite of the rather obvious difficulties, the incidence of recidivism is rather low. The program has proved its effectiveness in most cases by using service agencies in the community rather than seeking reinstitutionalization in the difficult cases. The program has also illustrated that in very many cases institutionalization is not the answer: The individual can receive effective service in the community and remain a part of the community.

The clients, themselves, are the most unique part of the program. It is gratifying to see their determination to remain in the community. Their willingness to cooperate with service personnel and their desire to learn have been the chief contributing factors in any successes we or Transitional Services may have had.

We also interviewed a number of shopkeepers to sample their opinions concerning how well the residents seem to be integrating into the neighborhood.

The owner of a business situated next door to Damon House expressed positive feelings about the residents and respect for one of the counselors he knew. However, he had some criticism:

Two come in regularly. One works here. The other fellow said he'd rather be in Polk (a state school) because at least there he had his bicycle to ride. Recreation should be provided. It must be confining to them.

They hang around a lot. If you're going to start one of these, this is the biggest problem. They stand out there even in the rain, with nothing to do. I suggested they move chairs out back and spoke to the counselors about it.

The owner of another establishment (a laundry) was quick to point out that he both understood the philosophy of independence and respected some of the counselors. However, he mentioned two aspects of the program that were problematic from his perspective: The neighborhood has become too saturated with residents from the system, and the supervision is uneven.

In sum, while persons in the community may have some (often justifiable) criticisms, their general support for a system that has added so many previously marginal persons to these neighborhoods is encouraging.

Follow-up

When residents move into their own apartments in the community, the follow-up staff of Transitional Services assumes some continued responsibility for them. At the time of our visit, the follow-up program consisted of crisis intervention work with approximately 60 ex-residents each month. The follow-up staff is alerted to the existence of a problem by the ex-resident himself or herself, by a roommate, landlord, or the base service unit.

Eight ex-residents were interviewed. All mentioned that the Transitional Services staff was responsible for finding their apartments and job placements. In addition, all felt that Transitional Services prepared them adequately for their move into the community. They agreed that living in a Transitional Services facility allowed them more freedom than did the state school, but less freedom than they were able to have living on their own in the community. There were considerable differences among these ex-residents in terms of their levels of functioning and the quality of their lives. Two of the men were elderly and lacked most of the skills necessary to survive in their apartment; in fact, their landlord was evidently doing their cooking and washing for them. Also, they had few friends in the neighborhood and no day activities. In contrast, the two couples we visited were doing quite well. The female member of each couple worked, and each of the men took responsibility for housekeeping duties and cooking. These relationships seemed to be stable and increased the residents' security and ability to participate in the community immeasurably.

Most ex-residents live in the immediate vicinity of the Transitional Services facility in which they last lived, undoubtedly to maintain friendships and to maintain contact with a familiar neighborhood. As a result, some community members of the two neighborhoods in which Transitional Services facilities are located perceive the area as being saturated with handicapped people. Also some outside agencies serving Transitional Services residents criticize the program for promoting a "ghetto" for the disabled. They charge that large numbers of residents congregated in the same area force the community to focus attention on the residents' differences, often resulting in protest. They feel that, in this way, a subtle form of discrimination develops against Transitional Services residents. The administration of Transitional Services, however, feels that residents and ex-residents have as much right to reside in the few neighborhoods that are anonymous and safe as any other member of the community. Charges of oversaturation or ghettoization, they feel, are forms of discrimination against disabled people.

Conclusions

The Executive Director of Transitional Services relies on a professional advisory board and a board of directors for assistance. Although these bodies are not at all involved in the day-to-day operation of the program, some of the observations of a board member about this comprehensive system are worth noting.

Opposition has come from those people rejecting our basic philosophy; they feel that those whose handicaps are other than physical should live in institutions under very strict supervision and control. Support has come increasingly as the board members and staff have explained programs; we have repeated evidence from landlords and supermarket personnel who go out of their way to help our people; there are churches, clubs, and community agencies who give help in kind, as well as approval and support to Transitional Services.

The agency is trying to get us away from the Dickens era, when we warehoused and isolated those who did not fit within a range of norms. This only reinforced ignorant attitudes toward them and practically ensured that they could never return to the society. Transitional Services is an effort to work toward a society accepting of differences within a broader range.

In general, it appears to us that one of the most distinguishing features of the system is that it represents a way of living for retarded and disturbed people and a way of serving them that runs counter to traditional myths about these populations (that they need total care, are unable to function in the outside world, and cannot manage the day-to-day business of living). It is not a goal of the program to create a perfect setting; residents must be motivated to go on to independent living. By helping thousands of residents develop self-sufficiency, Transitional Services makes a significant impact on the retarded population of western Pennsylvania.

Transitional Services – Buffalo

Institutions are used to thinking about people in terms of months and years; while we think in terms of days and weeks.

Director, Transitional
Services, Buffalo

The primary reason for choosing to visit Transitional Services in Buffalo, New York, was to explore the crucial issue of *replication.* It is unusual to find a model that has been implemented in its entirety in a second sociopolitical environment.

Origins

Transitional Services – Buffalo traces its inception to a report written by the Department of Mental Hygiene of New York State in 1971, which concluded that institutions were overcrowded with people who could function more appropriately in a community setting and that services that could prevent people from being placed in institutions in the first place were sorely lacking. In response to these identified problem areas, staff members from the Department of Mental Hygiene in Buffalo visited programs across the country during the summer of 1971. The visitors concluded that the model operationalized by Transitional Services – Pittsburgh was the most adaptable to their situation and had the greatest potential to meet their two major goals of emptying the institutions and preventing future admissions.

The current director of Transitional Services – Buffalo was then the assistant director at Transitional Services – Pittsburgh. In November 1971 he was invited to interview for the position of director of the proposed program in Buffalo. He was subsequently hired and began work in January 1972. (By this time a budget for the comprehensive system had been approved.) By April 1972, residents were living in Transitional Services facilities. Thus the period of time elapsing from the initial study to recommendations to implementation was less than 1 year, indicating that the Transitional Services program is a relatively easily transportable model, given the carry-over of the individual serving as director.

The total population of the county in which Buffalo is located is 1.2 million, and Buffalo itself has approximately 500,000 inhabitants. Buffalo is clearly defined by ethnic pockets that are not characterized by a great deal of openness to change. Therefore it was important to select neighborhoods for residential facilities that would not cause unnecessary difficulties for the residents. Most of the present facilities are located in a cosmopolitan area near the universities, a choice of location also followed to some extent in Pittsburgh.

The program in Buffalo differs from the original one in Pittsburgh in that New York lacks the equivalent of Pennsylvania's mental health–mental retardation base service units that were mandated to provide medical care and psychiatric, social, and vocational services. The residents in Buffalo, instead, have to rely on local hospitals, private physicians, and preexisting community services to meet their needs. The base service unit seems to be a more organized and uniform method of providing service, thus putting the program in Buffalo, at least initially, at a disadvantage.

At the time of our visit, Transitional Services – Buffalo had 25 referral sources serving one county, although plans for expansion throughout western New York State were being considered. There were 118 residents in the program. Two additional apartment houses were projected to be opened by August 1974, bringing the total number of residents to 210. The staff, including administrators, counselors, secretaries, and maintenance workers, totaled 34 at the time of our visit.

Transitional Services – Buffalo is designed according to the original program, with three residential levels: (1) evaluation or assessment center, (2) supervised apartment buildings, and (3) independent apartment units. However, the Buffalo program developed these levels in a different order, beginning with supervised apartments. Independent apartments were created next, and finally the evaluation center was added. The staff viewed the supervised apartments as affording the optimal setting for rapid and thorough programming. By the time of our visit, 106 residents had moved through the program, only eight of whom had experienced such extreme problems adjusting to independent living that they were forced to return to the program for further training.

Effectiveness of the Replicated System

As we have indicated, Transitional Services – Buffalo has made an extremely strong start, both from the perspective of actually implementing the program and in terms of the numbers of residents served. We were also interested in the qualitative success of replication – how residents and staff would evaluate its effectiveness. The five residents we interviewed were extremely positive in their assessment of Transitional Services. They consistently mentioned that they had many friends in the program, and they were happy to live in a Transitional Services facility for reasons such as, "I like having my own place" and "everyone's been so good to me here." Reflecting the program's practical emphasis, residents noted that they had learned skills like cooking, sewing, cleaning, laundry, shopping, and handling money since they had moved to Transitional Services. The positive attitude of these five residents may reflect the feelings of the majority, although there have been some problems, including several arrests.

Residents in Transitional Services – Buffalo participate in the process of hiring staff members. The director cited an instance in which an applicant for the position of Resident Counselor had been approved by the three staff members who had interviewed her, but after being interviewed by the committee of residents, withdrew her application. Evidently the residents can effectively influence the selection of staff members.

Staff members of Transitional Services are concerned with maximizing the effectiveness of each model in the system and, at the time of our visit, there was much discussion about the evaluation center. Staff members had become concerned that this model, originally called a group home, was seen by referral sources as a cozy place to live rather than a place for assessment and planning. The change of name to "evaluation center" was seen by some staff members as inconsequential. In the words of one: "Nothing substantially different is going on there than before. The evaluation is not more precise and a sense of autonomy is difficult to convey to a large group of residents." Another cited two functions of the evaluation center, mobility training and minimizing the confusion of residents who had just recently returned to the community, and questioned whether these services were actually being provided. In general, the staff felt that the evaluation center could be more effective if it were not set up as a group home but rather as apartments for smaller groups. The apartment structure would not hinder their meeting the goals of mobility and orientation to the community, and they believed it would actually enhance the process. It was impressive to find that staff members on all levels of the hierarchy were concerned with building a more effective and training-oriented system. Their attitude of constructive criticism seemed to indicate the potential for growth and diversification of the program.

Conclusion

The experience of Transitional Services – Buffalo indicates that this model of a comprehensive residential system is replicable in different sociopolitical environments. Yet to implement a comprehensive residential system, the cooperation of typically competing agencies in the geographic area is necessary. In addition, a single agency must be designated as the coordinator and planner for all models of residences. The example of Transitional Services both in Pittsburgh and Buffalo suggests that a nonprofit corporation is an effective sponsoring agency. Another necessary but not sufficient condition for implementation of a comprehensive residential system is a commitment to planning; obviously, administering such a large agency in the absence of long-term planning and funding commitment would ensure failure.

The Transitional Services system could well serve as the basis for expansion and elaboration because its structure is flexible. Other models could be added to the system without changing its philosophy of operation. Indeed, the addition of more graduated steps should help the agency do its job even better. At the time of our visit, Transitional Services in Pittsburgh was planning to add a new residential model at the upper end of the continuum. They envisioned the possibility of (and had assessed the need for) operating apartment buildings and renting most units to typical people in town, saving a few apartments for those ex-residents who had some difficulty functioning totally independently. To provide the needed assistance, a janitor-counselor would be hired who would be trained to respond to ex-residents' needs. For example, the janitor-counselor might be called on to help with coin-operated washing machines or to assist deaf individuals by installing a lightbulb that would flicker when the doorbell is pressed. More typically, though, the ex-residents would feel free to turn to this janitor-counselor to ask questions and receive assistance on daily living problems as they arise.

This new residential model allows Transitional Services to accept a more retarded or multihandicapped population for which partial independence is an option if they need it. The possibilities for even further expansion are evident: boarding homes for elderly retarded people and respite services for retarded people living with their families, to name just two. Planners of community residences should find it encouraging that flexibility is a salient characteristic of this type of a comprehensive system.

III. Issues

13. Sponsorship

PERHAPS the very first decision to be made in beginning either a single community residence or a comprehensive system concerns its sponsorship. Sponsorship refers to an agency or body of people that serves as the administrative and/or financial overlay of a community residence. Patterns of sponsorship vary. The administrative leadership may or may not be separate from the sources of support, which may come from public or private monies, and monies may be allocated on a program or per-person basis. The method of sponsorship affects both the nature of the program developed and the type of residents admitted to a particular community residence. Also, it is the most important factor in determining how a community residence becomes associated with the political and social structure of a particular state or region.

Private Funding and Sponsorship

Some community residences are private corporations that receive virtually no public funding and thus derive most of their support from residents' payments and private donations. Examples of such facilities in our sample are sheltered villages, which may or may not be sponsored by private nonprofit corporations. Although these community residences are usually licensed by a state agency, they are typically autonomous in determining how the program will operate. Frequently, privately sponsored community residences attract residents who are the adult sons and daughters of economically successful parents. These parents, concerned about the quality of their handicapped children's future lives, especially after their own deaths, seek to secure this future by placing their retarded children in a comfortable, stable residential setting. In response to the concerns of these parents, privately sponsored facilities are often permanent homes for these residents. The monthly fee is usually quite high.

Privately sponsored community residences receive limited monitoring from public agencies; they are freer from state and local government constraints that may discourage innovation and experimentation. However, freedom from such constraints does not imply that innovation is the norm. To the extent that the facility is dependent on funds from individuals who are often more interested in maintaining the security of the resident than in exploring his or her potential for development, private sponsorship may well limit the program's pursuit of certain options, such as integration into the community and other forms of risk taking.

Public Funding and Sponsorship
Community residences that receive their financial support from the state and are administered by state agencies, usually departments of mental health, are considered to have public sponsorship. Sometimes state institutions sponsor community residences for their discharged residents. In addition, there is a growing trend to establish training residences on the grounds of state schools to ease the transition for residents from the institution to the community (e.g., Quarter-Way Cottage program).

Whereas eligibility is determined by the resident's ability to pay in privately sponsored residences, it is determined by the law in publicly sponsored facilities. Residents in privately sponsored homes typically come from their family homes in the community, whereas publicly sponsored community residences have, predominantly, formerly institutionalized residents. While most privately sponsored community residences are seen as a permanent placement, a salient feature of publicly sponsored houses is the expressed commitment to training residents for future independent or semi-independent living in the community. The phrase "making retarded citizens taxpaying citizens" helps sell publicly sponsored community residences to state legislatures. However, truly competent programming is often impeded by state restrictions, such as civil service regulations that govern hiring, firing, and promotion. Recognizing this, and also desiring to marshal local community support, some planners initially involved with community residences that have public sponsorship have since opted for the development of private, nonprofit corporations that, while receiving public monies, maintain administrative control and have a local power base.

Private Sponsorship of Facilities Receiving Public Funds
In the private sponsorship of facilities that receive public funding, the administrative direction comes predominantly from a private, nonprofit corporation, while the funding comes partly from state agencies. Because this type of sponsorship is the most common, it will be discussed in greater detail. There are several options available through which state agencies can fund private community residence facilities. Generally, each state chooses one of the options, and thus the benefits that might be derived from differing alternatives are not usually available to consumers in any one state.

One common way that public funds are channeled to a community residence is through single start-up grants to pay for the cost of opening and furnishing a house. If a community residence receives a start-up grant from the state, the corporation must be prepared to abide by the regulations established by the state, which may include anything from physical plant requirements to staffing patterns, and some states have been known to dictate even how a resident must spend his or her day.

Following the start-up grants, a state may provide funding by paying the staff members' salaries (while resident payments cover the cost of food, utilities, and part of the mortgage installments). The consequences of funding staff salaries are quite important. For example, if the staff members receive their salaries from the state but are hired by a private corporation, for whom are they working? Since the state may withhold checks from the corporation if it disapproves of the staff members, it might appear that the state is the more powerful employer. In response to this situation, corporations usually follow the state guidelines for hiring staff and thus do not often come into conflict with the source of funding. In this way, state agencies have the potential to exert a considerable amount of control over the quality of life in a community residence.

A second method through which state agencies can fund private residences is by paying a flat sum of money to the corporation per person per day (e.g., Transitional Services and foster family care homes). Although a per diem payment typically constitutes a much greater expenditure on the part of the state than does the payment of salaries of the staff members, it places the state in the position of directly purchasing services rather than staff members. Residents in this method of sponsorship typically pay some room and board. Often, the residences funded on a per diem basis have a larger amount of money to support their programs and, consequently, may provide a wider and richer range of services; they certainly have more flexibility in budgeting.

A brief visit was made to an interesting state-wide, privately sponsored program that receives public funding as well as funds from parents. The Guardianship Trust program in New Hampshire seeks to fill some of the service gap in this state, which generally provides very meager services to its citizens. (New Hampshire is the only state that, at this writing, has neither a sales tax nor a personal income tax to generate revenue.) Under this program, parents can secure the future of their retarded children by purchasing an insurance policy that claims the trust as one of the beneficiaries. Also, parents may bequest their home to the trust as a part of the contractual arrangement between both parties, thus defraying part of the cost of the insurance policy. Federal funds were instrumental in the establishment of the program and state funds help pay some of the operating costs. The long-range goal of the Guardianship Trust program is to become financially independent of public funds, relying totally on monies from the trust. By 1975 the Guardianship Trust had developed seven community residences, all small group homes.

The final variation of public payments to private facilities is one that, to our knowledge, has not yet been tried: a voucher system. A voucher for a set amount of money could be made available to every retarded adult who wishes to live in a community residence. With varying degrees of support and guidance (depending on the capabilities of the resident) the resident might select the house he or she wishes to live in and, if accepted to this program, might purchase his or her own services. This type of sponsorship is, of course, highly controversial. Both the state and the corporation lose some degree of control over the services, while the retarded person gains some control over his or her life. Many people would justifiably question the ability of many residents to make a reasonable choice of a living situation. However, the concept of having citizen advocates for retarded people (Wolfensberger and Zauha, 1973) may make it possible for the more severely retarded residents to share much of the responsibility for such decisions with a person whose primary loyalty is to that retarded person.

The use of vouchers would place the business of running a community residence into a fee-for-service framework, which also has drawbacks, such as less monitoring and planning by state agencies; the possibility that no community residences will be begun in an area due to unexpressed consumer needs; the possibility that retarded people may be exploited and coerced into using their vouchers in particular residences; and the possibility that the use of vouchers in purchasing services for retarded persons may prove to be as inflationary as Medicare and Medicaid have been in the purchasing of health services. However, even with these possible liabilities, vouchers would be an innovative and potentially normalizing method of sponsorship to explore, at least on a limited basis.

In each of the three methods of public payments to privately sponsored programs, the state could, and probably should, exercise some administrative and decision-making control over these private, nonprofit corporations. Few states, however, have developed evaluation methods sufficient to guide judgments about community residence programs. Thus state contracts to these sponsors are often renewed based on a need for continuing the "service" rather than on an accurate assessment of the quality of the program.

Funding Implications

The sponsorship option chosen for a community residence determines much about funding. Despite the differences already discussed, some similarities do exist among sponsorship options. Therefore to further understand sponsorship options we need to examine what the cost of operating community residences was at the time of our study and also the specific breakdown of these costs.

Practically all community residences in the sample (92 percent) derived some part of their budget from resident payments, and in 1973 the average monthly fee was $183. This average, however, contains much variability (s.d. = $103). In some community residences the fee covers the entire cost of the program, although in most programs a part of the budget is obtained from other sources.

Annual budgets were reported by 196 community residences, but these figures must be regarded quite cautiously. The reliability of reported budgets is dubious; in many cases the person completing the survey questionnaire did not have full knowledge of the community residence budget, and some reported that the amounts seemed out of line, almost always too low (given other information available, such as staffing patterns). Also, while it is often argued that the cost per resident in a community residence is less than that in an institution, two factors are overlooked: (1) The budget usually does not include personal expenses, such as clothing or vacations; and community services, such as medical care, training programs, recreational programs, or workshops; while the institution budget more accurately reflects the real costs within that setting; and (2) costs vary with the resident's level of functioning. Costs of care for the resident who is profoundly retarded, physically ill, or multiply handicapped are apt to be higher, thereby increasing the average institutional costs. The institutional cost for the more capable residents who have thus far moved into community residences was always less than the institutional average.

The true costs of community residence alternatives must be estimated with a long-term perspective. It may well be that annual community residence costs per resident, if more accurately compared, are as high as or higher than institutional ones. However, this short-term cost of community residences is not only justifiable on humanistic grounds by the improved quality of life in these facilities but on economic grounds as well. Community residences have much higher resident turnover than institutions, with many residents moving on to self-sufficiency or to less costly alternatives.

Having argued that budget estimates do not include all services, are not comparable to those of institutions, and are generally unreliable, we will report them with the hope that the reader will keep these cautions in mind. The average reported annual budget for 1973 was $56,000, or $4,680 per resident. There was considerable variability in budget per resident across and within models, as seen in Table 13-1.

Small group homes, semi-independent units, and sheltered villages appear to be the most costly, although as we have noted, even these amounts

Table 13-1
*Mean Budget Per Resident, by Model**

	Mean Budget per Resident	*N*
Small group home	$5,690	86
Medium group home	$4,080	37
Large group home	$3,380	12
Mixed group home	$3,480	8
Group homes for older adults	$2,060	14
Foster family care	$2,240	11
Sheltered village	$5,200	5
Workshop-dormitory	$3,450	13
Semi-independent apartments	$5,440	11

**Mini-Institution (MI) is not included, since only one reported a budget.*

underrepresent the actual costs of the programs. Foster care and group homes for older adults are the least expensive services. The cost per resident in group homes decreases significantly with increasing size of the house.

A common problem faced by the community residence staffs is the delay between the time funds are spent and when reimbursement arrives from the state. At least one community residence we visited ran out of funds waiting for state reimbursement; they had to resort to a sit-in at the office of the state financial officer to get payment quickly enough to avoid closing down. Coping with such problems is a pervasive problem and drains off much of the staffs' time and energy. Perhaps more problematic than the delays in payment, however, is the fact that many potentially good sponsors are discouraged from beginning a house for fear of having reimbursement problems.

Fiscal and Administrative Responsibility

The previous discussion concentrated mainly on the economic aspects of sponsorship. What are the issues surrounding the administrative aspects? What is the role of the corporation of the community residence? Prior to the opening of the residence and in its early stages of operation, the corporation finds itself faced with daily crises. Problems range from zoning disputes and furniture purchases to recruiting residents and hiring staff. However, once the community residence begins to function effectively, members of corporations find that they are no longer in constant demand and should at this point define a more long-term role for themselves. Although it may be obvious to an outsider that the appropriate role for a corporation is handling administration, finances, and community relations, it is difficult for many members of corporations to relinquish the control they had earlier exerted over day-to-day operations, perhaps because many members of boards of directors are either parents of retarded people or professionals in the field of retardation.

A further sponsorship issue arises with respect to associations for retarded citizens as sponsors. Traditionally, these associations have functioned principally in an independent advocacy role. They maintained their ability to criticize programs and demand improved services because they were primarily a consumer group and not extensively involved in the provision of services themselves. Now, however, with the advent of state programs that provide funding for community residences, many associations have become involved in service provision, resulting in an uncomfortable liaison between the associations for retarded citizens and the departments of mental health.

Perhaps the main impetus for the associations' involvement in the provision of community residential services was that when state funds were made available, very few other (nonparent) groups came forward to form corporations. The reluctance of others may have been due to the risky nature of starting one or several community residences, as well as a less intense investment in the problem. As a result the associations for retarded citizens may have lost some of their previous effectiveness as advocacy groups; it is certainly difficult to criticize, demand improvement in, or possibly recommend the closing of a program that one is sponsoring. A $40,000 mortgage is a large investment and the emotional investment may become even greater.

Taken at face value, the problem seems insoluble. Who will provide the services if the associations for retarded citizens do not, and who will provide the advocacy if the associations cannot? Two solutions have been proposed: In the United States, many associations for retarded citizens have recruited citizen advocates, volunteers who represent the interests of retarded persons on a one-to-one basis (Wolfensberger and Zauha, 1973). These citizens presumably will advocate for the improvement of services for their retarded friends. However, the extent to which volunteers can be given the responsibility for knowledgeable and continuing program advocacy is questionable. The second solution has been used extensively in Denmark, where parent groups have set up community residences and then subsequently have turned the established programs over to the state for continued funding and operation.

Conclusion

It seems that private sponsorship of facilities receiving public funding is the most promising method of sponsorship when a comprehensive system is being developed. It has proved to be a flexible method of sponsorship, providing backing for diverse programs such as small group homes, workshop-dormitories, community preparation programs, semi-independent units, and comprehensive systems.

To further promote flexibility, it is suggested that public funding be given on a per-day, per-person basis rather than as annual program support. With such funding, programs can diversify and expand more rapidly (as each new resident brings in new monies) instead of having to wait for the next fiscal year for approval of funds.

The drawback of choosing private sponsorship with public funding for a comprehensive system concerns the security of the program's future. Public sponsorship probably ensures a more stable future in terms of funding than does private sponsorship, because with the former, civil service positions are involved and property is purchased. In fact, we have seen that the prototype of public sponsorship – state institutions – are nearly impossible to close down. Yet this secure future can quickly foster a stagnant program, which is less likely with private sponsorship programs that are continually open to evaluation by the funding agencies.

14. Staff

Normalization is what the houseparents think is normal.

A houseparent

IN any community residence the two most crucial factors determining the success of the program are the staffing pattern and the characteristics of individual staff members. These are especially important to the extent that community residences are autonomous from statewide guidance or accountability within a comprehensive system. A sponsoring agency can attempt to control the influence of individual staff members' personalities, skills, and orientations through hiring, training, and evaluation, but of greater programmatic importance are the initial decisions about the staffing pattern and therefore staff roles within the community residence.

Staff Roles

We have seen a number of staffing patterns that are characteristic of community residence models. These include young (or less frequently older) married couples functioning as houseparents, three (or more) single individuals serving as housemanagers, professional staff filling specialized roles, individuals serving as a foster family, operators of group homes for older adults, and staff members who work and live with retarded people as a result of a spiritual commitment. The particular staffing pattern chosen is largely determined by the philosophical orientation and the size of the program.

Decisions concerning staff roles should be preceded by the determination of staff function: Should the staff primarily be teachers, counselors, or substitute parents? This decision will dictate many of those to follow. Teaching staff members need specific skills and often include persons with special education or public health or vocational rehabilitation backgrounds. Counselors may require skills in interpersonal relationships as well as a sophisticated awareness of community resources. Substitute parents must fill a generalized function, teaching at times, but supporting and protecting the residents most of the time. Each of these staff roles results in a different kind of program, and each has distinct implications for the residents.

The size of the program also has an influence on these decisions. With fewer than 10 residents, unless a program is "experimental" and thus especially well funded, a program budget usually cannot afford more than three staff members, who must serve generalized functions. A major criticism of the generalized staff pattern is its inability to meet its implicit goal of providing all the skills and support the residents need. The incredible array of specific duties and responsibilities of houseparents is typified by the list from one small group home, outlined below.

I. Houseparents are responsible for instruction of living skills on a group or an individual basis
    A. Grooming
        1. Care of hair
            a. Combing
            b. Washing
            c. Dandruff removal
            d. Style and length
        2. Clothing
            a. Cleaning
            b. Proper size and fit
            c. Matching
            d. Selection
            e. Purchase
            f. Polished shoes
            g. Tied laces
    B. Hygiene
        1. Toilet
            a. Flushing
            b. Menstruation
            c. Cleaning of tub
            d. Use of deodorant
        2. Shaving
            a. Armpits and legs for females
            b. Face for males
            c. Proper use of safety razor
            d. Change of blade
    C. Housekeeping
        1. Proper procedure of bedmaking
        2. Vacuuming
        3. Sweeping
        4. Cleaning sinks
        5. Dusting
    D. Meal preparation
        1. Setting tables
        2. Preparing food
    E. Etiquette
        1. Table manners
        2. Social manners

II. Houseparents aid residents in learning about the community and the use of community facilities
   A. Medical facilities
   B. Department stores
   C. Specialty shops
   D. Value and budgeting of money
   E. Use of public transportation

III. Medical care
   A. Obtain medical or dental care
   B. Accompany residents to clinic, hospital, or place where medical or dental assistance will be administered
   C. Dispense medicine to residents
   D. Renew and purchase prescriptions

IV. Other duties
   A. Schedule and prepare meals and eat with residents
      1. Prepare weekly menu to be presented to the director
      2. Order food
   B. Provide transportation
   C. Conduct tours of residence
   D. Responsible for high standards of cleanliness throughout residence
      1. Responsible for own living quarters
         a. Make bed
         b. Clean room
   E. Make sure that residents are accounted for and in appropriate rooms
   F. Make sure that residents follow through on assigned duties and that they understand these duties
   G. Deal with immediate resident problems with serious problems being referred to the director
   H. Handle petty cash, keep receipts, and return to the director
   I. Receive and distribute mail
   J. Participate in resident case conferences as requested
   K. Assist in keeping records on residents
   L. Set curfew hour
   M. Set an example of good, clean living
   N. Teach clients to prepare bag lunches and set up schedule for doing so
   P. See that all bills are forwarded to the director or his assistant
   Q. Other duties as assigned by the director of adult services

---

An alternative to a generalized staff becomes possible in larger community residences, where more staff members can be hired, each with a specialized job description. Examples of specialized roles include: teacher of community survival skills, counselor, job finder, teacher of homemaking skills, and follow-up counselor. Most often, specialized staff members bring previously developed skills to their work at the community residence and treat their work there as a job rather than as a way of life. Typically, they do not live at the community residence, in contrast with their generalized counterparts.

For residents, the implications of being supervised by generalized as opposed to specialized staff are important. Raush and Raush (1968), in their survey of halfway houses for former mental hospital patients, noted that professional or specialized staff tended toward risk taking with residents more often than less well-trained, generalized personnel. Generalized staff, while offering the support of substitute parents, also often create familial dependence in residents, which causes their behavior to be more immature than necessary. In contrast, specialized staff members might maintain more impersonal relations with residents and at the same time cause them to develop self-reliance and competence, and thus act more like adults. Certainly, both staffing patterns have desirable qualities, and large community residences or comprehensive residential systems have the financial ability to hire both generalized staff (to provide support) and specialized staff (to provide training and counseling). Transitional Services (see Chap. 12) is a good example of how a combination of both kinds of staff members works to the advantage of the residents and the program alike.

Training

The need for a trained staff is common to all staffing patterns and is articulated by community residence workers frequently. Although 84 percent of the staff members in the community residences we visited were educated beyond the high school level, only 33 percent said that they had previous training or experience relevant to their work. Almost all reported they were interested in learning new skills to do their work more adequately; they mentioned that they would be eager to take courses or practice teach.

What is needed is an on-going mechanism for staff training, either on a regional level or within a large comprehensive system. Funding for staff training should not be directed toward purchasing services for a one-shot program but, rather, spent to develop resources that will provide a variety of training programs over the course of many years. This is particularly important in light of the fact that staff turnover is very rapid (average length of time on the job was 1.83 years among staff members interviewed) and with one-shot training, the net effect after a few years could be zero. An association of community residence staff members would have great potential as the locus of some of this continual training, as well as providing staff with much needed support in this often isolating line of work.

Staff Morale

A frequently mentioned complaint of staff members in the community residences we visited was a lack of privacy and time for themselves. Indeed, 42 percent said they had less privacy than they had initially expected. This issue was particularly important to staff members who lived in the residence and had no home elsewhere. Of the settings visited, only Transitional Services, the Apartment Project, the Quarter-Way Cottages, and the Young Adults program had staffs who did not live in.

The implications for staff living in the community residence are numerous. They are practically never off duty because they have no other home to go to. For the same reasons, vacations are difficult without large expenditures of money for accommodations. Indeed, over half the staff members interviewed had not taken a vacation since they began working at the community residence, and those who had vacationed worked primarily in non–live-in settings. Even the option of spending free time within the community residence is not satisfactory because residents typically continue to approach staff members with questions. Live-in staff members frequently have only their bedroom for privacy, yet this room is occasionally used as their office too, and the omnipresent reminders of work constantly distract them. Lack of privacy and free time is particularly a problem for married couples who serve as houseparents. They may see each other all day but rarely be alone together.

Marital Status. This is an unusually problematic issue. Our overwhelming experience – one attested to by the numerous divorces of ex-houseparents – is that the staffing pattern of young married couples is a poor idea. Several community residence directors and many single relief persons repeatedly elaborated on the problems caused by this staffing pattern: (1) If the houseparents' relationship is unstable, it creates a tense atmosphere in the community residence. (2) When the houseparents quit or are fired, or if they go on vacation, suddenly the community residence is left with most, if not all, its staff gone. (3) Typically, the wife works full time while the husband attends school or works elsewhere during the day. There have been several cases in which the husband's interest in the community residence was minimal, and the wife in actuality performed both their functions (e.g., Arcade House and Town House).

Salary. This is another factor that contributes to low staff morale. What is typically found with generalized staffing patterns (houseparents and housemanagers) is that the pay is extremely low. Full-time staff members could likely be earning better salaries working fewer hours elsewhere. The staff members interviewed were generally young and well educated. Only four settings had an average staff age of over 40 years, and fully 84 percent of staff members had some education past high school. Hence, a further issue that arises is job mobility. Young, educated, skilled men and women have options in the labor market other than direct care positions. They can expect to be upwardly mobile, but *not* in community residences. Only in larger agencies, like Transitional Services, can staff members expect to advance over time. Typically, there are no positions for staff members to advance to. Only 60 percent of community residences' staff members said they would remain on the job for one more year, and only 19 percent said they would stay for 5 years. A certain amount of staff turnover is healthy in any program, but it seems essential to encourage some staff members, the more proficient ones, to plan careers in the field of community residential services.

Conclusion

What should be clear by now is the need for a reconsideration of a variety of staff-related issues. A number of community residence directors have recently noted that it is becoming increasingly difficult to recruit staff, especially for live-in positions, despite the high unemployment rate. These considerations lead us to make the following recommendations:

1. That staffing young married houseparents who live at the community residence usually be considered a last, rather than a first, option
2. That within larger programs, specialized staff be hired to provide residents services not available from the generalized houseparent
3. That staff within larger programs be required to maintain a residence separate from the community residence, be paid to work a 40-hour week, be paid for overtime, and be required to take vacation time
4. That salaries be competitive to attract competent staff and to provide incentives for the staff to remain at the community residence
5. That married couples both working and living at the community residence be avoided as house staff; that if the job is live-in, three (or more) single people be hired
6. That within the structure of the comprehensive system, job mobility be made possible.

15. Community

THE assumption in relocating services in the community was that a more dignified, normalized way of life would be provided for retarded citizens. However, the concept of *community* was not well defined in this assumption. Where is the community? Who comprises the retarded adult's community?

It seems obvious that the geographic unit is not all that is meant by "community"; for example, we do not know of a single neighborhood in which the citizens met and decided that it was in their best interest to have a community residence within their town boundaries. Rather, a combination of separate forces (parent groups, professionals, and the courts) have pressed for provision of community-based services. Thus a disparity exists between the interests of the community of people concerned about the retarded and the geographic community to which the retarded are to return. About a third of the community residences surveyed reported some opposition to their opening from the local community, although this opposition diminished as the programs became established.

Opposition

Opposition to community residences on the part of their surrounding communities typically is expressed as resistance to the particular location chosen, not to the concept of community residences per se. Surprisingly, among the residences surveyed there was no relationship found between a community residence's likelihood of receiving opposition and the size of the residence or the degree of retardation of the residents. Although we have no statistical data to account for why neighborhoods oppose community residences, Table 15-1 indicates which groups voiced opposition.

Of all the community residences surveyed, 35 percent reported some resistance, with many of these indicating several sources. Since the survey did not include any houses that were prevented from opening or that had closed

Table 15-1
Sources of Community Opposition (percent of all community residences surveyed)

Neighbors who complained	24%
Zoning dispute	12
Political leaders	5
Parents of retarded people	4
Mental health and mental retardation associations	2
Other	4

because of community resistance, the opposition found in 35 percent of the sample is most definitely an underrepresentation of true opposition.

A very powerful form of opposition comes from parents of retarded people, usually parents whose adult sons and daughters live in institutions. This opposition is directed less at a particular community residence than at the state's plans to develop community residences in general. These parents typically argue that a community residence cannot offer the wide range of services provided by a state institution and, in particular, the protection and security of an institutional program. This stance can better be understood by examining these parents' histories of dealing with professionals. Years ago they followed the advice of their pediatricians and others who told them to institutionalize their children. Over the years they remained active in the parent groups associated with the institutions, doing what they could to improve the services delivered to residents there. Over time they adjusted psychologically to their decision to remove their child from the family and the community. To reduce the dissonance between wanting to "do right by" their child and the realities of institutional existence, they quite naturally came to see more benefits to the institution than others did. To be confronted now with a reversal in professional opinion – that the institution is not even a safe place to live, much less a therapeutic environment – puts these parents in a very difficult position.

The 4 percent of residences reporting opposition from parents of retarded people also underrepresents this form of opposition. Some parents who kept their children home *against* the advice of professionals resist community residences as they resisted institutions in the past. For example, some do not want their now adult sons and daughters to live in community residences, although they feel that residents of state institutions can benefit by returning to the community. Thus their opposition is not to community residences as a deinstitutionalization mechanism, but to residences as living units for their own children; and as such they are not in *active* opposition to opening community residences for others.

An example may help to highlight more passive parent opposition.

Mrs. Rose is a parent of a moderately retarded young adult who has lived at home all his life, despite professional opinion that he would be better off in an institution. Over the years, Mrs. Rose had become increasingly more active in parent groups and, in fact, several years ago was appointed director of the group home sponsored by the local Association for Retarded Citizens. Since then she has developed three new community residences, primarily for residents of state institutions.

When Mrs. Rose hires her staff, she brings her son along to the interview. Later she asks him if he thinks he would like to live with this applicant, but she always reassures him that he will never have to live in a community residence.

Mrs. Rose would never be characterized as being in opposition to community residences but her automatic exclusion of her own son indicates that her support for this service is not unequivocal.

Preparation

Fully 77 percent of residences reported that they did something to prepare communities for the presence of the community residence. The frequency of the various preparatory activities is shown in Table 15-2.

Table 15-2

Types of Community Preparation (percent of all community residences surveyed)

Talked to neighbors	45%
Talked to professionals	44
Talked to local businesses	38
Talked to city government	37
Media publicity	35
Talked to parent groups	34
Talked to clergy	32
Other	14

All these efforts to prepare and educate members of the community were intended to improve the reception of the community residence on opening and to reduce potential or actual opposition.

We unexpectedly found a slight (but statistically significant) positive relationship between preparation and opposition; that is, a house reporting preparation was more likely to report opposition too. This relationship may imply that some preparation efforts backfire, because they alert the community to the community residence's presence and spark opposition. An equally plausible explanation is simply that preparation is often in response to incipient opposition. The causal link is impossible to uncover in correlational data. However, it may, in fact, be safer for a community residence to maintain a low profile on entering a neighborhood so as not to risk the possibility of sparking opposition. This may especially hold if the community residence is definitely "legal"; i.e., if it is not in violation of any local zoning ordinances and therefore does not need to seek special consideration from neighbors or government. After the community residence is established, reaching out to the community seems to have generally been very satisfying.

Community Involvement

The relationship between a community residence and its surrounding neighborhood certainly does not limit itself to the period of time in which the residence begins operation. It continues to develop and change as time passes. Often, staff members reported that the neighbors who at first were most strongly opposed to the house eventually became loyal friends. Very few community residences (6 percent) reported that their respective communities held negative attitudes about the house at the time of the survey (on the average almost 5 years after opening), and therefore we can hypothesize that familiarity with the program and its residents, or at least the realization that the community residence is indeed here with no disastrous consequences, improves the relationship between a community residence and its neighbors.

Citizens in the community may become actively involved with the operation of a community residence, as volunteers, board members, etc. Models varied significantly with respect to the amount of community involvement in the community residences (Fig. 15-1). (This scale included volunteers, parent involvement, community boards, etc.) Workshop-dormitories and small group homes were especially high in community involvement and foster family care and group homes for older adults were especially low.

The scale in Figure 15-1 includes the involvement of parents of retarded people, because they are the most important advocacy community of the residents. From this point of view it is easy to understand the relatively high community involvement score of sheltered villages, in which parents are encouraged to become involved but neighboring citizens are not. The type of community involvement in sheltered villages, then, is quite different from that in small group homes, in which community involvement is high because integration with the geographic community is actively sought.

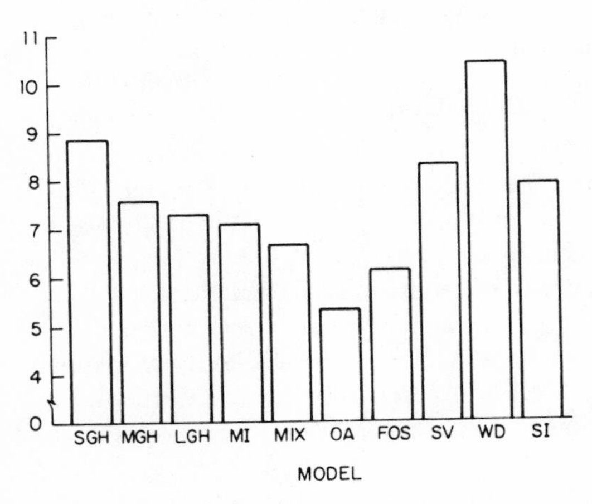

Figure 15-1
Community involvement scale by model.

Conclusions

In this section we have explored the relationship between community residences and two very different kinds of communities: geographic and advocacy. But neither of these communities offers the third and perhaps most important aspect of community living, namely, the *psychological sense of community* (Sarason, 1974). What we truly strive for with the return to the community is that a retarded person would then be able to develop a "readily available, mutually supportive network of relationships upon which one could depend and as a result of which one did not experience sustained feelings of loneliness . . . ." (Sarason, 1974, p. 1).

We must question here if the mainstream of the community residence movement actually enhances a resident's psychological sense of community. The sheltered villages do seem to bring a sense of community to the retarded, although at the expense of another aim – that of integration with the broader community. Most typical community residences intend that residents eventually become more independent, and the ultimate sign of success is indicated by ex-residents living in independent apartments, alone or with peers, with just a social worker or a citizen advocate for support. This goal can be realized by many retarded adults who do, in fact, develop an interpersonal network that gives them a sense of belonging, as witnessed by the examples presented earlier. Yet some ex-residents spend meaningless and lonely lives, and others are recognized by service providers as needing additional supports and are returned to community residences, or even to institutions, as failures.

We raise the possibility that independent living is an isolating experience for some retarded adults, which is not to suggest the abandonment of this goal. Rather, we would suggest alternative supports to help enhance a psychological sense of community for ex-residents. First, we would recommend increased attention to interpersonal experiences in the community-residence training program itself. Furthermore, while some programs do well in following ex-residents over time, providing continuing friendship and help in finding resources, few community residences consider this a formal part of their program. As we suggest better follow-through, we also advocate the development of meaningful work options and recreational centers, as well as access to "typical" community activities and, perhaps most importantly, an improved acceptance of the retarded citizen by others in the geographic community.

16. Program

THE primary importance of program issues is how they affect the residents. This chapter attempts to highlight issues related to two stages in the "career" of a resident who is living in a community residence, namely the process of moving into one and the quality of life in the community residence. Despite their obvious importance, issues related to the future (moving out and long-range plans) are not included because the present study does not have sufficient data in this area.

Beginnings: Moving in

Two major issues that are related to moving into a community residence concern the resident's role in the decision-making process and the resident's preparation for the move. The process of determining where a retarded person will live is more often dependent on the needs and opinions of parents and professionals than on the needs and desires of the retarded person. The decision as to who will live in community residences has been made in some states by legislation or administrative decision, which gives preferential treatment to retarded persons from institutions. As a result, this group is overrepresented in the community residences we surveyed (49 percent) relative to their percentage in the total population of people who are retarded (about 5 percent). Also contributing to the imbalance is the reluctance of many parents, who have adult-aged retarded children living at home, to place their sons and daughters in community residences. Parents' reluctance may be partly caused by fear, but also often stems from their years of struggling against professional opinions that recommended institutional placement (see Chap. 15). As we have seen, parents of institutionalized adult retarded people, who are still in contact and involved with their children, may also resist placement in community residences for a variety of reasons.

Once selected for placement into community residences, individuals are prepared for their move in a variety of ways. Some visit the prospective community residence for a day or a weekend before moving in, while others are visited in their current residence (institution or parental home) by community residence staff. Sometimes residents recommend that their friends from the institution or the community be invited to move into the house. A small number of residents from institutions participate in preparatory training programs, such as the Quarter-Way Cottages (see Chap. 9). More often than not, residents arrive at the community residence unprepared for the kind of life they will be leading and often without having indicated a desire to be there.

Residents were quite vocal about their feelings toward their previous placements and about moving into community residences. Seventy percent of residents interviewed said, with varying degrees of conviction, that they wanted to leave the institution for the community residence. Their comments follow.

I didn't like it there too long. It's an awful place. It's hard when you're put away.

I wanted to leave. I wanted to learn to live on my own. Too many girls there who couldn't take care of themselves . . . . I've been wanting to get out on my own for a long time.

I wanted to get out of there . . . . I didn't like it there. Mother put me there. I used to pray every night to get out. I don't miss it.

I don't know, not sure. I'm going back to visit [the institution] *Friday. I miss them.*

You'd want to leave if you were there for forty-five years.

A common theme among the residents who expressed dissatisfaction about moving into the community residence was their sense of having been persuaded to move.

I liked it at the school. My mother talked me into it [leaving].

They wanted me to come here so I came . . . . I had more friends at the school.

I didn't want to come. I came because my parents wanted me here.

I go everywhere they take me. I don't really have much choice . . . whether state school or here . . . no real choice.

These responses are particularly striking when one takes into consideration that often retarded people have been socialized into not complaining about their life situation. Thus, the discontents expressed by these residents might very well represent a wealth of more complex feelings that are left unvoiced.

Present: Life in the Community Residence

Fully 75 percent of the residents said that they preferred living at the community residence to their previous living arrangement.

You bet. I've been here five months and like it much better. The outside life is better than the institutional life which I gave up on. I can do what I want and I go as I please.

There's more freedom . . . more civilized like other people. You can do things for yourself like civilian living. You can earn money for spending. Clothes had to last three years in the institution.

In general, most of the residents said that they liked the community residence better because of the new skills they had learned, the new people they had met, and the additional freedom and privacy they were experiencing. Yet 25 percent of the residents were dissatisfied with living where they were now as compared with their previous arrangement.

I still wish I was in the institution. It's hard to take care of an apartment, going shopping, finding money. I'm not satisfied being in an apartment.

I hate it here, the people. I don't know.

Actually, I'm a changeable person. I'm having a hard time adjusting here and I have just about given up.

Several personal and setting characteristics seemed to be predictive of resident satisfaction in the community residence. Concerning *resident characteristics,* those residents who were younger, borderline retarded, and/or new to the community residence seemed to have the most difficulty in adjusting; this seemed to be the case in a variety of models, such as workshop-dormitories (Town House), sheltered villages (Coventry), and even semi-independent apartments (Apartment Project). Possibly if, in the future, persons who are borderline retarded receive ample education and training before reaching adulthood, then supervised community residential living will be less necessary. However, it also seemed that the small proportion of borderline retarded persons who moved into community residences were a subgroup characterized by emotional and behavioral problems that had impeded their unsupervised living.

We have also considered throughout this book *setting characteristics* that seem related to the residents' adjustment. One additional source of information is the questionnaire about program environment that was administered to staff members and residents in all settings visited. The items were divided for scoring into four subscales: (1) program organization; (2) staff (versus resident) control; (3) clarity of and emphasis on rules; and (4) feelings toward the community residence and interaction between members. When the rankings of community residences on all these scales were examined, it was not clear which residents were most satisfied and which were most dissatisfied. However, when the extent of staff-resident agreement in their response to the questions was determined (regardless of whether the community residence was high or low on given scales) the resultant ranking was very consistent with expressed resident satisfaction, as illustrated in the following:

Highest staff-resident agreement	Quarter-Way Project
	Transitional Services – Buffalo
	Halfway House
	Transitional Services – Pittsburgh
	Apartment Project
	Arcade House
	Hickory Manor
Lowest staff-resident agreement	Coventry Village
	Town House

You may recall the tension we observed in Town House (workshop-dormitory), the regrets about leaving home and the desires for a more independent future expressed by some residents at Coventry (sheltered village), and the general malaise at Hickory Manor (group home for older adults). It may be, then, that the extent to which the staff and residents share common perceptions of the community residence program is as good and perhaps a better predictor of resident satisfaction than the specific characteristics of the program.

Two further dimensions of the resident's experience while living at a community residence are of utmost importance and warrant special consideration here: leisure and work.

Leisure. Leisure time activities have a great impact on how a resident experiences life in a community residence. Residents may spend their free time watching television and listening to the radio; doing chores around the house and washing clothes; swimming, fishing, and playing badminton when weather permits; sitting around smoking cigarettes and going to sleep early; talking to other residents; walking around the neighborhood and hanging out; visiting friends and families; going to church; going bowling; going to movies; and going shopping. Indeed, the range of their activities, although limited by the often small amount of spending money they have, can be as broad as any person's in the community. Like most other community dwellers they spend their leisure time most often with peers they know from work, the community residence, and their previous residences.

Similar to other groups, retarded persons might prefer to participate in leisure time activities oriented toward their particular interests and capabilities. Indeed, some community residence staff members report that separate recreational programs developed with the needs of the retarded in mind provide a pragmatic option for many of their residents. Some residents we saw were not going swimming or playing Ping-Pong, but were sitting in front of the television or walking around the neighborhood, much as they had previously done in the institution. These residents lacked not only the social skills to make appropriate overtures toward others and to maintain relationships, but also the ability to hit a Ping-Pong ball or do the crawl stroke. And even if the YMCA down the street had a Ping-Pong table and a swimming pool, a resident might have been fearful of entering on his or her own. Too, the experience of taking classes to learn these recreational skills might be an exercise in frustration and failure, since the level of instruction might not be appropriate for them.

More socially sophisticated residents benefit as well from separate programs. Finding a date or friends might be facilitated through an organized social group. Although one might look askance at the idea of a club made up of retarded members, other groups in our society form clubs based on shared interests and common characteristics; examples are churches and synagogues, exclusive country clubs, and the VFW. Also, some of the groups for the retarded already in existence are beginning to have more than a recreational value. In Massachusetts, a group of retarded men who have been members of a social group (the Mohawks) for many years are currently acting as paid consultants to persons who are planning to open community residences. A second example is the group who organized the Our Life Conference (for retarded persons to come together to discuss their needs) in England.

The organization of these social clubs does not decrease the necessity of making general community recreational activities accessible to retarded people. Operators of these activities must be made more receptive to including retarded people as members, rather than (as we witnessed in a large city we visited) making subtle moves to prevent them from joining. To enhance this process, the retarded persons might benefit from the assistance of community residence staff members or citizen advocates, at least for the first few times they participate.

Work. Although we found that 20 percent of residents were in competitive employment, this figure is somewhat misleading. Some settings, in fact, require a job or eligibility for employment as a criterion of admission, and have more than 80 percent of their members in competitive employment. Most community residences, however, have none or one person employed in the labor force; in the programs we visited, only 10 percent of residents were competitively employed. Also, those employed in the labor force are typically in marginal jobs that will be immediately affected by fluctuations in the economy.

Fully 27 percent of residents interviewed worked only at the community residence or had no work placement at all. This was especially a problem in the small group home, where, for example, one resident might remain behind in the community residence each day while the others went to day or work placements. This situation results in an isolating and lonely day for the unemployed resident and an additional burden for the staff, since these programs plan to have the community residence empty during some daytime hours. In larger settings, persons not employed can get together for daytime leisure activities; in fact, Transitional Services places a low priority on work and considers relying on welfare or supplementary security income payments for an income as an acceptable alternative for persons with minimal skills and a long history of institutionalization.

Most residents interviewed, however, attended a day activity center or sheltered workshop (63 percent). The heavy reliance on sheltered workshop placements may become a problem over time. Currently, many sheltered workshops express difficulty in obtaining and keeping sufficient contracts; larger workshops with directors who have business and management expertise tend to fare better. Surely, though, these contracts too will be affected by economic trends. Several residents interviewed had been intermittently layed off from their workshops because of the decline in contracts. One must question whether sheltered workshops will remain a viable model in the future, as progressively more community residences open and seek work placements for their residents. When one or two sheltered workshops can barely obtain enough contracts in a given area, it does not bode well for expansion to 10 or 20 more.

Sheltered workshops experience constant conflict between the pressure to complete contracts on time and the residents' need for training in new skills. Within larger workshops with multiple contracts work tasks can be assigned more according to individual abilities and training needs, and persons can, theoretically, be "brought along" toward more complex tasks. Yet in any of these settings, there are residents who could spend their day better, either in a vocational training program (for those with the potential to move into competitive employment) or in a living skills training program (for those who lack many of the basic living skills needed for community living and who should be spending at least part of their day acquiring them).

Fully 33 percent of the residents interviewed stated that they did not like their present day activity and 69 percent said they would rather have been doing other kinds of work. Typically, residents would have preferred being employed in competitive jobs, being janitors, nurse's aides, babysitters, and garage attendants. Often residents felt that their work was repetitive and boring and that they were underpaid. Some of these feelings may not be inconsistent with the attitudes of many other, nonretarded persons toward their work, especially those in unskilled and semiskilled jobs. However, it did seem that many of the persons interviewed had the potential to move into more interesting work roles if the systematic training were available to them.

An in-depth, comprehensive study is greatly needed to delineate future economic trends, how they might affect retarded workers, and the types of employment for which these individuals might be best suited. Planning agencies must come to see vocational training as a high priority if residents are indeed to move closer to the community in a genuine way.

17. For Parents: Choosing a Community Residence

THIS chapter is directed to parents who now are, or at some time in the future will be, faced with the prospect of placing an adult son or daughter into a community residence. However, it should also be useful to professionals working with and planning for retarded adults. A series of questions suggest the kind of information needed to make a considered decision about the most appropriate type of community residence for a prospective resident. Each question raises a host of issues that have been dealt with earlier in this book, and we will assume here that you are already familiar with the complexity of those issues.

Prior Considerations

Before we can discuss specific questions, some general considerations should be addressed. Making a decision about your son's or daughter's future is indeed difficult, beset with both aspirations and anxieties. For your child, this change in lifestyle is likely to be quite dramatic: new friends, a new home, perhaps a new neighborhood, and certainly new expectations. But you as a parent will be faced with changes as well, and as a participant in the placement process, your needs and hopes must be clearly articulated for you to be comfortable with the lifestyle chosen for or by your child.

Who decides what is best for your child is really the most basic question — *Who* should choose? Making their own decisions will be possible and practical for some retarded adults and less so for others. Yet irrespective of how much you are each involved in the final decision about community residential placement, it must be acknowledged that often the needs of parents and those of their adult sons and daughters do not exactly coincide. Herein lie the conflicts of independence versus protection, proximity to resources versus the quality of the neighborhood, and integration versus separation among others. You might want to make a list identifying important goals for community residential placement, a list that integrates your point of view with that of your child.

Also, prior to considering specific questions, an assessment of the specific needs of your son or daughter is crucial. You can then evaluate residences in terms of their potential to enhance your son's or daughter's strengths (to identify the kind of atmosphere that will promote personal growth) and to reduce his or her skill deficiencies (to determine the degree of training and support necessary). This assessment of needs would best result in a second list of goals; this time the list would not be as much value-oriented and subjective as skill-oriented and concrete.

Once general goals and specific needs are clearly articulated, the questions that follow can be asked from your own, personal context. We can suggest many directions to follow in tracking down the information needed: Visit community residences and talk to staff members, board members, parents of residents, residents themselves, neighbors, and other concerned citizens to whom the staff may direct you. Bring the prospective resident along to solicit feelings about the community residence, and to observe current residents' reactions to him or her. Investigate several residences to gain some idea of their diversity. Get yourself invited to eat dinner wtih the residents and staff so you can gain a true feeling for the quality of life in the house. Read your state's plan for community residences to see how any single house fits into the larger picture. Perhaps also solicit advice from your state's Association for Retarded Citizens or Department of Mental Health and Retardation. Later in this chapter we present a list of articles, books, and pamphlets that may prove to be useful in making placement decisions.

We can certainly recognize the complexity of the issues raised here for parents of retarded adults. The motivation for placement usually comes more from you than from your son or daughter, and elements of uncertainty may make your decision about the need for placement seem more like "pushing out" than "moving ahead." Although the information gathering and placement processes may seem difficult, time consuming, and emotionally taxing, we feel it is necessary to spend the effort and time to best match your son or daughter with an appropriate program. If a comprehensive system is available in your geographic area, then both information gathering and decision making will be that much easier, because a clearly defined route to a general goal is articulated in the program's philosophy. However, in the absence of a comprehensive system, a parent making a placement must use the initial entrée into the community residence system in a careful way, because future options remain more ambiguous when a residence is not formally associated with others. Although we urge caution and care in making community residence placements, we recognize that the options available in some parts of the country are extremely limited. Even where choices are limited, however, informed parents, who know what to look for and ask about, can strongly influence a community residence to move toward better programming. With these considerations in mind we turn to the following questions.

Are there specific criteria for admission to this residence? Admission policies vary widely. Some community residences exclude the physically handicapped retarded adult because of architectural barriers, and most exclude persons who have chronic medical problems other than epileptic seizures. Others require that a work placement be assured prior to admission. Two common exclusionary policies limit those who are not fully independent in their self-help skills (dressing, grooming, and eating) and those who have behavior problems that are difficult to control. In some community residences the admission criteria are clearly stated, and you will be able to determine easily whether your son or daughter is eligible, whereas in other residences the admission criteria may be inferred only from the characteristics of the present residents.

Where did most of the residents live prior to moving to this community residence? The answer to this question might suggest an admission criterion, one that often is only implied. If all but one or two of the present residents share a common background (such as having lived in institutions), then you know something about who will most likely be admitted in the future. Preferences for residents with certain backgrounds might be a reflection of house policy or of state policy. For example, in some states class action suits* have led to requirements for provision of community alternatives for institutionalized retarded persons; frequently, the result has been the partial or total exclusion of those who have never lived in an institution.

Quite apart from the issue of admissions, it is necessary to consider the background of the present residents in terms of the chances of your son or daughter fitting in with the group. We found that if all but one or two residents had shared a common background, the remaining ones were not likely to become friendly with the larger group and thus were isolated. They were left out of day-to-day experiences (like discussing or visiting friends back at the institution) and of the more abstract experience of having a common frame of reference. This factor alone should not rule out a community residence as an appropriate place for your son or daughter, but it is an important consideration nonetheless.

What is the policy on length of stay in this community residence? This question is one of the most important ones you should ask, and the answer may not be easy to determine. You will first have to decide if you are seeking a permanent or a transitional home for your son or daughter, and if transitional, then toward what goal? A common problem you will face is that often the policy on length of stay in a community residence may not reflect well the reality of resident turnover. As we showed earlier, many self-designated permanent homes have considerable (and presumably unplanned) turnover. Ask therefore

*Class action suits are court suits brought in behalf of an entire class of individuals, such as retarded adults living in a particular institution.

about residents who have left the community residence in recent years. Ask where those ex-residents now live, so you can differentiate between houses that promote self-sufficient living on the part of ex-residents and those that have a high rate of reinstitutionalization. Asking about ex-residents will usually give you an indication also of how well the community residence follows up its residents once they leave and if staff members show an interest in providing continuing support to them. When a residence has the goal of providing a permanent home for residents and yet has a high rate of turnover *or* when a residence is set up to be a transitional facility and has infrequent turnover, the incongruity should be explored further.

Where is the residence located? The location of a community residence determines much about the quality of daily life and future options that are offered. To answer this question, it will be necessary to spend time walking about the neighborhood, finding the bus stop, talking to shopkeepers, and, in general, gaining a sense of the immediate community. Seek a community residence located in a community where neighbors, shopkeepers, and local agencies are accepting of (or at least not actively opposed to) the community residence. Look for a neighborhood relatively free from crime and yet not so affluent so as to adapt the resident to a lifestyle that is impossible for him or her to continue after leaving the community residence. Assess the availability of public transportation, because this is a factor in holding a job or reaching community resources. See what resources (stores, movies, etc.) are in close proximity to the house. An appropriate setting, then, is one that can provide for the resident's particular needs for access to jobs, training, facilities, and other people.

Is the physical quality of the house itself appropriate to the needs of your son or daughter? The physical environment gives out many messages: This is a place the residents care about (they keep it clean); this is a place where one can have privacy (there is one toilet per bathroom); this is a place where residents' individual identities have room for expression (they choose their own decorations); this is a place where people enjoy one another's company (there is a large dining room table, and an often-used living room). However, none of these factors is necessarily good or bad. For example, many residents who have previously lived at home prefer single rooms, whereas residents from institutions often prefer to share a bedroom, at least at first. Ask yourself, then, if the physical environment is appropriate to your child's likes and needs, whether it provides adequate opportunities for furnishing according to his or her own wishes, and whether it is consistent with your long-term goals. Like the surrounding neighborhood, the physical quality of the house may promote or hinder these goals. A relatively luxurious and comfortable house may be more appropriate in a community residence that provides a permanent home for residents, whereas more transitional community residences would be wise to furnish the rooms to be similar to the kinds of places residents will be likely to move next.

What administrative connections exist between this residence and other community residences? Connections may be formally defined, as in comprehensive systems, or less so, as in associations among group home staff members. There are potential advantages to placing your son or daughter in a community residence with formal connections with other programs if such an arrangement is available to you. If the residence is administered by an agency that also sponsors other types of community residences, such as a group home and semi-independent apartments, there is room for planned movement within this system if another placement seems, in time, to better match your son's or daughter's needs. Also, a formal connection with a day program, such as a workshop, a work training program, or even a recreational program, implies more ready access for residents to these services, access that otherwise is often difficult to secure.

What arrangements have been made to provide the community residence with backup resources? At various times a resident may need professional services, such as medical, dental, psychological, vocational, or legal. Resources available to a community residence may include something as simple as an informal agreement with the local physician to provide medical care to residents or more extensive and formalized arrangements, such as contractual agreements with specialized psychiatric or vocational facilities. Backup resources are provided in a variety of ways. Residences may have in their yearly budgets monies designated to purchase specialized consultant services. Other programs, typically larger community residences or those sponsored by large agencies may have staff members who have specialized skills, and thus the specific needs of your son or daughter can possibly be met in the community residence itself. Still other community residences may rely exclusively on community-based resources, but may have staff to help the resident make use of such resources. Whatever the arrangement, you should be confident that your son or daughter will be provided with adequate and appropriate services before making a final placement decision.

What is the staffing pattern of the community residence? As discussed in earlier chapters, the staffing pattern of a community residence determines to a large extent the quality of life experienced by the residents. In small, autonomous community residences, the staff may also totally determine the nature of the program. Many concerns about staff have been addressed at length in earlier chapters, and the implications of various staffing patterns have been discussed. We will not try to review all these issues here. We should note, however, that perhaps the two most important considerations – whatever the staffing pattern – are staff *competence* and *stability* on the job, and these characteristics are especially difficult to assess. Seek the opinions of parents of present residents and of professionals who are familiar with this residence. And certainly do not discount your own impressions about the staff's competence.

Staffing is less of a problematic issue when the community residence program and its staff are monitored regularly by some outside group, such as a local association for retarded citizens, which can independently suggest changes in the program. Of course, with a comprehensive system, the potential for some in-agency monitoring exists because of the graded levels of staff responsibility.

How much autonomy can a resident expect to have in this community residence? Autonomy, defined as freedom from specific imposed rules and restrictions, is a difficult issue for parents and professionals to resolve. The community-residence movement is associated with an ideological commitment to increased autonomy for retarded persons that is greater than they have been afforded previously in their residential settings. Yet as we have seen, almost all community residences place some restrictions on the personal activity of residents, and most often the restrictions are house-wide policies, not adapted to individual needs.

What you have to consider in evaluating this issue is the amount of autonomy in specified areas that your son or daughter can successfully handle now. If a community residence has rules that result in less autonomy for him or her than before, this may pose a very real problem. The ideal arrangement is certainly *not* the house that places no restrictions on the resident, but rather one in which decisions about autonomy are made individually, based on each person's needs and capabilities. A commitment by the community residence staff to take some considered risks seems more desirable than sheltering the residents totally.

How do residents in the community residence continue to develop skills? Skill enhancement should be a particularly important area of concern in choosing an appropriate community residence. Some residences are philosophically opposed to continued teaching of community living skills for adults, whereas others passively neglect this function. This is generally more often the case in residences that provide a permanent home than in those that have residents who are in transition.

If you are seeking a community residence with a strong training component, however, there are several points to consider. Find out *when* the skill teaching occurs. In most small group homes, for example, residents spend their weekdays in work or other day placements, leaving only the evenings and weekends for skill teaching sessions. For highly skilled residents this may be sufficient; however, for those individuals who have many skill deficits, learning might well be impaired by the lower priority that teaching sessions are assigned. If your adult son or daughter needs to learn a wide variety of community living skills, you might want to consider a residence that provides skill building sessions during much of the day and that only later introduces a full day of work.

Another point to consider is *what kinds* of skills are emphasized. Many community residences focus on basic living skills, such as cleaning, cooking, traveling, and using money. These programs are often more suited to individuals who previously lived in institutions than to those who grew up in their family homes. The latter, who often have been exposed to these activities as part of growing up in the community, might benefit more from the development of social interaction skills, independence and decision-making skills, and community participation skills. Community residences that are larger in size often have the resources to offer diverse skill teaching, whereas smaller programs must to some degree limit their focus. The backgrounds of the staff members are also relevant here; a staff member with a special education background may stress different skills than would a social worker.

Finally, ask about *how* skills are taught and how progress is evaluated. Is the description of teaching goals general and vague, or do the staff members talk in terms of specific objectives with clear-cut and perhaps written programs? Can the staff show you examples of continual record keeping and evaluation?

In considering the issue of skill teaching, it is important to *observe* firsthand what is taught on a typical day rather than to rely on staff reports. A list of skills taught may sound impressive, but often you will find that teaching of some skills is infrequent or poorly executed and thus is of little benefit.

What is the policy on work in this community residence? The normalization principle stresses that spending one's day doing some form of meaningful work is an important way of becoming integrated into community living. Almost two-thirds of the residents in our sample worked in either competitive or sheltered settings. One of the first things to find out about a community residence therefore is whether the residents work. If they do not, find out why not and what else they do during the day. In one house some residents may not be working because they are participating in a well-structured community-living skills training program, whereas in another house working might simply be precluded by a lack of transportation to jobs.

If work is stressed in a community residence, try to find out how much flexibility there is in job placement. Who helps the residents find an appropriate work setting? Are all residents required to work to continue to live in the community residence? If a resident loses a job, is there a limit to how long he or she can remain in the house while unemployed? Do all residents start out in the same sheltered workshop? These and other examples of inflexibility are not uncommon and may pose problems for a resident who quits a job or who may not be able to work for a period of time. Similarly, what plans are made for residents who become chronically ill and are thus unable to work again? Are they automatically excluded from the residence, and if so, are options other than institutions provided for?

Another point to consider is the type of job typically held by residents. Most retarded people in community residences end up in factory or factory-like jobs, or service positions in cafeterias, hospitals, etc. This limited focus excludes other very realistic work possibilities, such as clerical work, house painting, and gardening, to mention just a few. It is helpful when a community residence has contacts with a wide variety of work options so that placements can most closely fit the residents' abilities and choices.

How viable is this community residence? What is its potential longevity? These questions are bound to be of concern to parents when making decisions about the future living arrangements of their retarded adult son or daughter. These are also difficult questions to answer, and information must be used inferentially. No program, public or private, is ultimately assured of a secure and permanent future, yet there are indications of security that should be pursued. The following questions should be asked: How secure are funding sources? How receptive is the community to the continued existence of the community residence? Is the community residence legally well established (i.e., no zoning ambiguities)? Does this community residence fit in well with the state plan for community services for the retarded?

While the goal of a secure future is certainly an important one, it alone does not ensure an adequate quality of life for a resident; certainly state institutions at the present time are far more secure than any community residence is, but when security is steeped in stagnation, it loses its desirability.

Viability also involves a stable future of program excellence. A community residence that determines its program on the basis of the skills of its current staff is certainly less secure than one in which the program philosophy is well articulated and the staff recruited have skills that are compatible with that philosophy. Similarly, a relatively long-term commitment to the job on the part of the staff members ensures a more stable future. Yet guaranteed job permanence, as in civil service, is known for its propensity to produce mediocre staff performance, and this too should be avoided.

Are there costs associated with living in a community residence? In the overwhelming number of community residences there is a monthly fee that covers rent and usually food as well. In *most* private nonprofit community residences the fee is expected to be paid out of the resident's Supplemental Security Income (SSI) and/or wages. In the more expensive private programs, substantial parental contributions are expected. If parental payments are required, it is important for you to find out what plans are made for the resident whose parents can no longer pay (loss of income, old age, or death), since few private community residences guarantee that the resident will be allowed to continue to live there. For most families it is a more secure arrangement when the resident fee is small enough for the resident to pay it out of his or her own wages or SSI.

Conclusions

If you do find a community residence that satisfies most of your concerns and if admission can be secured, then we suggest that you and your son or daughter together develop a written agreement with the staff members, which includes a statement of goals as well as a plan describing the ways in which the community residence program will meet them. Hopefully this agreement will serve as a guide to planning for your son's or daughter's stay in the residence and should be therefore flexible and open to regular review and modification. In considering the implementation of this program plan, it might be wise to see if it is possible to arrange for your child to be assigned a citizen advocate who could monitor progress in specified areas and seek additional services where needed. Check with your state's Association for Retarded Citizens to find out if there is an advocacy program available in your area.

If, however, after visiting many programs you are unable to find one that satisfies your son's or daughter's needs, what are your options? Placement into a community residence is presently not considered the right of all retarded adults, and there is no formal appeal procedure known to us that would result in the creation of a community residence that is appropriate for an unserved individual. Unfortunately, this leaves parents in the position they have customarily been in – gaining time-limited admission for the child in a program that most closely, though inadequately, meets his or her needs, while at the same time advocating for the creation of new and more appropriate services. Sometimes it is even necessary for parents to initiate services themselves, through the auspices of a local, private, nonprofit organization, such as an association for retarded citizens. Advocacy is certainly the preferred option and in the past has been somewhat successful in making state and local agencies more responsive to the needs expressed by consumer groups. Effective advocacy encompasses a variety of activities, such as exerting political pressure, building a solid consumer base, attracting media coverage, and most important, gaining an extensive understanding of the issues involved. To this end the following is a bibliography of articles, books, and pamphlets we have found useful in understanding various components of the task of starting, operating, and evaluating a community residence.

Bibliography

Background Research

Begab, M. J., and Richardson, S. A. *The Mentally Retarded and Society: A Social Service Perspective.* Baltimore: University Park Press, 1975.

Edgerton, R. B. *The Cloak of Competence: Stigma in the Lives of the Mentally Retarded.* Berkeley: University of California Press, 1967.

Community Residences: Theory and Research

Blatt, B. *Souls in Extremis: An Anthology on Victims and Victimizers.* Boston: Allyn and Bacon, 1973.

Cherington, C., and Dybwad, G. *New Neighbors.* Washington, D.C.: President's Committee on Mental Retardation, 1975.

Edgerton, R. B., and Bercovici, S. The cloak of competence: Years later. *American Journal of Mental Deficiency,* Vol. 80, No. 5, 1976, 485–497.

Kugel, R. B., and Shearer, A. *Changing Patterns in Residential Services for the Mentally Retarded* (rev. ed.). Washington, D.C.: President's Committee on Mental Retardation, 1976.

Kugel, R. B., and Wolfensberger, W. *Changing Patterns in Residential Services for the Mentally Retarded.* Washington, D.C.: President's Committee on Mental Retardation, 1969.

O'Connor, G. *Home is a Good Place: A National Perspective of Community Residential Facilities for Developmentally Disabled Persons.* Washington, D.C.: American Association on Mental Deficiency, Monograph No. 2, 1976.

Wehbring, K., and Ogren, C. *Community Residences for Mentally Retarded People.* Arlington, Texas: National Association for Retarded Citizens, 1975.

Wolfensberger, W. *Normalization: The Principle of Normalization in Human Services.* Toronto: National Institute on Mental Retardation, 1972.

Practical Applications

Biklen, D. *Let Our Children Go: An Organizing Manual for Advocates and Parents.* Syracuse, N. Y.: Human Policy Press, 1974.

Friedman, P. R. *The Rights of Mentally Retarded Persons: An ACLU Handbook.* New York: Avon Books, 1976.

Residential Services and Facilities Committee. *The Right to Choose.* Arlington, Texas: National Association for Retarded Citizens, 1973.

Wolfensberger, W., and Zauha, H. *Citizen Advocacy and Protective Services for the Impaired and Handicapped.* Toronto: National Institute on Mental Retardation, 1973.

References

Baker, B. L., Brightman, A. J., Heifetz, L. J., and Murphy, D. *Steps to Independence.* Champaign, Illinois: Research Press, 1976.

Bandura, A. *Principles of Behavior Modification.* New York: Holt, Rinehart and Winston, 1969.

Bank-Mikkelsen, N. E. A Metropolitan Area in Denmark: Copenhagen. In R. B. Kugel and W. Wolfensberger [Eds.], *Changing Patterns in Residential Services for the Mentally Retarded.* Washington, D.C.: President's Committee on Mental Retardation, 1969. Pp. 227–254.

Birenbaum, A. The Changing Lives of Retarded Adults. Unpublished paper, 1974.

Blatt, B. *Exodus from Pandemonium: Human Abuse and the Reformation of Public Policy.* Boston: Allyn and Bacon, 1970.

Blatt, B., and Kaplan, F. *Christmas in Purgatory: A Photographic Essay on Mental Retardation.* Boston: Allyn and Bacon, 1966.

Butterfield, E. C. Basic Facts about Public Residential Facilities for the Mentally Retarded. In R. B. Kugel and W. Wolfensberger [Eds.], *Changing Patterns in Residential Services for the Mentally Retarded.* Washington, D.C.: President's Committee on Mental Retardation, 1969. Pp. 15–33.

Chigier, E. The Peer Group Principle. In M. Cohen [Ed.], *International Research Seminar on Vocational Rehabilitation of the Mentally Retarded.* American Association on Mental Deficiency, Special Publications Series No. 1, 1972.

Clark, G. P., Kivitz, M. S., and Rosen, R. A transitional program for institutionalized adult retarded. *Vocational Rehabilitation Administration Project No. 1275P.* Elwyn, Pennsylvania: Elwyn Institute, 1968.

Cobb, H. V. *The Forecast of Fulfillment: A Review of Research on Predictive Assessment of the Adult Retarded for Social and Vocational Adjustment.* New York: Teachers College Press, 1972.

Conley, R. *Economics of Mental Retardation.* Baltimore, Maryland: Johns Hopkins Press, 1973.

Dybwad, G. *New horizons in residential care of the mentally retarded.* Presented at the annual conference of the National Association for Retarded Children, Cincinnati, Ohio, 1959.

Dybwad, G. *Challenges in Mental Retardation.* New York: Columbia University Press, 1964.

Dorgan, J. Foster home care for the psychiatric patient. *Canadian Journal of Public Health,* Oct. 1958, 49(10), 411–419.

Eagle, E. Prognosis and outcome of community placements of institutionalized retardates. *American Journal of Mental Deficiency,* 1967, 72(2), 232–243.

Edgerton, R. B. Issues Relating to the Quality of Life among Mentally Retarded Persons. In M. J. Begab and S. A. Richardson [Eds.], *The Mentally Retarded and Society: A Social Science Perspective.* Baltimore, Maryland: University Park Press, 1975.

Fairweather, G., Maynard, H., Sanders. D., and Cressler, D. *Community Life for the Mentally Ill: An Alternative to Institutional Care.* Chicago: Aldine Publishing Co., 1969.

Fernald, W. E. After-care study of the patients discharged from Waverly for a period of 25 years. *Ungraded,* 1919, 5, 25–31, 119–120.

Fields, S. Asylum on the front porch, II: Community life for the mentally retarded. *Innovations,* 1974a, 1(4), 11–14.

Fields, S. Asylum on the front porch, III: A medieval tradition. *Innovations,* 1974b, 1(4), 15–16.

Fritz, M., Wolfensberger, W., and Knowlton, M. *An Apartment Living Plan to Promote Integration and Normalization of Mentally Retarded Adults.* Downsview, Ontario: Canadian Association for the Mentally Retarded, May, 1971.

Gardner, W. I. *Behavior Modification in Mental Retardation: The Education and Rehabilitation of the Mentally Retarded Adolescent and Adult.* Chicago: Aldine Publishing Co., 1971.

Glasscote, R. M., Gudeman, J. E., and Elpers, R. *Halfway Houses for the Mentally Ill: A Study of Program and Problems.* Washington, D.C.: American Psychiatric Association, 1971.

Goffman, E. *Asylums: Essays on the Social Situation of Mental Patients and Other Inmates.* New York: Doubleday and Co., 1961.

Greenblatt, M. Massachusetts Department of Mental Health Interoffice Memo, 1972.

Grunewald, K. A Rural County in Sweden: Malmohus County. In R. B. Kugel and W. Wolfensberger [Eds.], *Changing Patterns in Residential Services for the Mentally Retarded.* Washington, D.C.: President's Committee on Mental Retardation, 1969. Pp. 255–288.

Hansen, C. E. The work crew approach to job placement for the severely retarded. *Journal of Rehabilitation,* May–June 1969, 35(3), 25–27.

Hunt, N. *The World of Nigel Hunt.* New York: Garrett, 1967. P. 40.

Kadushin, A. Child Welfare: Adoption and Foster Care. In R. Morris [Ed.], *Encyclopedia of Social Work.* New York: The National Association of Social Workers, 1972.

Kanter, R. M. *Commitment and Community: Communes and Utopias – Sociological Perspective.* Cambridge, Mass.: Harvard University Press, 1972.

Kimball, W. Human warehouses: An inside look at the Fernald school for the retarded. *Boston After Dark,* May, 1972.

Kugel, R. B., and Wolfensberger, W. *Changing Patterns in Residential Services for the Mentally Retarded.* Washington, D.C.: President's Committee on Mental Retardation, 1969.

Lent, J. R. Mimosa cottage: Experiment in hope. *Psychology Today,* 1968, 2(1), 51–58.

Martin, G. L. The future for the severely and profoundly retarded: Kin Kare? foster homes? *The Canadian Psychologist,* 1974, 15(3), 188–241.
Martin, G. L., and Lowther, G. H. Kin Kare: A Community Residence for Graduates of an Operant Program for Severe and Profound Retardates in a Large Institution. Presented at the International Symposium on Behavior Modification, Minneapolis, Minn., 1972.
Mass, H., and Engler, R. *Children in Need of Parents.* New York: Columbia University Press, 1959.
New York State Association for Retarded Citizens and Parisi v. *Carey,* No. 72-C-356/357 (E.D. N.Y., April 30, 1975), approved 393 F. Supp. 715 (E.D. N.Y. 1975).
Nirje, B. The Normalization Principle and Its Human Management Implications. In R. B. Kugel and W. Wolfensberger [Eds.], *Changing Patterns in Residential Services for the Mentally Retarded.* Washington, D.C.: President's Committee on Mental Retardation, 1969.
Nirje, B. The Normalization Principle and Its Human Management Implications. sium on normalization). *Journal of Mental Subnormality,* 1970, 16, 62–70.
Raush, H., and Raush, C. *Halfway House Movement: A Search for Sanity.* New York: Appleton-Century-Crofts, 1968.
The Right to Choose, National Association for Retarded Citizens, Residential Services and Facilities Committee, Oct. 1973.
Rivera, G. *Willowbrook: A Report on How It Is and Why It Doesn't Have to Be That Way.* New York: Random House, 1972.
Sarason, S. B. *The Psychological Sense of Community.* San Francisco: Jossey-Bass Publishers, 1974.
Schrader, P. J., and Elms, R. R. *Guidelines for Family Care Home Operators.* New York: Springer Publishing Co., 1972.
Slingerland, W. H. *Child-Placing in Families.* New York: Russell Sage Foundation, 1919.
Timbers, G. D., Fixsen, D. L., Phillips, E. L., and Wolf, M. M. Teaching-family Homes: Community-based, Family Style Treatment Programs for Adolescents with Severe Behavior Problems. Presented at the 81st Annual Meeting of the American Psychological Association, Montreal, Sept. 1973.
Ullman, L. P., and Berkman, V. C. Judgments of outcome of home care placement from psychological material. *Journal of Clinical Psychology,* 1959, 15, 28–31.
Windle, E. The prognosis of mental subnormals. *American Journal of Mental Deficiency* (monog. suppl.), 1962, 66, 1–180.
Winspear, C. W. The protection and training of feeble-minded women. *Proc. Nat. Conf. Charities and Correction,* 1895. Pp. 160–163.
Wolfensberger, W. A New Approach to Decision-making in Human Management Services. In R. B. Kugel and W. Wolfensberger [Eds.], *Changing Patterns in Residential Services for the Mentally Retarded.* Washington, D.C.: President's Committee on Mental Retardation, 1969a. Pp. 367–381.
Wolfensberger, W. Twenty predictions about the future of residential services in mental retardation. *Mental Retardation,* Dec. 1969b, 7(6), 51–54.
Wolfensberger, W. The Origin and Nature of Our Institutional Models. In R. B. Kugel and W. Wolfensberger [Eds.], *Changing Patterns in Residential Services for the Mentally Retarded.* Washington, D.C.: President's Committee on Mental Retardation, 1969c. Pp. 59–171.
Wolfensberger, W. Will there always be an institution? II: The impact of new service models: Residential alternatives to institutions. *Mental Retardation,* Dec. 1971, 9(6), 31–38.

Wolfensberger, W. *Normalization: The Principle of Normalization in Human Services.* Toronto: National Institute on Mental Retardation, 1972.

Wolfensberger, W., and Glenn, L. *PASS: A Method for the Quantitative Evaluation of Human Services.* Toronto: National Institute on Mental Retardation, 1973.

Wolfensberger, W., and Menolascino, F. J. Reflections on recent mental retardation developments in Nebraska, I: A new plan. *Mental Retardation,* Dec. 1970, 8(6), 20–28.

Wolfensberger, W., and Zauha, H. *Citizen Advocacy and Protective Services for the Impaired and Handicapped.* Toronto: National Institute on Mental Retardation, 1973.

Wyatt v. *Stickney,* 325 F. Supp. 781 (M.D. ALA) and 334 Supp. 1341 (M.D. ALA, 1971).

Appendix I

The PARC Project
Planning Alternatives for Retarded Citizens

Read House
Harvard University
Cambridge, Mass. 02138

Dear Friends:

As you know, the PARC Project is currently engaged in gathering vital information about community residences for retarded people in the United States. Very little is known about such residences. For example: How do these residences become established? Who are the residents? What are the staffing patterns? What are the architectural characteristics of the houses? What types of rules exist for residents? How are the houses financially supported? How do residents spend their days and evenings? What kind of relationships do residences have with their communities?

This survey is an attempt to answer the above and other questions. We realize that completing this questionnaire is an added strain on your already demanding work load. However, we are asking you to fill it out because, as pioneers in the emerging field of community residential living, you are the only people who can provide this important information.

The results of this survey will not merely collect dust on the shelves. We are determined to use the information that you and other respondents provide to facilitate the development of new residences and make it possible for them to benefit from your experiences. In addition, your information could assist new residences in establishing fruitful relationships with their communities.

Without your help, we will not be able to develop a complete picture of the ways in which community residences operate. Therefore we ask that you fill out the questionnaire as soon as possible, and return it to us in the enclosed stamped envelope. We would also be interested in receiving any additional information about your house that you may want to share with us. To cover the cost of mailing such materials, we are including a dollar bill. If you have any questions, feel free to call us. We look forward to receiving your completed questionnaire soon, and thank you in advance for your cooperation.

Sincerely,

The PARC Project

If You Would Like to Comment More Fully on Any Question, Use the Margins or Last Page of Booklet.

Name of residence (if any) ______________________

Address ______________________
No. Street City State Zip

Telephone ( ) ______________________
Area code

Name of person filling out this form ______________________

Position within residence ______________________

Length of time you have been working at the residence ______________________

Developmental History of Residence

1. Date of opening of residence ______________________
Month/day/year

2. Where did the primary impetus come from to form the residence? (Choose 2: Place "1" next to *most* important and "2" next to *second most* important.)

   Actions taken by:
   a. Individuals _____
   b. A parent group _____
   c. An institution or a state school for the mentally retarded _____
   d. A mental health association _____
   e. A private, nonprofit corporation _____
   f. Other (specify) ______________________

3. How did the house prepare the community for its presence? (Check all that apply.)
   a. Local newspapers/TV/radio gave publicity _____
   b. We spoke to:
      Parent groups _____
      Professionals in retardation _____
      Local business people _____
      Clergy _____
      Neighbors _____
      City government representatives _____
   c. Other (specify) ______________________
   d. We did not prepare the community _____

4. Opposition to the house came from? (Check all that apply.)
   a. Political leaders _____
   b. Zoning dispute _____
   c. Neighbors who complained _____
   d. Mental health or retardation association _____
   e. Parents of retarded people _____
   f. No opposition _____
   g. Other (specify) ______________________
   ____

5. The house is set up primarily to provide a home for residents for a period of:
   a. 1–6 months _____
   b. 6–12 months _____
   c. 1–3 years _____
   d. Permanent home _____
   e. Other (specify) ______________________
   ____

6. Is there a minimum or maximum age, above or below which you do not normally accept a resident?
   Yes ______ No ______
   If yes, what is the minimum ______ and maximum ______ ?

7. Is the house associated with an institution or state school for the retarded?
   Yes ______ No ______
   If yes, what is the name of this institution? ______________________
   ____

8. Religious affiliation of the house, if any: ______________________

9. What is the total number of residents who have lived in the house since it opened? ______

Resident Population

10. How many residents currently live in the house? ______

11. What is the resident capacity of the house? ______

12. Residents for your house were selected by: (Check all that apply, and star [*] the one that is most influential.)
    a. An institution for the mentally retarded ______
    b. A parent group ______
    c. The staff of the house ______
    d. State mental health or retardation services ______
    e. Community mental health or retardation agency ______
    f. Other residents ______
    g. Other (specify) ______________________

13. Does a resident under consideration for admission visit the house to discuss his admission with:
    a. A staff member:
       Always ______
       Usually ______
       Sometimes ______
       Never ______
    b. Other residents:
       Always ______
       Usually ______
       Sometimes ______
       Never ______

Questions 14–19

The following questions are designed to gather specific information about the current residents. Please indicate the number of residents who fall into each appropriate category in the questions in this section. If you are not sure of the exact number in any of the items presented, just give an estimate.

14. How many of the residents are in each of these age categories? (Use numbers.)
    a. 0–5 ______
    b. 6–12 ______
    c. 13–17 ______
    d. 18–21 ______
    e. 22–30 ______
    f. 31–40 ______
    g. 41–50 ______
    h. 51–60 ______
    i. 61–65 ______
    j. Over 65 ______

15. How many of the residents are: Male _____ Female _____

16. How many residents are:
   a. Mildly retarded _____
   b. Moderately retarded _____
   c. Severely retarded _____
   d. Multiply handicapped _____
   e. Other (specify) _____________
   ____
   f. Not sure of level of retardation _____

17. Before coming to this house, how many residents lived: (Use numbers.)
   a. In an institution or state school for the retarded _____
   b. At home with family _____
   c. In a foster home _____
   d. At another community residence _____
   e. At a hospital _____
   f. Independently in the community _____
   g. Other (specify) _____________

18. Previous to their *last* placement, how many residents lived: (Use numbers.)
   a. In an institution or state school for the retarded _____
   b. At home with family _____
   c. In a foster home _____
   d. At another community residence _____
   e. At a hospital _____
   f. Independently in the community _____
   g. Other (specify) _____________

19. When residents have left your house, how many have gone to live: (Use numbers.)
   a. In own apartment _____
   b. With family _____
   c. With foster family _____
   d. At an institution or state school for the retarded _____
   e. At another community residence _____
   f. At a hospital _____
   g. Returned to your community residence _____
   h. Other (specify) _____________
   i. Not applicable, all residents still live in house _____

20. After a resident leaves the house: (Check all that apply.)
   a. The resident has the option of visiting the house on his/her own _____
   b. There is an automatic follow-up within 6 months _____
   c. The resident is expected to have no further contact with the house _____
   d. Other (specify) _____________
   e. Not applicable, all residents still live in house _____

21. Who decides when a resident is ready to move out of the house? (Check all that apply and star [*] the most influential.)
   a. Board of directors _____
   b. House staff _____
   c. The resident _____
   d. Other professionals _____
   e. Other residents _____
   f. Other (specify) _____________
   ____
   g. Not applicable, all residents still live in the house _____

22. Does the house have legal responsibility for any of the residents?
   Yes _____ No _____

23. Of the following descriptions, indicate the item that *most* accurately describes your house (indicate with a "1") and the item that *least* accurately describes your house (indicate with a "0").
    a. Accommodation only ____
    b. Training in basic living skills ____
    c. A supportive atmosphere ____
    d. Training in work skills ____
    e. Counseling for personal adjustment problems ____
    f. Placement help for employment and future living arrangements ____
    g. Some degree of shelter and protection from the outside community ____
    h. An education program (e.g., reading) ____
    i. Recreational activities ____
    j. Other ____________________

24. The residents of the house need: (Choose the *three most* important.)
    a. Independence ____
    b. Training ____
    c. Exposure to new experiences ____
    d. Protection ____
    e. Friends ____
    f. Respect ____
    g. Security ____
    h. Guidance ____
    i. Dignity ____
    j. Support ____
    k. Freedom ____
    l. Responsibility ____
    m. Confidence ____

25. Do residents meet in groups without staff members? (Choose one.)
    a. Never ____
    b. Occasionally (less than once a week) ____
    c. Once a week ____
    d. Other (specify) ____________

Staff

26. How many staff members are currently working at the house? ____

27. How many of these live in the house? ____

28. Please list the positions the staff members fill: (Indicate number of staff members in each position, e.g., houseparent, director, etc.)

    ____________ ____________
    ____________ ____________
    ____________ ____________

29. What professionals outside the house either consult with staff or provide services to the residents? (Indicate number of staff members in each position, e.g., social worker, vocational counselor, etc.)

    ____________ ____________
    ____________ ____________
    ____________ ____________

30. At least one staff member is in the house: (Choose one.)
    a. Twenty-four hours a day ____
    b. Only when the residents are in the house ____
    c. Part of the time when the residents are in the house ____
    d. Other (specify) ____________

31. Do staff meet with natural or foster parents? Yes _____ No _____

32. How many staff members also work at an institution or state school for the retarded? _____

33. How often are staff meetings scheduled?
   a. Never _____
   b. Occasionally (less than once a week) _____
   c. Once a week _____
   d. Other (specify) _____

34. Do staff and residents have joint group meetings?
   a. Never _____
   b. Occasionally (less than once a week) _____
   c. Once a week _____
   d. Other (specify) _____

Physical Plant

35. In what type of building is the residence housed? (Choose one.)
   a. Some apartments in an apartment building _____
   b. Ex-apartment building now totally occupied by the residents _____
   c. Big old house _____
   d. Big new house _____
   e. Ex-hospital or convalescent home _____
   f. Ex-hotel or motel _____
   g. Town house _____
   h. Rural farm buildings _____
   i. On hospital grounds _____
   j. Other (specify) _____

36. What is the area directly next to the residence? (Choose one.)
   a. Hospital or state school _____
   b. Business district _____
   c. Factory _____
   d. Urban residential area _____
   e. Suburban area _____
   f. Rural area _____
   g. Farmland _____

37. How many rooms are there in the residence (counting kitchen and bathrooms)? _____

38. How many of these are bedrooms for the residents? _____

39. How many of the following facilities are there in the house? (Use numbers.)
   Toilets _____
   Bathrooms _____
   Sinks _____
   Showers _____
   Bathtubs _____
   Closets _____

40. Are there any rooms that are off limits for residents? Yes _____ No _____
   If yes, which are these rooms? _____

41. Can the bathrooms be locked from the inside? Yes _____ No _____

42. Can the bedrooms be locked from the inside? Yes _____ No _____

43. Where is the telephone(s) located? ______________________________

____

44. Is the main telephone a pay station? Yes _____ No _____

45. If the telephone is listed in the phonebook, under what name(s) is it listed?

____

46. Public transportation is available within: (Choose one.)
 a. 5 blocks of the residence _____
 b. 1/2 mile of the residence _____
 c. 1 mile or more from the residence _____
 d. No public transportation is available _____

47. Does the residence own or have daily use of a car? Yes _____ No _____

Rules and Policies

48. Who performs the following tasks? (Check all that apply.)

Task	Houseparent	Resident	Other (specify)
a. Cleaning bedrooms	_____	_____	_____
b. Cleaning living and dining rooms	_____	_____	_____
c. Cleaning kitchen	_____	_____	_____
d. Maintenance of grounds	_____	_____	_____
e. Preparation of meals	_____	_____	_____
f. Setting the table	_____	_____	_____
g. Serving meals	_____	_____	_____
h. Doing dishes	_____	_____	_____
i. Food shopping	_____	_____	_____
j. Shopping for supplies for residence	_____	_____	_____
k. Laundry	_____	_____	_____

49. Are the residents permitted to drink alcohol within the house?
 a. Yes _____ b. No _____ c. No policy, the issue never came up _____

50. Can residents entertain nonresidents of the opposite sex in the house?
 a. Only during certain hours (specify) _____ to _____
 b. Only in specific areas of the house (specify which rooms) __________

 ____
 c. Yes, no restrictions _____
 d. No _____
 e. No policy, the issue never came up _____

51. Residents are expected to be in the house by:
 a. 8 P.M. _____
 b. 10 P.M. _____
 c. Midnight _____
 d. Other (specify) ______________________________
 e. No policy _____

52. Residents are expected to go to bed by:
    a. 10 P.M. _____
    b. Midnight _____
    c. Other (specify) ______________________________
    d. No policy _____

53. What provisions are made for vacations, overnight "leaves" from the residence, etc.?
    ____
    ____
    ____

54. Do residents bring guests for dinner to the residence? Yes _____ No _____

55. Do residents have keys to the front door of the house? Yes _____ No _____

Financial Arrangements

56. How is the residence supported? (Check all that apply.)
    a. State funding _____
    b. Association for Retarded Citizens _____
    c. Church supported _____
    d. Private industry _____
    e. Nonprofit foundation _____
    f. Resident payments _____
    g. Private donors _____

57. What percentage of total operating expense is covered by resident payments?
    a. None _____
    b. 1–24% _____
    c. 25–49% _____
    d. 50–74% _____
    e. 75% or more _____

58. Indicate the monthly fee paid to the house by each resident, if there is one ____________. If there is no set fee, what is the average monthly amount paid by each resident? ____________

59. What is the annual budget for the residence for the current year?
    $____________

60. Who takes primary responsibility for the residents' money? (Check all that apply.)
    a. Houseparents _____
    b. Residents _____
    c. Family _____
    d. Other (specify) ______________________________

61. How many of the residents derive their *primary* sources of income from each of the following items? (Use numbers.)
    a. Parents _____
    b. Social Security _____
    c. State aid to disabled people _____
    d. Wages _____
    e. Other (specify) ____________
    ____
    ____

62. How many residents are provided with medical services by each of the following? (Use numbers.)
    a. Private physician ______
    b. Out-patient department of hospital ______
    c. Community or public health clinic ______
    d. Institution or state school for the retarded ______
    e. Other (specify) ______________________________

63. How many of the residents have their medical services paid for by each of the following? (Use numbers.)
    a. Medicare ______
    b. State health insurance (e.g., medicaid) ______
    c. Residents pay out of their own income ______
    d. Benefits provided by place of employment (e.g., Blue Cross/Blue Shield) ______
    e. Other (specify) ______________________________

Day Activities and Night Activities

64. How many of the residents are presently placed in each of the following work situations? (Use numbers.)
    a. Sheltered workshop ______
    b. Farm ______
    c. Working in the residence itself ______
    d. Competitive employment ______
    e. Day activity center ______
    f. Not yet placed ______
    g. Other program (specify) ______ ______________

65. How are group recreational activities planned? (Check all that apply.)
    a. By houseparents ______
    b. By residents ______
    c. No group recreational activities ______

66. Please list the three most recent recreational activities in which at least half the residents participated (if any).

    ____
    ____
    ____

67. Indicate how many of the following items are currently owned by the house, staff, or by any of the residents: (Use numbers.)

	Home-owned	Resident-owned	Staff-owned
a. TV	______	______	______
b. Radio	______	______	______
c. Record player	______	______	______
d. Records	______	______	______
e. Books	______	______	______
f. Magazines	______	______	______
g. Musical instruments	______	______	______
h. Clocks	______	______	______
i. Telephones	______	______	______

Community Relations and Resources

68. Which of the following are on your board of directors? (Check all that apply and star [*] the chairman or president of the board.)
    a. Parents ______
    b. Association for Retarded Citizens representatives ______
    c. Professionals in retardation ______
    d. Lawyers ______
    e. Politicians ______
    f. Local business people ______
    g. Clergy ______
    h. Other (specify) ______________________________

69. How do you feel the community views the house? (Choose 2: Place "1" next to the item that *most* clearly applies and "0" next to the item that *least* applies.)
    a. They are interested and concerned ______
    b. As a place for rehabilitated retarded people, and therefore safe ______
    c. They feel it reduces the property value around the house ______
    d. They feel the residents may cause unpleasant incidents ______
    e. Neutrally, or without knowledge or interest ______
    f. Community attitude unknown ______
    g. Not applicable (specify why) ______________________

70. How many members of the community currently volunteer at the house? ______

71. In conclusion, is there anything unique or especially effective about the residence that you would like other people to know about? (Use back if necessary.)

72. To help us gain information about as many facilities as possible, please indicate the names and addresses of any other community residences with which you are familiar.

73. We are eager to receive any written materials about your house that you may have available. Below are examples of the types of information we are interested in. In order to facilitate your sending these materials, we have enclosed a dollar bill to cover postage charges.
    –Letter telling us about the house
    –Written description about the house
    –Research or evaluations of the house
    –Progress reports
    –Newspaper articles about the house
    –References of written works that you have found helpful in running the house
    –State guidelines
    –Applications for funding
    –List of board of directors
    –Photograph of house
    –Annual budget
    –Architectural plans of the house

74. In the body of our report, no names will be associated with the information collected on this questionnaire. However, a list of participating community residences will be included in the appendix of our report. Would you be interested in having the name of your house on this list?
Yes ______ No ______

Thank you very much for filling out this questionnaire.

Appendix II

Intercorrelations among Variables for 226 Group Homes (includes small group homes, medium group homes, large group homes, and mini-institutions)

	Size (no. res.)	*Retard*[a]	*Age*	*Percent male*	*Popu-lation*	*Length open*
Community						
Length open	0.10	−0.01	−0.01	−0.15[b]	0.06	–
Population of municipality	0.15[b]	0.03	−0.16[b]	0.06	–	0.06
Community preparation	0.01	−0.03	−0.19[c]	0.07	0.03	−0.11
Community opposition	0.05	0.01	0.06	0.19[c]	−0.11	−0.07
Community involvement	0.12	−0.09	−0.12	0.05	0.03	−0.06
Institution						
Institutional involvement	−0.07	0.05	0.22[c]	−0.02	−0.05	−0.11
Percent from institution	0.04	−0.06	0.32[d]	0.03	−0.11	−0.12
Residents						
Age	0.09	−0.07	–	−0.12	−0.16[b]	−0.01
Percent Male	0.04	−0.04	−0.12	–	0.06	−0.15[b]
Retardation	0.04	–	0.07	0.04	−0.03	0.01
Staff						
Staff-to-resident ratio	−0.33[d]	0.07	−0.20[c]	0.00	0.05	−0.04
Professional-to-resident ratio	−0.40[d]	0.06	−0.16[b]	0.08	−0.06	−0.14[b]

	Size (no. res.)	*Retard*[a]	*Age*	*Percent male*	*Population*	*Length open*
Finances						
Fee	0.21[c]	−0.15[b]	−0.08	−0.11	0.03	0.14[b]
Budget per resident	−0.28[d]	−0.04	−0.18[b]	0.12	−0.05	−0.18[b]
Program						
Autonomy	−0.22[d]	0.03	−0.07	0.06	0.01	−0.22[c]
Responsibility	−0.17[d]	0.09[c]	−0.31[d]	0.04	0.04	−0.34[d]
Work	−0.20[c]	0.20[c]	−0.43[d]	0.18[c]	0.25[d]	−0.14[b]
Percent competitively employed	0.06	0.34[d]	−0.22[c]	0.08	0.26[d]	−0.08
Percent in sheltered workshops	−0.20[c]	−0.06	−0.10	0.11	0.03	−0.11
Desturn	−0.22[c]	0.25[c]	−0.20[b]	0.10	0.09	−0.13

[a]High retardation score means *less* retardation.
[b]$p < 0.05$
[c]$p < 0.01$
[d]$p < 0.001$

Index

Index